THEORY AND PRACTICE OF MONEY

Jennie Hawthorne
Senior Lecturer in Economics,
South West London College

Heinemann : London

William Heinemann Ltd

10 Upper Grosvenor Street, London W1X 9PA

LONDON MELBOURNE TORONTO

JOHANNESBURG AUCKLAND

Printed in Great Britain by
Biddles Ltd., Guildford & King's Lynn

Editor's Foreword

The *Heinemann Accountancy and Administration Series* is intended to fill a gap in the literature that caters for accountants, company secretaries, and similar professional people who are engaged in giving a vital information service to management. As far as possible, due recognition is given to the fact that there are two distinct bodies of readers: those who aspire to professional status – the students – and others who are already managing and/or serving management.

Theory and Practice of Money is an up-to-date account of the use of money and credit in the modern world as well as the operation of the major financial institutions. Written in a concise manner and covering all the essentials, it should allow the student to see a broad, yet detailed, account of how the financial system operates. Jennie Hawthorne, the author, has made a special study of the subject and in particular has looked at the requirements for the major professional bodies, particularly the Institute of Bankers. As part of this process, she has included typical examination questions and suggested answers, thus enabling the student to study through practical work which will allow him to pass examinations.

In recent years the importance of money as a method of control has gained considerable prominence, both economically and politically. For this reason a new book on the subject is extremely welcome. For students it can be recommended without reservation. Businessmen, accountants, financial advisers and managers should find a great deal of value from reading the book or using it as a work of reference.

J. Batty

Preface

The aim of this book is to provide in a brief and readable form, the material necessary to meet the requirements of examinations in monetary theory and practice (Applied Economics). The book will therefore be useful for students taking the Institute of Bankers' examinations and for 1st year students on Business Studies and similar degree courses where certain options require knowledge of monetary and fiscal policy and business finance.

The disadvantages of covering an examination syllabus in one volume are obvious. No segment can be treated in great depth. There abound exhaustive books on topics which here form only small chapters. But the advantages of the comprehensive approach are obvious too. Instead of the student being unable to see the wood for the trees, (a not uncommon symptom) s/he can identify not only the wood, but each individual tree and choose where, when and if to linger.

Although the book has been written mainly for examination candidates, it will also interest those who wish to know more about money, monetary terms and the relative merits of different forms of saving and investment. Each chapter concludes with typical questions taken from the Institute of Banker's past examination papers, with one question answered in full, as a suggested 'model'.

Acknowledgements

Among the many people and institutions who have helped in this book's fruition, mention must be made of the Economics Intelligence Department of the Bank of England, the Economics Departments of other banks, particularly Barclays for their charts, the Midland in Sheffield for research; the Institute of Bankers for their examination questions; the Stock Exchange, World Bank, National Association of Pension Funds, Building Societies Association, Finance Houses Association, Banker Magazine, Investors Chronicle, Bankers Clearing House; and Phillips and Drew (especially Stephen Lewis) ... all for facts and figures.

I also wish to thank my past and present students in the U.K., Africa, Hong Kong, Malaysia, the Bahamas, the West Indies and South America for their stimulating ideas; Mr F.D. Staples, librarian at South West London College for that perquisite of all librarians: a quiet and courteous efficiency; and lastly my family; those away: Francine, Jennifer, Jeremy, Kathy; those at home: Stephanie, for her knowledge of E.E.C. law; Michael and John. They, like my husband, provided a welcome source of inspiration, encouragement ... and distraction, without which no book is ever written.

Jennie Hawthorne

Contents

CONTENTS xiii

1 Money

In markets all over the world, money can be seen changing hands. These transactions show money in its passive role as a medium of exchange.

Many economists, however, suggest that money plays a dynamic role in modern societies. Yet money is not a force like gravity. Its power is limited. It works only in areas where there are economic goods.

Our first query, then, about this substance must be, what *is* money? Our second will be, what does money do? In other words, what is the nature of money and what are its functions?

1.1 THE NATURE AND FUNCTIONS OF MONEY

The nature of money may become more apparent if we look at the reasons why people *want* money. They want money because it is a liquid asset. It can be stored. It can be spent. How it is spent does not matter. The different purchases made all emphasize the sameness of money's nature as anything generally acceptable in payment of debt.

1.1.1 MEDIUM OF EXCHANGE

From the nature of money, we can deduce one of its functions. If it is acceptable in settlement of debt, it must serve as a medium of exchange. In a barter economy, where no acceptable medium of exchange exists, trading works by a series of 'swaps'. There is no purchase and sale, but an exchange of one wanted good for another wanted good. Without this 'coincidence of wants' (each person wanting what the other has to offer), no exchange can take place. Trade must be limited. It can take place only at a certain time, and only with a certain person or persons.

Money splits any transaction into two parts, purchase and sale. The buyer gives money for a purchase. The seller gets money for a sale. They are using a medium of exchange acceptable to both and they are using it *now*.

1.1.2 STANDARD FOR DEFERRED PAYMENTS

The invention of money also enables buyers and sellers to make arrangements for *future* transactions. A barter arrangement for the delivery of future goods could prove very unsatisfactory for all sorts of reasons. The promise of a future delivery of wheat or livestock against a future delivery of some other goods or services, is fraught with hazards. But the promise of a future money payment can be guaranteed, if the credit standing of the payer is good. And if it is not, and the money for the bargain is not forthcoming, the seller need not deliver. Money in this kind of transaction is acting as a standard for deferred payments, a very important function in modern societies, and one which has led to the development of many diverse financial institutions concerned with saving and the provision of credit.

1.1.3 UNIT OF ACCOUNT

There is another important way in which money functions: as a unit of account. In a barter economy, the worth of one good is measured against the worth of another. If the parties to the transaction believe that their respective goods are of equal worth, the exchange will take place. But there is no guarantee that those goods will exchange for similar things tomorrow or the next day. No buyer or seller may turn up for years. The goods may rot or perish. It will be hard to guess their value, if any. The use of money, however, provides some kind of measuring standard. It measures the worth of goods and services. As a ruler measures widths and lengths, so money measures values. It compares dear and cheap in price terms as the ruler measures distances in linear terms. Without money, transaction of any kind could be a long and belligerent business. With money, comparisons of worth (both now and in the future) can be made. Costing and accounting become possible. Machinery is set up and industries develop from the use of money as a unit of account.

1.1.4 STORE OF LIQUID WEALTH

A fourth function of money is to act as a store of liquid wealth. Wealth can be held in many forms: paintings, land, buildings, machinery, even human skills and talents. These forms of wealth are illiquid. They are not always quick or easy to convert into cash of the required amount. Inflation erodes the 'store of value' function of money for the value of the 'store' falls when prices rise. People then seek an alternative 'store'. Pictures, stamps, bullion take the place of money. This is a reversion to customs of earlier times when money was not invented, and goods and chattels served as a store of value.

Any kind of article can serve as money, providing it fulfils the functions of money. The most important of these functions is to act as an acceptable medium of exchange. What makes any particular commodity acceptable in this way? The reasons can be grouped as follows:

(a) Its inherent or intrinsic value. A gold sovereign made of valuable metal will prove more 'acceptable' than a paper note of nominally the same value.

(b) Enforcement through law. Such money is known as fiat money. When offered in the right quantity (legal tender)* it discharges debt. During times of unstable government, or hyperinflation such as occurred in Germany after World War 1, even fiat money may prove unacceptable and people will turn to other forms.

(c) Custom or common consent. Cigarettes or coffee were generally acceptable as exchange media in Germany after the Second World War. In primitive societies, all manner of exchange items varying from knives and furs, to beads and bells, have been accepted as money.

(d) The qualities or attributes of money. They can be listed as follows:

(i) Portability. Slabs of iron or concrete would not prove generally acceptable in exchange, although the Spartans used iron as money to impede the transport and accumulation of wealth. In the sixteenth century, the Swedes used copper coins which weighed over 40 lb. This exception to the general rule of portability was due to the fact that Sweden was then very rich in copper.

(ii) Scarcity. The supply of money must be stable: not too much or its value falls; not too little or another medium of exchange will be found to take its place. Thus, in the nineteenth century when the quantity of coins circulating in America, New Zealand, Britain and Australia proved insufficient for trade, private tokens became a method of payment until they were declared illegal.

(iii) Divisibility. The unit used as money must be able to be divided so that the sum of the parts is equal to the whole. There are few commodities which fit this specification. Animals do not. Neither do precious stones. By contrast, British coins have a weight/value relationship. Thus, not only are 8 halfpence or 4 pence equal in value to 2 twopence units; they are equal in weight, too. In this regard, they are like the silver pennies of William of Normandy, 20 of which eventually became a standard of both weight and value.

(iv) Homogeneity. Each unit of money must be uniform. A deposit in one bank must be as 'spendable' as a deposit of the same amount in another bank. Coins with the same face value must have the same worth. If coins of the same weight and face value were struck in gold and lead, the gold coins would be stored, the lead ones spent. The hoarding of one species, the spending of another is due to the fact that they are not uniform; not homogenous. Queen Elizabeth I's monetary adviser, Sir Thomas Gresham understood the idea of homogeneity very well and enshrined it in a principle now known as Gresham's law: "Bad money drives out good". When two kinds of money circulate together, that which is regarded as 'good' will be spent (if spent it is) far more slowly than the 'bad'. In time only the 'bad' will circulate at all.

---

*Bank notes are legal tender up to any amount; 50p up to £10; 5p up to £5; bronze coins $\frac{1}{2}$p, 1p, 2p, up to 20p.

(v) Recognizability. Money must be readily recognized for what it is. Trying to evaluate the worth of every coin before using it, would cause lengthy delays when buying and selling goods and services. If precious stones were used as money, who would be able to tell the difference between a real diamond and a fake? By contrast, bank notes are easily recognizable.

(vi) Durability. Anything used as money must be able to last. It must not fall to pieces in one's hands. Coins of copper or gold take 5000 years to wear out, but these metals are now too precious to be used as common currency. Before decimalization in 1971, the Bank of England used to issue over 8 million notes a day (five times as many as were issued in Western Germany,) and more than were issued to the whole of the United States. The average life of a £1 note was only 8 months in 1966, and of the ten shilling note, only five months. This lack of 'durability' was one of the reasons why the ten shilling note was abandoned and a new ten shilling (50 pence) coin struck when decimalization was introduced.

Summarizing, it can be said that money is anything commonly acceptable in payment of debt. To be acceptable in this way, it must perform certain functions and possess certain qualities.

But what precisely comprises the money supply (or money stock as it is referred to by the Bank of England) in the U.K.? And elsewhere? It is easy to see that in the U.K., coins and notes fulfil all the functions and possess all the qualities of money. So do notes and coins in other (including developing) countries. But bank deposits? How do they qualify as money? And if they do, why should building society deposits not so qualify. . .or the deposits of any financial institution? How can it not be money that is taken out when it is money that is put in?

To answer these questions we must first look at the definition of the money stock in the U.K. and elsewhere. We must try to see why some items are included, and others which seem the same, are not.

1.2 U.K. MONEY SUPPLY (THE COMPOSITION OF THE MONEY STOCK)

In 1970 there were three definitions of the money stock, in the U.K.
Excluding: DCE = Domestic Credit Expansion (data presented May 1969) there was:
(i) M1 = notes and coin in circulation with the public plus sterling current accounts held by the public sector.
(ii) M2 = M1 plus private sector sterling deposit accounts with the banks and discount houses.
(iii) M3 = M2 plus all other deposits (sterling and non-sterling) held by the U.K. banking sector.
In June 1972, M2 was excluded from the definitions. M1 and M3 only remained. The terminology was also altered. 'Sight deposits' replaced

current accounts, in May 1975. Sterling deposits were distinguished from non-sterling. The total money stock was divided into three groups as follows:

(i) M1 = notes and coins in circulation with the public

plus

non-interest-bearing sight deposits in sterling by the U.K. private sector with the banking sector

less

60% of transit items

plus

interest-bearing sight deposits in sterling.

(ii) Sterling M3 = M1

plus

sterling private sector time deposits with the U.K. banking sector

plus

sterling public sector sight deposits with the U.K. banking sector

plus

sterling public sector time deposits with the U.K. banking sector.

(iii) M3 = Sterling M3

plus

U.K. residents' deposits in other currencies with the U.K. banking sector.

(In monetary discussions the following terms are used, though they do not appear in the official money stock: Retail M1 = M1 less interest-bearing deposits; M4 = Sterling M3 + accepted commercial bills and non-bank holdings of Treasury bills; M5 = M4 + Building Society deposits.)

Figures for the U.K. Money Supply are given below.

The Money Supply: U.K.: January 1980

	£m. unadjusted	£m. seasonally adjusted
(a) Notes and coin in circulation with the public	9,319	
(b) U.K. private sector sterling sight deposits (current accounts) after deducting 60% of transit items		
non-interest-bearing	14,379	
interest-bearing	3,798	
Money stock M1 = total of a + b	27,496	27,620
(c) Private sector sterling time deposits including U.K. residents' holdings of certificates of deposit	27,353	

	£m. unadjusted	£m. seasonally adjusted
(d) U.K. public sector sterling deposits	1,169	
Money stock Sterling M3 = M1 + c + d	56,018	56,180
(e) U.K. residents' deposits in other currencies	4,857	
Money stock M3 = Sterling M3 + e	60,875	61,040

The monetary aggregate (or total) M3 of £61,040 is over six times as large as the total of notes and coin (£9,319). The importance of bank deposits in the money supply can thus clearly be seen.

1.2.1 MONEY STOCK DEFINITIONS OF OTHER COUNTRIES

Nigeria. 'Total monetary liabilities' comprises money supply plus quasi-money. The money supply itself is made up of demand deposits plus currency outside banks.

Malaysia. 'Private sector liquidity' comprises money supply plus quasi-money. The latter is made up of fixed savings and other deposits of the private sector; the money supply comprises currency held by the private sector plus demand deposits of the private sector.

The United States of America. In 1980, the U.S.A. changed its methods of measuring the money supply. The old measures concentrated on money within the banking system. But important changes in financial techniques have brought forth many non-banking institutions, such as money market mutual funds which, in 1980, controlled around $40,000m (£17.5m) assets. The new money definitions aim to take these into account.

M1 used to include currency plus demand deposits. It is now divided into M1A and M1B.

M1A comprises currency plus demand deposits minus deposits held by foreign banks and official institutions.

M1B is the broader definition. It comprises M1A plus all deposits in current accounts in United States building societies and other financial institutions.

M2, which used to be roughly the same as the U.K.'s M3, has been broadened. It comprises M1B plus almost all savings accounts plus overnight Eurodollars and money market mutual funds.

M3 has also been broadened. It now includes M2 plus large-denomination time deposits at all institutions. A new measure is also to be introduced called '1' which will include almost all financial liquidity in the economy. M1A and M1B figures will be published weekly; M2, M3 and '1' figures once each month.

1.3 MONEY CREATION

Banks are unique in their ability to create money. This money-creating power arises from the fact that banks keep only a fraction of the money deposited with them. The rest is used for loans to customers, and for other types of investment. Money lent out comes back in the form of new deposits. Providing the bank has enough liquid assets to meet any likely demands for repayment by depositors, this process can continue to a predictable amount. *Example* Assume £100 deposit is paid into Bank A. Bank A, by law or custom, must keep 20% of its deposits in liquid asset form. Bank A starts off with the following balance sheet:

Bank A

£	£
Liabilities	Assets
100 deposit	100 cash reserve

The manager of Bank A is unlikely to allow the £100 to remain in the vaults, but he must keep the required reserve asset ratio of 20% in liquid form. (In the U.K. the required reserve asset ratio for banks is $12\frac{1}{2}$% but it was reduced to 10% in January 1981 to increase liquidity during the tax gathering season.) The manager of Bank A lends out £80 from his new deposit, thus:

£	£
Liabilites	Assets
100 (deposit)	20 (cash)
	80 (loans/advances)

The £80 is spent by the borrower. It comes back to another bank, Bank B. The manager of Bank B does exactly the same as the manager of Bank A: he accepts the deposit of £80, and keeps 20% of it in liquid asset form, while investing/lending the rest. Bank B's balance sheet now looks like this:

Bank B

£	£
Liabilities	Assets
80 (deposit)	16 (cash)
	64 (loans/advances)

The £64 lent by Bank B will be spent on goods/services and the recipient(s) of the £64 will deposit the cash into Bank C. The balance sheet of Bank C will follow the same pattern as that of Bank A and B, thus:

Bank C

£	£
Liabilities	Assets
64 (deposit)	12.8 (cash)
	51.2 (loans/advances)

If we stop to consolidate the accounts of the three banks at this point (and the credit creating process can go on still further), we get a combined balance sheet as follows:

		Liabilites		Assets		
		£		£		
Bank A		100	(deposit)	20 (cash)	80 (advances)	
	B	80		16	64	
	C	64		12.8	51.2	
		244		48.8	195.2	

The above figures show that out of the initial deposit of £100, Banks A, B and C have together created additional deposits of £144. But out of their new total combined deposits fo £244, they have only £48.8 (20% liquid asset ratio) to meet the demands of their depositors. The process of money creation is not yet completed for the £51.2 in Bank C will be lent, passed to Bank D and so on. The final totals when this multiple lending is finished, will be as follows:

Liabilites	Assets	
£	£	
500 (deposits: all banks)	100 (cash)	400 (advances)

Thus an initial deposit multiplies by 100/Reserve Asset Ratio. With a ratio of 25%, £1 deposit grows into a total of £4. With a ratio of 10%, a £1 deposit multiplies into a total of £10. With a ratio of $12\frac{1}{2}$ %, a £1 deposit multiplies into total deposits of £8. The ratio by which an initial deposit will expand, is sometimes referred to as the bank deposit multiplier (Figure 1.1).

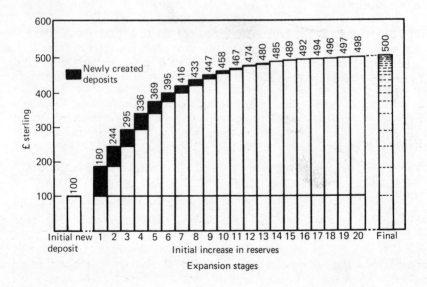

Figure 1.1 Cumulative effect of 100 initial deposit with 20% reserve requirement.

Monetary Expansion created by initial deposit
Mathematically, this can be shown by treating the sum of deposits as a geometric progression to infinity thus:
Let A = the initial deposit
  b = the reserve asset ratio (expressed as a decimal)
  S = the final monetary expansion (sum of deposits plus initial deposit.)
Then,
$$S = \frac{A[1-(1-b)^{\infty}]}{1-(1-b)}$$
As $(1-b)^{\infty} \to 0$, the formula reduces to:
$$S = \frac{A}{1-(1-b)}$$

Example
(i)
Let initial deposit A = £100
reserve asset ratio b = 20% = 0.2
Then $1-b = 0.8$
$$S = \frac{100}{1-0.8} = \frac{100}{0.2} = £500$$

Example
(ii) (U.K. reserve asset ratio)
Let initial deposit A = £100
reserve asset ratio b = $12\frac{1}{2}$% = 0.125
Then $1-b = 0.875$
$$S = \frac{100}{1-0.875} = \frac{100}{0.125} = £800$$

1.4 CONSTRAINTS ON THE CREATION OF CREDIT

There are some obvious limitations to the creation of credit by the banks, e.g. (i) *the demand for loans by customers*. Changes in demand for loans may be the result of the level of interest rates; of inflationary expectations; of Government directives; the level of business confidence. But if customers do. not want loans, the credit-creating process of the banks is curtailed. Loans create deposits. Fewer loans means fewer deposits. Equally obvious as a limit to the creation of credit by the banks is (ii) *the necessity* for them *to keep* to such *reserves* as the law, custom or prudence dictates. The bank's assets must show a level of profitability, security and liquidity. They must also comply with government directives.
Less obvious as restraints are leakages from the banking system such as (iii) *the preference of the public to hold cash rather than deposits*. The more cash the public holds in relation to deposits, the less the ability of the banks to create credit from these diminishing deposits. A similar leakage can be caused by the public preferring to hold their assets in forms (such as physical assets; bonds) other than bank deposits. Initially, this may involve merely a change of ownership of deposits. But demand for bonds raises their price and lowers their yields. This makes them less profitable for banks to buy. It also cheapens the cost of alternative sources of finance. In both cases, the

opportunity for profitable further expansion by the banks, grows less.

(iv) *Transfers to the public sector* similarly create a leakage from the system which restricts the bank's ability to expand credit. A purchase of government securities by a bank will be paid to the Government through the bank's account at the Bank of England. The bank's cash base at the Bank of England falls. If the base goes below a safe minimum, the bank will have to reduce its deposits.

Transfers to the public sector are also caused by higher taxes or a greater volume of import buying or a switch from bank deposits to savings in Government media. All of these transfers reduce the volume of bank deposits. Unless they are balanced by a similar volume of spending by the Government, bank deposits will fall, and restrict the ability of the banks to expand.

(v) *Inter-bank transactions*. Individual banks lose and gain deposits to other banks. An expansionary bank never gets all its own created deposits back. Some are transferred to other banks. The expansionary bank settles with them through the clearing house. This means drawing on its account at the central bank. Its reserves will fall. If they fall below the minimum level, the bank's expansionary policy will have to stop. The total of bank deposits are unaffected—but are redistributed among individual banks.

1.5 MONEY AS A CLAIM

Because bank deposits are bookkeeping entries, it is not always easy to regard them as money. They are obviously less tangible than cash. But they are claims, too, just as a bank note itself is a claim against the bank that issues it. A pound note is a claim against the Bank of England. The Bank acknowledges the claim by the words, "I promise to pay the bearer on demand the sum of one pound", signed by the Bank's Chief Cashier.

A bank deposit is a claim against the bank which accepts it. The deposit becomes a liability against which the bank has a corresponding asset. The bank's liability to its depositor can be used directly as a medium of exchange. It is immediately 'spendable.'

1.6 OTHER FINANCIAL CLAIMS

Why are deposits in a building society not regarded as equally 'spendable'? When money is withdrawn from a building society, it is the same as money drawn from a bank. Why make any distinction? Why should building society deposits not comprise part of the money supply? (They do in some countries.)

The first reason is that bank deposits create money. Building society deposits create houses. The building society passes on the money received from lenders to borrowers who want houses. The bank passes on money received from lenders to borrowers who want money. Some part of this money comes back to the banks and is relent to start a new cycle of lending.

Banks thus play a special role as creators of money. Building societies and similar savings institutions merely pass on funds which have been created elsewhere.

The second reason for suggesting that the liabilities of the banks are money, while those of the building societies are not, is as follows: The liabilities of banks are money because they are acceptable in payment of debt. The building society depositor might argue that his savings are no different from a current account in the bank. He can withdraw them (often more conveniently), just as he can withdraw his current account money from the bank. So where is the difference? It can be summed up by the word *transferability*. The bank account is immediately transferable in payment of debt or as a medium of exchange. The use of the cheque highlights the difference. An account holder in a building society cannot transfer his savings to another person for payment of goods and/or services. He must first take out his money and then use it for the purpose(s) desired. Because the owners cannot directly transfer their savings in building societies, and similar financial 'intermediaries' that are not banks, such deposits are classed not as money, but quasi-money — nearly money but not quite.

Technically, money in the U.K. should consist of M1 only, with the additional items making up M3 being classed as quasi-money. The latter, consisting of time and public sector deposits and non-sterling deposits lack what might be called immediate 'spendability'. The International Monetary Fund emphasizes this distinction between M1 and M3. To aid international comparability, it defines the narrow aggregate M1 as money, and the extra items in M3 as quasi-money.

Nevertheless, in the U.K., it has been found easier to class as money, all those direct claims against the banks, which are listed in the U.K. money supply. Deposits in other financial institutions such as building societies, are excluded. Their totals do however provide additional liquidity in the economy and thus reduce the demand for bank money.

1.6.1 EXAMPLES OF FINANCIAL CLAIMS

Payment can be made from the money stock by means of the *cheque*. This is not money but a claim to it: a written instruction to the bank or National Giro to pay money owed to a depositor or to his nominee.

Postal Orders act like cheques in that they transfer a certain sum to a named person. One person pays for the order over the post office counter and transfers this claim for money to another.

Less important means of payment include *luncheon vouchers* which are similar to meal tickets, but have the advantage to the employee of being at least partly tax-free. There are also *gift tokens* of various kinds by which a person buys a paper claim to goods of a specified amount. The advantage of such tokens is that the claim for goods which they represent can be transferred to other persons and look more attractive than postal orders which are claims for money. *Standing Orders* are instructions to banks or the National Giro to pay out certain sums at regular intervals to specified persons or groups.

Most means of payment in use are in the form of promises to pay in the future. *Credit cards* are issued by credit card organizations as well as the commercial banks. They enable goods bought today to be paid for over a period of time at a higher total cost. The difference between the cash and credit price is the payment made to the credit company or bank that lends the cash.

A Bill of Exchange is a promise to pay on or before a certain future date, a certain sum of money to a specified person. Their use today is governed by the Bills of Exchange Act 1882. The primary function of the Bill is to enable a seller to obtain cash immediately he has despatched his goods whilst, at the same time, the buyer can defer payment until the goods reach him. A charge is made for this service by specialized institutions known as merchant banks.

Another form of a promise to pay a certain sum in the future is the *Treasury Bill*. The promise is made by the Government, and there is not, as with the Bill of Exchange, a direct link between goods and payment; hence the Treasury Bill is regarded as a loan to the Government for a period of 91 days on terms the Government tries to arrange to its best advantage.

1.6.2 FINANCIAL CLAIMS REGARDED AS MONEY

Financial claims can only be regarded as money if they perform the four functions of money.

Assets which have some money functions such as a store of value or standard for deferred payments are classed as 'near' or quasi-money. In the U.K., they include Bills of Exchange, foreign currency deposits in banks and sterling deposits in institutions other than banks. However, from a public policy viewpoint, the classification of money is not quite so simple. Some quasi-money is very easily 'translated' into the real thing: building society deposits are a good example. They can be taken out as quickly as can M1 bank deposits, often with more convenience for the retail customer. They add to the volume of total liquidity. A collective spending spree by holders will fuel inflation as much (or as little) as the use of any equivalent purchasing power. To their owners, at least, they are as much 'money' as time deposits in the bank. Purists might argue that if M1 exists in isolation and yet M3 includes M1 then a new version of money stock M4 should include building society deposits plus M3. The hazard here is not one of analysis alone but of accounting, and double counting. Can we pinpoint exactly the proportion of building society deposits already included in M3?

Building societies provide housing finance but, like other saving agents, they must keep their surplus funds somewhere. If those funds are not exchanged for physical assets and are not allowed to seep overseas then they must end up as public or private sector bank deposits in the U.K.

Money provides a mechanism for the liquidation of debt: payments for goods and services. It has grades of acceptability for this purpose, depending on (i) the time needed for convertibility into an acceptable medium and (ii) the value received in exchange. Legal tender money is immediately acceptable and suffers no loss in exchange. Other financial debts and claims such as stocks and shares, insurance policies and building society deposits, need time for conversion or transference; some may suffer loss in the process. Hence, technically they are regarded as quasi money — just as a £1 note is regarded as money and a Treasury bill is not.

1.7 THE ECONOMIC IMPORTANCE OF MONEY

Modern economists give far greater weight to the role of money in the economy than did the classical economists. Thus, John Stuart Mill wrote, "There cannot, in short, be intrinsically, a more insignificant thing in the economy of society than money: except in the character of a contrivance for sparing time and labour. It is a machine for doing quickly and commodiously, what would be done, though less quickly and commodiously, without it; and like many other types of machinery, it only exerts a distinct and independent influence of its own when it gets out of order".

Money makes possible the price system and so avoids the disadvantages of barter. It helps adjust production to the wants of the community as expressed through their purchases. In this way, resources are maximized and specialization takes place. In its store-of-value role, money enables liquid wealth to be stored and transferred. Investment and saving become possible and lead to the development of financial institutions. These play a *passive* role in the transference of claims and assets. They also play a *dynamic* role by supplying or restricting credit and so expanding or contracting the supply of money and the growth of the economy.

When money functions inadequately, or its distribution is fossilized into extremes of wealth and poverty, grave social and economic repercussions result. Both from the viewpoints of social justice and of economic efficiency, it is therefore necessary to ensure that money serves the community and does not paralyse or destroy it.

SOURCES OF CAPITAL

See attached list of groups willing to lend (Figure 1.2).

TYPICAL QUESTION

Examine the effects of an increase in the supply of money on the level of prices, employment, interest rates, and foreign exchange rates.

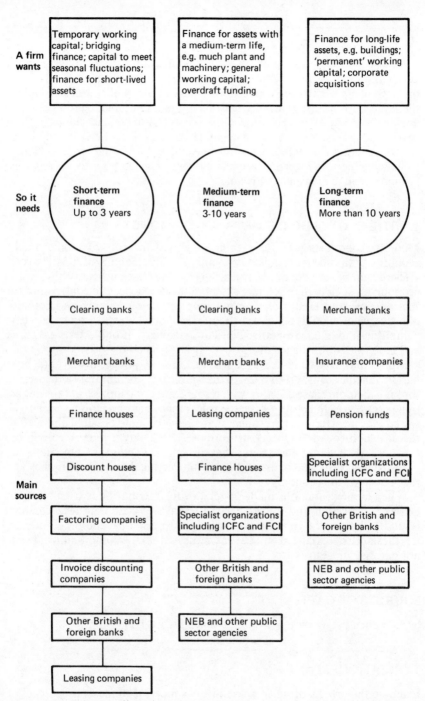

Figure 1.2 Quick guide to sources of finance (from *Money for Business*, pp. 26 – 27, Bank of England and City Communications Centre).

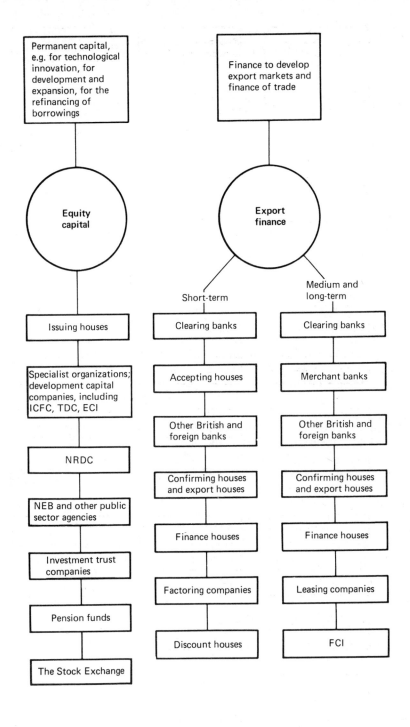

Permanent capital, e.g. for technological innovation, for development and expansion, for the refinancing of borrowings

Finance to develop export markets and finance of trade

Equity capital

Export finance

Short-term

Medium and long-term

Issuing houses	Clearing banks	Clearing banks
Specialist organizations; development capital companies, including ICFC, TDC, ECI	Accepting houses	Merchant banks
NRDC	Other British and foreign banks	Other British and foreign banks
NEB and other public sector agencies	Confirming houses and export houses	Confirming houses and export houses
Investment trust companies	Finance houses	Finance houses
Pension funds	Factoring companies	Leasing companies
The Stock Exchange	Discount houses	FCI

SUGGESTED ANSWER

An increase in the supply of money raises price and employment levels and lowers interest and exchange rates. The extent of such changes depends on the state of the economy.

During a situation of full employment, an increase in the money supply will mean more money being available for the same amount of goods. Prices tend to rise, with real national product unchanged. During a period of low resource utilization, however, an expanded money supply affects output more than prices.

The usual effect of an increased money supply on interest rates is to bring them down. The community holds its liquid claims in the pattern it considers best. When money supply expands, bank deposits increase and, as a consequence, liquidity preference falls. The public, preferring to hold less money, exchanges it for other assets. This results in bond prices going up and interest rates going down.

Exceptional factors operated during the period from Autumn 1971 onwards, so that, though the money supply rose during the last quarter of 1971 by $5\frac{3}{4}$ % to reach a total of £20,280 million, interest rates did not fall. Credit expanded as a result of (a) structural changes in the banking system in 1971, (b) more issues of certificates of deposits. This expansion meant that the Government had to finance its requirements through the non-bank public to avoid further inflating the money supply.

Government securities must have a sufficiently attractive interest rate to compete with other investment opportunities and to induce the public to part with money in exchange for bonds. People will not lend capital unless the rate of interest compensates for the erosion of real value caused by inflation. This is why, during a period of monetary expansion, Bank rate kept at 5% and interest rates did not fall. It also explains the high level of interest rates in 1979 – 80.

Finally, the effect on a country's exchange rates of an increase in the supply of money, is to lower them. If the inflation rate is higher in the home country (prices are rising there more quickly) demand for that country's goods and therefore for that country's currency, will fall. At the same time, there will be an increased demand, due to higher home prices, for cheaper imported goods again causing a strain on exchange rates which any outflow of capital will exacerbate. The result will be a lowering of the country's exchange parity when a floating rate is operating, or a drain on the country's reserves to bolster up a fixed exchange rate.

ADDITIONAL QUESTIONS

1. In what ways does the existence of money facilitate the working of an economy?

2. Define the measure of the money supply known as M3.

3. (a) State both the narrow and broad definitions of the money supply as used by many central banks.

(b) Many British firms issue luncheon vouchers to office staff. These vouchers can be exchanged only in cafes and restaurants for food. In what ways, if any, can such vouchers be considered to be money?

4. What forms of asset are generally regarded as being money? Why are others excluded? Illustrate your answer with reference to any country with a developed monetary system.

5. 'Official control of the money supply should be aimed at the level of bank deposits, leaving the note issue to find its own level.' Discuss, with reference to communities in different stages of development.

2 Theoretical Aspects of Money

This chapter looks at some theoretical aspects of money: the raw materials which those institutions discussed in Chapters 3 and 4, deal in and create.

2.1 NATIONAL INCOME

We begin with the concept of national income. This can be defined as the money value of the flow of goods and services produced in a given period of time. Many economists, particularly the Monetarists, link changes in the money supply with changes in National Income.

In a modern economy, money exchanges for goods and services and therefore flows in the opposite direction to them. Thus:

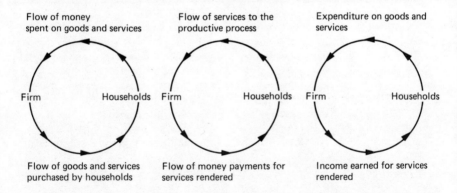

Flow of money spent on goods and services — Firm — Households — Flow of goods and services purchased by households

Flow of services to the productive process — Firm — Households — Flow of money payments for services rendered

Expenditure on goods and services — Firm — Households — Income earned for services rendered

Money passes from households to firms in exchange for goods and services. It is passed on by firms in payment for services rendered. The flow of money is a circular one. It passes out of firms as wages, profit, interest, rent. It goes back again as spending on products. This concept of a flow shows one man's spending as another man's income. Payments by one group are receipts by another. National income equals national expenditure.

If households receive no income, they can do no spending. If they do no spending, firms will have no customers. If they have no customers, firms will not produce. If the firms do not produce, there will be no goods and no wages paid and so on. So, unless the government steps in as a purchaser, taking the place of the absent private purchaser, national income will fall.

The aggregate expenditure of households and firms equals the aggregate income of households and firms which equals the money value of the aggregate output. In other words, national expenditure equals national income equals national output. (Another phrase for national income is net national product: that is gross national product after an allowance has been made for depreciation).

The level of the circular flow of income/expenditure may rise or fall. Changes in the levels affect saving, investment and employment. The flow remains static, neither rising nor falling, when withdrawals from the flow equal injections into the flow, or viewed another way, when aggregate monetary demand equals national income.

Spending on consumer goods is called consumption (C). Consumer goods are those which are lost to the economy after the time period over which the national income is being measured. Spending on capital goods is called investment (I). Capital goods are those which add to the capital stock of the economy and are not used up over the time period. Spending by government (G) is another form of spending and covers any type of spending by the public sector.

The circular flow of income can grow larger by injections (J). These are additions to the income of households which do not arise from the spending of firms, and additions to the income of firms which do not arise from the spending of households. Government spending is such an injection. Investment adds to incomes without any change in the spending of households on goods and services. It is thus classed as an injection. Exports provide extra income for households and firms (X). They are also injections.

The circular flow of income diminishes when there are withdrawals (W). Withdrawals occur when income is not passed on in the circular flow to firms through spending by households; or to households through spending by firms. Savings (S), taxes (T) and imports (M) are withdrawals.

Suppose, for example, households do not spend all the income they receive, but save some. Further suppose, that the institution where they deposit those savings finds no suitable investment medium for them, and holds on to the money. National income will fall. There has been a leakage by savings from the circular flow. Aggregate spending still equals aggregate income, but the circle of flowing money is smaller. If the government imposes taxes, the income received by households and firms will be less. Unless the government spends the taxes in public works, the circular flow of income will again contract.

Finally, some part of the flow of income may seep abroad. If money is spent on imports, foreigners receive the cash. That is yet another leakage from the national circular flow.

The circular flow will increase when there is more spending by households, government or business investors. Export earnings will also add to the circular flow. This analysis means that the Government can counteract a leakage from the system by an injection, or counteract an inflationary trend by a withdrawal.

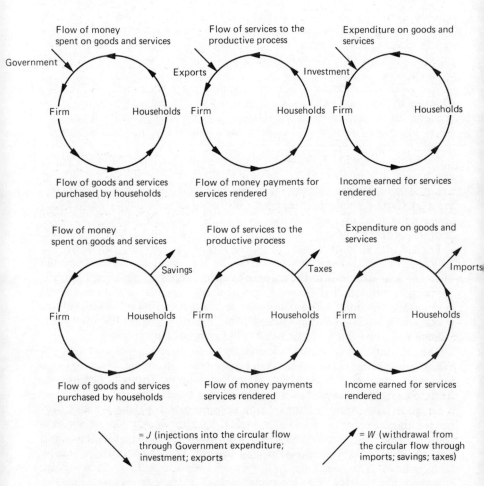

If total injections (J) are greater than total withdrawals, the total or national income expands. If total withdrawals are greater than total injections, the circular flow will diminish. Equilibrium occurs when injections equal withdrawals. Equilibrium need not coincide with full employment level and will persist until W or J alter. On this point of equilibrium between demand and supply, whether for goods, for money or for labour, Keynes moved away from the classical economists. Theirs was a long-run analysis. Keynes was interested in finding short-run solutions to the problem of unemployment, i.e. the disparity between the demand for and supply of labour; and equally interested in what caused an equilibrium between the demand for and supply of money.

People could alter their ideas on how much to save. Investors could alter their plans on how much they intended to invest. The balance of payments would sometimes be in deficit, sometimes in surplus. The Government could have a budget surplus with their revenue exceeding expenditure; or a deficit, with their expenditure exceeding revenue. Any such changes increased or diminished the circular flow. A rise in W or a fall in J reduced aggregate (national) income. A rise in J or a fall in W raised national income. But injections into and leakages from the system had a *compounded* effect. They increased or decreased national income by more than the sum injected/withdrawn. They had a *multiplier* effect.

The Multiplier measured changes in the size of national income brought about by changes in J. Savings and consumption depend largely on income levels. If income rises, a proportion of the extra income will be spent on consumption. This proportion is known as the marginal propensity to consume (*MPC*). The proportion saved (or withdrawn) from the extra income is known as the marginal propensity to save, or withdraw (*MPS* or *MPW*). What is not consumed is saved, so that *MPW* + *MPC* equals 1, and the multiplier equals 1/*MPW*. Mathematically, the multiplier was

$$\frac{\text{the change in national income}}{\text{the change in injections}}, \text{ i.e. } \frac{\Delta Y}{\Delta J}$$

Thus, if as a result of extra Government spending of £10m, national income reached a new equilibrium £100m higher than previously, the multiplier would be 10.

Example

Assume an economy is in equilibrium. There are idle resources. The Government now raises its spending by £10m. J exceeds W by £10m. The economy is in disequilibrium. How is it to be brought into equilibrium again? National income must rise until an extra £10m has been withdrawn from the circular flow and J again equals W. If the marginal propensity to save (withdraw) is 1/10 the multiplier will be 10 and national income will rise by £100m as follows:

	National income £m	Marginal propensity to consume 9/10 £m	Marginal propensity to withdraw 1/10 £m
(a)	10	9.0	1.0
(b)	9	8.1	.9
(c)	8.1	7.29	.81

	National income	Marginal propensity to consume 9/10	Marginal propensity to withdraw 1/10
	£m	£m	£m
(d)	7.29	6.561	.729
(e)	6.561	....	.....
(f)	....	....	.....
etc.			
Total	£100.00	£90.00	£10.00

(a) £10m has gone into the circular flow. Of this 1/10 is withdrawn by taxes, imports or savings (£1m). The rest is spent (£9m). This consumption spending is received by another group (b) who spend 9/10 of the £9m (£8.1m) while 1/10 (£9m) is withdrawn. This process continues until the circular flow reaches £100 and withdrawals total £10m, which equals the amount of the original injection.

The multiplier also works negatively so that withdrawals (saving, taxation, imports) are multiplied in the same fashion.

The idea of the circular flow of national income meant that budgets could be used to steer the economy in the direction that a government wished it to go. During a period of falling prices, the budget had to be reflationary (a budget deficit). During a period of rising prices, the budget had to be deflationary (a budget surplus). Governments thus had the power through their revenue and expenditure to change the level of national income and of employment.

Until Keynes expounded these ideas, the reaction to falling prices and unemployment, was to save money. In the U.K. in the depression years, teachers and civil servants were asked to take cuts in their pay to help the nation. Keynes insisted that deflation was caused by too little purchasing power, by a lack of income, not too much. The government could raise the level of national income. If they did, the result would be firstly a decrease in unemployment. As full employment was reached, the effect of an increased national income would be felt on prices. The money value of the national income would rise. So there had to be some fine tuning to get the effects desired.

The Accelerator is another form of geometric expansion. It is seen in the capital goods industries where a change in consumption leads to a multiplied or accelerated change in the number of machines needed to make those consumption goods.

Investment is a function of change in income. If income changes, so will consumption and investment. Demand for capital goods derives from the demand for consumption goods. Changes in the latter lead to changes in the former, but at an accelerated rate. This is because investment in machines consists of two elements (a) replacement, (b) the purchase of new machines to meet the higher demand.

Example

A factory has 50 machines. Each produces 400 chocolates. Ten machines are replaced each year.

	Demand for chocolates	Machines needed	New machines needed	Replacement machines	Gross Investment
Year 1	20,000	50	—	+ 10	10
2	24,000	60	10	+ 10	20
3	28,000	70	10	+ 10	20
4	30,000	75	5	+ 10	15

Note

(i) In Year 2 demand for chocolate increases by 20% but gross investment increases by 100%.

(ii) To maintain the new level of investment, the demand for chocolates must increase by the same absolute amount, that is by 4000 per year.

(iii) If the rate of increase in the demand for chocolates slows down, the investment level will fall.

2.2 ECONOMIC FLUCTUATIONS

Fluctuations in economic growth which the accelerator theory tried to explain were sometimes grouped into 3 types: (a) business or trade cycles of about 9 years' duration from peak to peak; (b) an inventory cycle lasting 18 months to 3 years and (c) a long-wave cycle of around 50 years.

2.2.1 BUSINESS OR TRADE CYCLE

Four phases were distinguished in the trade cycle:

(a) Depression with heavy unemployment; unused resources; a fall in price levels and in profits.

(b) Recovery when the lower turning point is reached and employment, income, profits and spending rise. New investment takes place. Prices no longer fall but stay constant or rise.

(c) Boom. Resources become fully utilized. Prices rise. Shortages appear. Demand for investment funds rise and so do interest rates.

(d) Recession. After the upper turning point, the boom gives way to recession. Demand, profits, prices and incomes fall. Depression sets in again.

2.2.1.1 *Causes of business/trade cycles*

Various theories have been put forward to account for trade or business cycles:

(a) The theory of *cumulative upswings and downswings* concentrates on the multiplier, accelerator and self-realizing expectations.

(b) That of *floors and ceilings* postulates a ceiling to national income in the form of full employment. Once that point is reached, only new investment will increase output. Similarly, national income never sinks to zero because in any economy there must be some minimum replacement level of investment.

(c) *The theory of instability* suggests that changes in investment before the top or bottom of a cycle, set up an endless cyclical instability in the economy.

2.2.2 THE INVENTORY CYCLE

The inventory cycle lasts for 18 months to 3 years and is explained mainly by the accelerator mechanism. Investment in stocks (inventories) is similar to investment in capital goods and is a function of income. When sales fall, stocks accumulate. Manufacturers cut production below the level of current sales to reduce stock. Income and sales fall still further. When stocks reach the desired level, production will be below the level of current sales. It will have to be increased. Output goes up. Recovery begins.

2.2.3 THE LONG-WAVE CYCLE

This long-wave cycle is sometimes called the Kondratieff cycle after the Russian-born economist of that name who described it. Schumpeter, too, investigated these long-term cycles of about 50 years, which were preceded by periods of great innovation.

Business or trade cycles were a long-term phenomenon. Keynes wanted a short-term solution to the problem of unemployment. He argued that governments could, by their budgetary decisions, raise the level of spending and thus of national income. A government could counteract a leakage from the system by an injection; could counteract an inflationary trend by a withdrawal. Governments had the power through their fiscal policies to stabilize the economy. If private investment were insufficient, the government should increase its own spending. National income would then rise; unemployment would fall. When resources were all fully utilized, the impact of increased Government spending would be felt on prices.

2.3 ECONOMIC GROWTH

Inflation has been ascribed to many causes: an increase in the money supply; increases in wages or commodity prices; lack of import controls; increases in aggregate demand. By a *reductio ad absurdam* method, some part of the truth can be clearly seen: Assume all output ceases. People continue to receive incomes. If incomes remain the same while the volume of goods diminishes, the price of the rapidly dwindling store of goods must go up. Eventually one group will have money; the other will have goods. Those goods which are not consumable will be brought over and over again through higher and higher offers of money.

There is a relationship between output, i.e. the production of goods, and the money available to buy them. But, money is used more than once. Hence, money supply cannot only be thought of as a stock: it must also be considered a flow which takes in the concept of velocity. On the other side, what causes output to rise? What stimulates production and economic growth?

If economic growth is defined as the growth of output of goods and services per head of population, it can be seen that this output depends on two factors: (a) natural resources and (b) human behaviour. About the former, little can be done. Countries are like people: some have more natural advantages than others. Even when natural resources are available for economic growth, their utilization depends on human behaviour and knowledge. The factors which influence human behaviour towards economic growth can be summed up as follows:

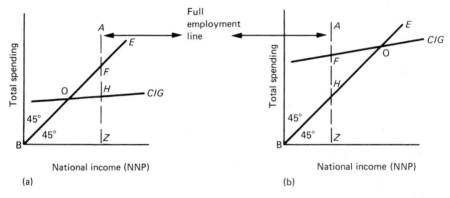

National income (NNP)

(a)

National income (NNP)

(b)

Figure 2.1 The diagrams represent the total income and spending of a country with neither exports nor imports. The only injections are investment and government; the only withdrawals, savings and taxes. In (a) and (b), the equilibrium level of national income (where total spending equals total income) is at point 0. But in neither case is the point 0 at full employment level.

(a) Deflationary gap. Total spending (consumption, government spending and investment = *CIG* line) equals total income at point 0. But this total spending is not enough to ensure full employment (the vertical line *AZ*). There is therefore a 'deflationary gap' at *FH* which measures the amount of extra spending necessary to bring total spending into equilibrium with total income (NNP) at the full employment level.

(b) Inflationary gap. Total spending (consumption, government spending and investment = *CIG* line) equals total income at point 0. But this total spending is greater than the full employment level (the vertical line *AZ*). There is therefore an inflationary gap at *FH* which measures the amount of extra saving necessary to bring total spending into equilibrium with total income (NNP) at the full employment level.

(a) The effort to economize, which means the effort to maximize output and minimize cost and all the effort which goes along with those aims such as risk-taking; innovation; geographical and occupational mobility.

(b) There must be institutions and attitudes which encourage the effort to 'economize'. Rewards in status or material benefits must be sufficient; conventions and attitudes must not act as a barrier to innovation.

(c) There must be governments and/or other institutions which encourage saving and investment.

W.W. Rostow gave five stages of economic growth through which countries passed to full development. Only in the third stage are savings and investment emphasized. The stages he outlined were

(a) the traditional society;
(b) the pre-take-off;
(c) take-off;
(d) maturity;
(e) high mass-consumption.

Maturity came for Britain around 1850; for France, Germany and the U.S.A. around 1910; Sweden around 1930, Japan around 1940, Canada and Russia in the 1950s.

These views link economic growth with innovation and investment. Capital stimulates and implements ideas. It does not create them. However, the infrastructure of a modern economy would be impossible without capital, as would the development of large-scale enterprises. But, in these cases, extra output results from an increased money supply; growth is matched by investment. The conclusion is simple. All forms of money must be exchangeable into something equally acceptable by the holder of the money. If money supply increases and the goods or services for which it can be exchanged, do not increase, or do not appear likely to increase in the future, then the prices of goods must rise and the value of money will fall.

2.4 SUMMARY

2.4.1 NATIONAL INCOME

Consumer demand determines output, and hence employment. If aggregate demand (expenditure) increases, so will output and employment. Aggregate demand/expenditure, sometimes called Aggregate Monetary Demand (AMD), consists of consumption (C) + injections (investment, government expenditure, exports) − withdrawals (savings + imports + taxation) = the money value of the Gross National product i.e. AMD = National Income. When there are more planned injections than planned withdrawals, national income expands; when there are more planned withdrawals than injections, national income contracts. Expansion leads to greater output and employment unless resources are fully utilized, when prices will rise.

2.4.2 SAVING AND INVESTMENT

Investment affects the size of the national income and the level of employ-

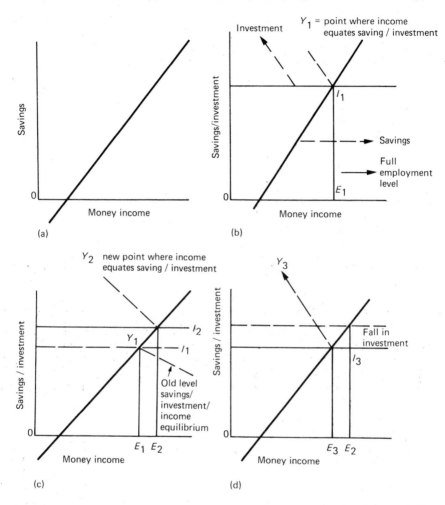

Figure 2.2   (a) People cannot save what they do not have. *Savings depend on income.* Aggregate savings depend on aggregate (national) income.

(b) *Investment depends* on the *rate of interest* and the *marginal efficiency of capital* — not on income. Only one level of national income will equate savings with investment (Y_1).

(c) If investment increases (I_2), higher incomes in (1) the capital goods industries result (accelerator effect) and then in (2) others. Savings get pulled up to equal investment at a new level (Y_2).

(d) Investment falls; pulls income down; savings equal investment at a new lower level (Y_3).

ment. Classical economists believed that changes in the interest rate corrected disequilibria between saving and investment.

Keynesian economists believe interest rate to play a minor role in adjusting saving and investment. If an economy is in equilibrium, they argue, any increase in investment causes national income to rise until additional saving equal to the extra investment was generated. The size of the change in the national income would be determined by the multiplier. Other influences on investment were the level of income, the rate of change of income (the accelerator) and business expectations. (See Graphical summary. . . . .)

Questions on saving, investment or national income are not often set in the *Applied Economics* examination of the Institute of Bankers, though they do appear in earlier examinations. A few short test questions therefore follow.

A FEW SHORT TEST QUESTIONS

1. What factors can affect the level of investment?
2. What function did the rate of interest perform in classical economics?
3. What conditions were necessary for the rate of interest to perform as in question 2?
4. Assume there is an increase in the desire to save. What would be the consequences according to (a) the classical theory (b) the Keynesian theory?
5. What would be the mutliplier if, of extra income received, the following amounts were spent: $\frac{4}{5}$, $\frac{3}{5}$, $\frac{2}{3}$ 1?

A FEW SHORT ANSWERS

1. The size of national income, the rate of interest, the rate of change of national income, and business expectations.
2. It equated savings and investment without any changes in national income.
3. If more is invested when interest rate falls; if more is saved when interest rate rises; if the investment curve is interest-elastic; if the interest rate can move freely.
4. (a) Interest rates would fall; investment would tend to rise until savings = investment.
   (b) Savings rise; national income falls. Savings decrease until once again they equal investment at the original level.
5. W = $\frac{1}{5}$ Multiplier = 5
   W = $\frac{2}{5}$ Multiplier = $2\frac{1}{2}$
   W = $\frac{1}{3}$ Multiplier = 3
   W = 1   Multiplier = 1

3 Financial Institutions in the United Kingdom: the Commercial Banks

3.1 WHAT IS A BANK?

A financial institution lends, accepts or transmits money. The *commercial banks* do all of these things. They also *create* money. This function, unique to banks, distinguishes them from other financial institutions. It makes them more important for two reasons (a) they can affect the growth of *individual industries*. Their ability to give or withhold credit, aids or restricts *specific kinds of development*. (b) The creation of credit also affects the *whole economy*, for 90% of the country's total money supply consists of bank deposits created by bank advances.

It is easy to see how important banks are; difficult to define what a bank is. The classic U.K. definition, "a body of persons, whether incorporated or not, carrying on the business of banking . . ."* adds nothing to our knowledge of banks or bankers. However, the Protection of Depositors Act 1963, provides a clue, for it forbids the use of the words, 'bank', 'bankers', or 'banking', in advertising except from institutions recognized as 'banks'.

Hence, there are obviously institutions recognized as banks. How did they achieve recognition? Until 1967, only two types of legal recognition counted (a) by the Inland Revenue for the purpose of distributing interest gross of income tax, and (b) a listing under Schedule 8 of the Companies Act, 1948.

A legal anomaly was revealed by the case of *United Dominions Trust* v *Kirkwood*, 1966. This led to a new basis of banking recognition. Under Section 123 of the Companies Act 1967, companies claiming to be banks, had to apply for certificates from the Department of Trade and Industry. These licenses exempted them from the provisions of the Moneylenders Acts 1900 – 1927. To obtain this most elemental recognition as a bank, companies needed (a) a minimum capital of £100,000, (b) competent management; (c) satisfactory banking experience and (d) a significant current account business.

---

*Bills of Exchange Act 1882.

Not surprisingly, an odd selection of companies crept in through Section 123 and came out as 'banks'. During a time of strict lending controls on other institutions, they expanded their activities.

More prestigious were the '127' banks. The Companies Act 1967, which had allowed the spawning of '123' banks, extended Schedule 8 (Section 127) to include any company satisfying the Department of Trade and Industry that it should be treated as a bank or discount company for the purpose of the Act.

Banks with '127' status had to obey various controls administered by the Bank of England and the Treasury, e.g. the percentage of assets which had to be held against liabilities; special deposits and directives.

There were thus two groups of commercial banks by 1967: those with '123' certificates and those with '127' status. Additionally, 'authorized' banks were allowed to deal in foreign exchange under the Exchange Control Act 1947. Finally, as a result of Competition and Credit Control 1971, came 'statistical' banks, an intermediate class from whom the Bank of England collected and collated information on such subjects as the money supply, level of advances and so on, and which were regarded as banks for the purposes of complying with official controls. Authorized and statistical banks overlapped the 123 and 127 category of bank.

Other ways of classifying U.K. banks have been attempted with varying degrees of success, e.g. wholesale and retail banking.

Wholesale banks cover all those banks which accept and lend large sums of money. They include merchant banks, overseas banks, foreign banks in London and other money market banks. They deal in the local authority market, certificates of deposit, the eurodollar market, the interbank market and similar large funds.

Retail banks are those such as high street branches of the clearing banks. They lend to and accept deposits from individuals and companies in smaller sums. Large deposits are not excluded from retail banks, but the interest paid is not competitive. By April, 1977, (Barclays Bank Briefing, April 1977) ordinary deposit accounts under £5000, provided one half of all interest-bearing deposits in the banks. In retail banking, loans are also of fairly small amounts, though a branch manager usually has discretion to lend up to £50,000 on his own authority. Larger loans need Head Office approval.

Perhaps the best way of defining a commercial bank, that is a bank which operates primarily for profit, is by its *function*. What does the bank *do*? The Banking Act 1979 created a system of recognized banks and licensed deposit takers. 'Recognized' banks can be categorized into the following groups: (a) Deposit banks; (b) Acceptance houses, also known as merchant banks; (c) Other British banks; (d) Overseas banks (American); (e) Japanese (f) Other (g) Consortium banks; (h) National Savings banks; (i) the National Giro; (j) The Trustee Savings banks. All these banks, save the National Savings Bank, maintain a minimum reserve ratio of $12\frac{1}{2}$%. (k) Discount houses keep other asset ratios. They are unique British institutions which act as bankers to the banks and as intermediaries between them and the Bank of England.

3.17 DEPOSIT BANKS

3.1.1.1 *London and Scottish clearing banks*

The functions of deposit banks are to accept deposits, to grant loans, provide account keeping and money transmission services. The largest and most important deposit banks in the U.K. are members of the centralized clearing system, the Bankers Clearing House, through which the majority of cheques are cleared. Until 1975, there were six English and three Scottish clearing banks covering 95% of the banking offices through 12,000 branches. The six English clearing banks are members of the Committee of London Clearing Bankers.

(i) Barclays Bank
(ii) Coutts and Co. (a subsidiary of National Westminster)
(iii) Lloyds Bank
(iv) Midland Bank
(v) National Westminster Bank
(vi) Williams and Glyn's Bank

The three Scottish clearing banks are members of the Committee of Scottish Clearing Bankers:

(i) Royal Bank of Scotland (a subsidiary of National and Commercial Group)
(ii) Bank of Scotland (part owned by Barclays)
(iii) Clydesdale Bank (subsidiary of Midland).

In October 1975, the Co-operative Bank became a functional member of the Clearing House, the first bank to join since 1936. This new entrant was followed a month later, in November 1975, by the Central Trustee Savings Bank acting as agent for the Trustee Savings Banks. Formerly purely savings banks, T.S.B.'s have developed into fully fledged domestic banks (see Chapter 3.1.21). Neither the T.S.B.s, nor the Co-op Bank are members of the Committee of Clearing Banks: they have direct clearing facilities but the Co-op Bank is listed by the Bank of England, like most other non-clearers with majority U.K. ownership, under *other British banks*.

Deposits are accepted from the public firstly by *current account*. No interest is paid on such accounts. Even the Co-operative Bank, which paid interest on such accounts, was forced in 1977 to give up the practice because of the high cost of maintaining and servicing current accounts.

In 1970, over half of the sterling deposits of the clearing banks were in current accounts. By 1977, the proportion had fallen to 40%. The decrease was due to (a) increasing sophistication of banking customers (b) higher interest rates and the greater attraction of interest-bearing deposits elsewhere (c) innovations such as credit cards which have led people to economize in the use of current accounts.

On *deposit accounts*, interest is paid, but it is not always competitive. As a result, the fastest-growing institutions for interest-bearing deposits have been the building societies. In their evidence to the Wilson committee, the clearing banks pointed out that the share of sterling deposits going to all the clearing banks fell from 49% to 35.4% over the period 1962 — 1976, while that of the building societies rose from 21% — 38%. It can be estimated that the proportion of total personal wealth (financial assets) held in the form of bank deposits was 10.3% in 1966 and 13.6% in 1976, whereas building society deposits accounted for 8.2% of personal wealth (financial assets) in 1966 but 17.7% in 1976. By January 1980, building society deposits totalled £45,601m; bank deposits (sterling) £76,886m.

Savings banks and insurance companies have fiscal and regulatory advantages for deposits which are denied to the banks. Building societies are favoured by the tax system. By 1978, they held 48% of the liquid assets of the personal sector compared with 30.5% for the clearing banks, 14.5% for National Savings and 7% for the T.S.B.s. Although the banks' profitability is usually higher, they have to achieve it on a much larger asset base. The following example illustrates this point. With a return on total assets of 1.36%, the Abbey National Building Society achieved £74m pretax profits; with a return of 1.44% on its total assets, the Midland Bank achieved £193m pretax profits (1977 figures). The profitability of the banks depends on the interest rate differential between their assets and liabilities times volume minus administration costs.

There are advantages to the banks in taking deposit accounts, even in small sums, for deposit accounts are relatively *stable*, but the competition is now for wholesale deposits. This development owes something to official restrictions in September 1973. Banks had to 'observe a limit of $9\frac{1}{2}$% on the rate of interest which they paid on deposits in amounts of under £10,000'. The purpose of this Bank of England directive was concern for the 'finance of housing', and to protect building societies from competition for deposits. The large flows of money resulting from the oil-price rises has also encouraged the development of the wholesale money market. As a result, clearing banks are competing for larger deposits. They have acquired stakes in hire purchase companies, and extended the whole range of their services to include factoring, merchant banking, insurance broking, computer payroll services, unit trusts and credit cards.

The money transmission and account keeping function of the deposit banks enables payment to be made at any bank in the United Kingdom. This is one of the advantages of economies of scale, as is the ability to use funds between branches to offset seasonal and other flows. In 1979, over 1,310 million debit clearings and over 195 million credit clearings went through the Bankers' Clearing House, while the Bankers' Automated Clearing Services dealt with 234 million standing orders and other credit transfers, value £49m, and 152 million direct debits worth £19m.

With the Scottish clearing system, dating from 1892, and applied to the banks in Scotland, this gives Britain one of the most sophisticated and efficient money transfer system in the world.

Loans by the banks provide a substantial source of funds for public companies. During times of high inflation, loan stock is not a good investment for lenders. Greater bank advances are needed to finance replacement of assets and stock at inflated prices, but high interest rates have some deterrent effect. During the years 1972 — 1974, bank borrowing provided 29 — 31% of companies' funds. By 1980, it ranged between 14% and 16%.

The problem for companies was not the difficulty of raising finance, as it had been earlier; it was that banks were trying to persuade companies to borrow/invest. Money was there (Figure 1.2 gives a list) from bank subsidiaries as well as public corporations, consortium banks, city institutions and insurance companies, though not always on the terms and for the length that companies require. Lending, primarily short-term, is the banks' business. If they cannot do this profitably at home because (a) depositors are switching their money elsewhere (b) companies are unwilling to borrow on the terms or for the time span offered, the banks will look for international and other business. Here, the competition is intense.

3.1.1.2 *The Northern Irish Banks*

Allied Irish Banks (including Provincial Bank of Ireland): Northern Ireland offices

Bank of Ireland (Northern Ireland offices)

Northern Bank Ltd., Ulster Bank Ltd.

Banking in Northern Ireland is carried on mainly by subsidiaries of London clearing banks. The Ulster Bank is a subsidiary of National Westminster: the Northern Bank is a subsidiary of the Midland. There is no exchange control betwen the United Kingdom, Northern Ireland and the Republic of Ireland. Banks such as the Bank of Ireland and the Allied Irish banks with head offices in the Republic, have offices in the U.K. for the benefit of their customers outside Eire. They all take deposits, grant loans, arrange money transmission services and create credit. As listed banks they keep a $12\frac{1}{2}$ % reserve asset ratio to their eligible liabilities.

3.2 MERCHANT BANKS

Merchant banks originally specialized in short-term trade finance. They now have many other activities. Seventeen merchant banks are members of the Accepting Houses Committee from which comes their alternative title Accepting Houses. The term 'accepting' explains the early functions of Accepting Houses or merchant banks as they are now more popularly called.

In the 19th and early 20th centuries, the Bill on London was a method of financing world trade. A British exporter would send a Bill for his shipload of goods going to a German importer. "Pay to British exporter the sum of £40,000 in three month's time." The German importer signed the Bill, a form of post-dated cheque and returned it to the exporter who took it to an

Acceptance House. The House 'accepted' the Bill. By accepting it, the House made itself responsible for the Bill at maturity. On the strength of the Accepting Houses's name, a discount House provided immediate cash, paying a lower sum than the £40,000. The difference would be the 'discount' rate, the price charged to the British exporter for receiving his money now rather than waiting for the full amount in 3 month's time. Sometimes, the Bill might be held by the Accepting House to maturity, but in any event they would charge a commission for lending their name to the Bill. The name of the Accepting House on the Bill gave it greater marketability.

When a buyer of goods arranges for a seller to draw a Bill on him direct, it is known as a Trade Bill. If the seller draws the Bill on an Acceptance House with whom he has an acceptance credit, it becomes a Fine Bank Bill. Trade Bills drawn by sellers on buyers are not so readily negotiable as Fine Bank Bills. Neither do they get discounted at the same rate, for the Accepting Houses, by 'accepting', make themselves responsible for the bill at maturity.

Established customers of merchant banks can have acceptance credits opened for them. They can then issue Bank Bills to the value of the credit. The bank pays the bill off at maturity and debits the customer for the amount, plus commission. Foreign firms buying from this country often use facilities of this kind. Re-imbursement credit is another form of acceptance credit. It is opened by a foreign bank with a British bank on behalf of a foreign company.

Merchant banks are now involved in many more activities than formerly. Part of this expansion has evolved from their knowledge of company finance; part has been forced on them in self defence. They are gradually being squeezed between the international banks and Big Four clearing banks. Fluctuations in exchange rates, and the huge flows of 'petro dollars' all increased the power of the giant international banks and the British clearers.

In spite of such competition, the merchant banks survive and flourish. They help in the raising of capital by new issues or other means as, e.g. Morgan Grenfell's organization of Davy International's £3bn. steel mill project for Brazil. They give advice on international contracts, organize mergers, manage unit and investment trusts; provide medium-term finance and deal in certificates of deposits and similar paper as well as euro-currencies.

Merchant banks are individualistic institutions. They all provide four main groups of services; short-term and corporate finance; investment advice and current and deposit accounts. They are also involved in all aspects of whole-sale banking.

The seventeen merchant banks who are members of the Accepting Houses Committee, a further 40, and some financial institutions such as the Industrial and Commercial Finance Corporation, belong to the Issuing Houses Committee and help in the flotation of new issues. Five of the merchant banks deal in bullion; several in commodities; others in leasing, factoring and export finance. Factoring is a form of debt collecting. The merchant bank buys up a customers debts for a given sum, or gets paid *pro rata* for the amounts recovered. For details of leasing see Section 10.10.6, p.000. Some merchant banks run their own unit trust services and the 17 Accepting Houses jointly own ARIEL (Automated Real-Time Investments Exchange, Ltd.) a computer-based share dealing system. Merchant banks provide a comprehensive financial expertise which the clearing banks, with their more rigid structure cannot do in the same way.

However, any new emphasis on liquidity by the Bank of England could alter this situation. If the reserve asset ratio of $12\frac{1}{2}$ % changed to a higher liquidity requirement for 'maturity uncertain liabilities' (a proposal suggested by the Bank of England's paper, The Measurement of Liquidity), the competitive position of merchant banks would worsen. It would also worsen if bills with Bank of England 'backing' — currently a perogative of accepting houses — were rationed out among all banks.

The more conformist that merchant banks have to be, in terms of liquidity, capital adequacy, matching positions in interest rates and currencies, the less opportunity will they have for their own special brand of entrepreneurial and management expertise.

3.1.3 OTHER BRITISH BANKS

This sector includes all other banks with majority U.K. ownership.

Thus, merchant banks which are not members of the Accepting House group are listed by the Bank of England within this group, so are many of the subsidiaries of the London clearing banks. The Co-operative Bank which is a member of the Clearing House, but not a member of the Committee of London Clearing Bankers, also comes within this sector. So do offices in Great Britain of Northern Ireland banks and the U.K. branches of three banks with head offices in the Republic of Ireland which are subsidiaries of U.K.-owned banks. It also includes any consortium banks which are entirely British-owned, and the Channel Island and Isle of Man subsidiary banks of U.K.-owned banks. In the latter group, comes the Isle of Man Bank, a subsidiary of Lloyds. Another subsidiary of Lloyds in this group of 'other British banks' is Lewis' Bank. The Scottish Co-operative Wholesale Society, Ltd. Bankers, C. Hoare and Co., and the Yorkshire Bank owned jointly by Barclays, Lloyds and National Westminster, are also listed.

Functions of banks in this sector are the taking of deposits, the granting of loans and money transmission services. But the banks are much more involved with international trade, finance and merchanting than are the smaller offices of the clearing banks. The total of their sterling deposits at January 1980 was over £15 bn. Other currency deposits at January 1980 amounted to over £19 bn.

3.1.4 OVERSEAS BANKS IN THE UNITED KINGDOM

There are more American banks in the square mile of the City of London than in the whole of New York. Their growth from 8 in 1960 to 62 in 1980 reflects the continuing attraction of the City as a financial centre. Nowhere in the world, does such a small area encompass so much financial expertise. By 1980, the current and deposit accounts of the foreign banks had reached £130bn. Their numbers, including representative offices, branches, subsidiaries and affiliates totalled 387 and, along with the Securities Houses, they employed some 30,000 staff. Those established before the 1939 — 45 war, serviced the needs of their domestic customers with interests in the U.K. Later arrivals were attracted to London by (a) the growth of the euro-currency markets and (b) the lack of restrictions compared with their own domestic financial markets. The American banks, unable to compete for deposits at home because of Regulation Q which restricted interest rates, found it easier to expand in London.

The post-war foreign banks have since diversified their interests. As well as dealing in the euro-currency market, which was partly why they came, they serve the needs of their domestic clients with European interests and participate in the sterling money market. They (a) act as international bankers to companies in England and overseas (b) finance international trade, overseas development projects, and domestic business operations: (c) operate as foreign exchange dealers and thus as an integral part of London's foreign exchange market; (d) grant loans to individual customers in Britain and overseas; (e) operate in the short-term money markets in sterling and foreign currencies.

Foreign banks in London are now establishing networks in other cities such as Aberdeen where they service the North Sea Oil industry. In the conurbations of Birmingham, Bradford and Liverpool they can cater for particular ethnic groups.

The total number of overseas banks listed by the Bank of England in January 1980, was 213. Additionally there were unlisted foreign banks and financial institutions directly and indirectly represented, giving London the highest number of foreign banks of any financial centre in the world. The listed banks, all of which keep to the minimum $12\frac{1}{2}$ % reserve asset ratio, are grouped in the following three categories.

3.1.5 OVERSEAS BANKS — AMERICAN

These include all the branches and subsidiaries of American banks in the U.K. including subsidiaries operating in the Channel Islands. Total sterling deposits at January 1980 amounted to £7 bn with other currency deposits at £50,670 m.

3.1.6 OVERSEAS BANKS — JAPANESE

This group comprises the U.K. branches of Japanese banks. There were only 4 such banks in London in 1950. In 1980, there were 22. Total sterling deposits at January 1980 amounted to 554m with other currency deposits at £28.035m.

3.1.7 OVERSEAS BANKS — OTHER

Into this sector go the principal European banks from France, Spain, Cyprus, Netherlands, Belgium, Greece, Switzerland, Hungary and Czechoslovakia. Banks from all over the world including the Moscow Narodny Bank and the Bank of China as well as Canadian, Australian, New Zealand, Hongkong, Arab and African banks jostle cheek by jowl in the City's square mile (and just beyond). Not all of them have shown the same growth as that of the American or Japanese banks. But as the Common Market becomes more a part of British life they will probably expand in much the same way as the American and Japanese banks have done. Branches and subsidiaries of all other overseas banks go into this sector as well as their Channel Island subsidiaries. Total sterling deposits at January 1980 came to more than £6 bn with other currency deposits at £45,172 m.

Almost all of the resources of the foreign banks come from foreign currency deposits, either from overseas residents or from other banks in London. Most of their assets are in advances to overseas residents or in 'balances with U.K. banks'. These balances are largely in foreign currencies. Few of the foreign banks compete with British banks for U.K. business. Their presence does, however, act as a stimulus to British banks by keeping them in direct touch with the continually changing needs of other countries and traders.

3.1.8 CONSORTIUM BANKS

These are banks owned jointly by several groups from different countries, but in which no one bank has a direct shareholding of more than 50%. To come within this sector and not Other British Banks, one shareholder at least must be an overseas bank. Consortium banks were first established in London in 1964. They developed more rapidly during the period around 1975 onwards, mainly because of the growth in oil revenues accruing to countries unable in the short term to use or recycle them. The major function of the consortium banks is to provide large-scale funds normally beyond the resources of an individual bank, for periods of 2 — 10 years. These funds are needed by international companies, governments and government agencies throughout the world. The total assets of the consortium banks range from around £200m for the smaller consortia to over £1,000m for the largest.

3.1.9 NATIONAL SAVINGS BANK

This bank was established in 1861 for small savings. It has no other function; does not lend or transmit money, and is the largest organization of its kind in the world. Over 21 million active accounts are in operation through the 21,000 post office which handle this business.

There are two types of account: *ordinary accounts* from which only fairly small sums can be withdrawn on demand; and *investment accounts* which are subject to one month's notice of withdrawal. The latter pay a competitive rate of interest compared with other small savings media. During the year ended 31 March 1978, Investment accounts more than doubled over the previous year with a jump from £671m to £1,541m. The Ordinary accounts rose from £1,548m to £1,731m, the highest figure for over 30 years.

Part of the increased inflow into National Savings was due to the fact that, whereas interest rates were falling fast in other financial institutions, the Treasury allowed the National Savings Banks to keep their much higher investment account interest rate until October 1977. Even when the rate had dropped 1.5 points thereafter, the NSB still offered a preferential return over its nearest rivals, the Building Societies. Indeed, the latter and other institutions were depositing their own receipts into the Savings Banks up to the maximum allowed. This trend was reversed in the first half of the financial year 78 — 79 when NSB investment accounts had a net outflow.

A number of other savings media also come within the National Savings markets though they cannot be classed as banks. They include Savings Certificates which give a higher rate than Building Societies and, being tax-free, have proved of particular benefit to higher tax taxpayers. Index-linked certificates, both for retirement and regular monthly savings have also proved popular. Premium bonds give no interest but the excitement of a lottery with money prizes.

Funds which come into the National Savings movement are lodged with the National Debt Commissioners who invest them in government securities. The National Savings Bank does not therefore operate a $12\frac{1}{2}$ % reserve assets ratio.

3.1.10 NATIONAL GIROBANK

Set up in October 1968 as a sector of the Post Office Corporation, the National Girobank began as a money transmission service operating through the postal system with cash facilities available at more than 20,000 post offices.

Girobank derives its powers from the Post Office Act 1969 and the Post Office (Banking Services) Act 1976. It must meet financial objectives set by the Government, pay commercial rates for the postal services it uses, and its own costs. The 1976 legislation reorganized Giro's capital structure and allowed for the development of general banking services including overdrafts.

In spite of increasing use by local authorities and Government departments, growth was initially slow. By 1978, however there were nearly $\frac{3}{4}$ m. customers, both corporate and private, with accounts held on a central computer system at Bootle, Lancashire. Girobank's money transmission service has proved particularly useful for rent collecting. As a result, it is used for this purpose by more than 160 of the 400 local authorities in the U.K.

The bank offers a current account banking service free (1980) to customers in credit, cheque guarantee cards (on which there are some restrictions) deposit and budget accounts, personal and bridging loans. It also operates a Postcheque service which enables customers with a Girobank guarantee card to draw cash in local currency at 75,000 post offices in 16 countries in western Europe.

Since Girobank received full banking status in 1978, it has been subject to the $12\frac{1}{2}$ % reserve asset ratio and credit controls.

3.1.11 TRUSTEE SAVINGS BANKS

Efforts at organizing savings banks began in the early part of the nineteenth century. After the Rev. Henry Duncan established the first at Ruthwell, Dumfriesshire, in 1810, an Act of 1817 settled their status. They then made great strides until Gladstone established the Post Office Savings Bank in 1861.

In 1973, the Page Committee which had been asked to report on National Savings, recommended that the Trustee Savings Bank should become a fully fledged bank in its own right. T.S.B.s should be able to provide lending and other services as well as receiving deposits.

As a result, in 1975, the Trustee Savings Banks were consolidated into 17 regional Trustee banks. By 1980, their total deposits were £5,430m from 8 million customers. This cannot compare with the £76m sterling liabilities of all U.K. banks, but T.S.B.s are a formidable force in personal banking. Furthermore, with only 1,641 branches (compared with Natwest's 3,200, Barclays' 3,000, Midland's 2,569, and Lloyds' 2,375), the usual overheads connected with retail banking tend to be lower.

Under the Trustee Savings Bank Act 1976, the T.S.B.s received powers to lend to corporate and personal customers and, in August 1977, launched a personal loans service. Some time elapsed before this scheme was actually afloat, but after only six months, loans amounted to some £25m. The lending ceiling has been raised and, for home improvements, amounts of £5,000 – 6,000 are available. T.S.B.s are also entering the home financing business. They will lend up to £30,000 at rates comparable with some of the building societies and by November 1980, some £166m had been lent to home buyers. Credit cards are handled by Barclaycard, and the Central Trustee Savings Bank, a member of the Bankers' Clearing House, acts for the Trustee Savings Bank in the clearing of cheques.

The final move to independence of the Trustee Savings Bank came in November 1979 when the assets of the 'ordinary' Department, till then included with the National Savings movement, were returned to the T.S.B. Under the Banking Act of 1979, it became an authorized bank with full status.

3.1.12 DISCOUNT HOUSES

These *are* not banks, but they form a very special link between the clearing and merchant banks and the Bank of England.

When a bill is 'discounted', it is bought or sold at less than its face value. The difference consists of the interest accruing from the purchase or sale date until the maturity date when the face value must be repaid in full. The rate of discount depends on (a) the standing of the 'acceptor', (b) the length of time to maturity of the Bill, and (c) market conditions.

Owners of bills who get them discounted for immediate cash, thus pay a price: the discount rate. The discounting of bills was the main function of discount houses in the nineteenth and early twentieth centuries.

With money borrowed 'on call' from the commercial banks they discounted bills for merchants who did not wish to hold them until maturity. In this way, discount houses helped finance trade with money which might otherwise have remained idle. They became expert in grading bills, an expertise which they still retain, and which is of great help to the commercial banks.

Discount houses form a link in the credit chain between the seller of goods who wants payment now and the buyer who wants to pay later. When a merchant bank 'accepts' a bill, it is more easily discounted. The discount house completes the work of the acceptance house (merchant bank) in the provision of trade credit.

Discount houses also deal in Treasury bills. These are promissory notes for fixed amounts of £5,000 – 1m. issued by the Bank of England on behalf of the government, and repayable in ninety-one days. The discount houses make a competitive bid for the weekly issue of new bills every Friday. The clearing banks may also tender for customers wanting a minimum of £5,000 worth of bills. Additionally, a few commercial companies hold Treasury bills as investments, and these will also tender.

Discount houses finance their operations by borrowing at short notice: (a) indirectly from the secondary money markets which have developed in the last decade; (b) 'on-call' from the commercial banks. Money so lent by the banks assures them of a liquid, yet profitable, asset. The discount houses also gain by paying to the banks at a rate slightly less than they receive on discounts and short-dated government stocks. On such margins they make their profits. Many, if not all, of their functions could be performed directly by the commercial banks, but the discount houses meet several needs of the monetary system and employ only a few hundred people. Some points in their favour are:

(a) Profits are low. They do their work with small, efficient staffs.

(b) By discounting trade bills they help to finance international trade.

(c) They provide the banks with a ready source of liquid assets, part of their $12\frac{1}{2}$ % reserve asset ratio, and a market for the sale of short-dated bonds if banks require further cash.

(d) They cover the government's short-term finance; in return for last resort facilities from the Bank, they undertake to buy, if necessary, the whole of the Treasury bill weekly tender collectively.

(f) They contribute to the creation of markets in financial assets such as certificates of deposit, short-dated government stocks, and local authority stocks.

(g) By borrowing on call and short notice from the banks, discount houses help to even out the flow of money, and save the banks from carrying too large a cash base.

(h) The discount houses act as a channel through which the Bank of England can provide additional cash if there is a demand for it, and without the possibility of a crisis – as might result if cash were provided direct to the banks.

(i) The discount houses form part of the mechanism through which the Bank of England can influence short-term interest rates.

There are 11 discount houses in London; together they form the London Discount Market Association. There are also a small number of firms known as 'running brokers', who specialize in selling 'parcels' of commercial or Treasury bills made up for maturity at convenient dates. As a result of this specialist business, a Bill may change hands several times. Holders include industrial companies, pension funds, finance companies as well as banks.

Since July 1973, the Bank of England has exerted control over the discount houses by requiring them not to allow their 'undefined assets' to exceed their capital by more than twenty times. 'Undefined assets' are all those except (a) balances at the Bank of England (b) Treasury and other public sector bills (c) Public sector stocks of less than five years to maturity. These restraints are laid on discount houses because they are *not* banks for the purposes of Competition and Credit Control, though grouped as part of the banking sector for statistical purposes. Public sector assets such as Treasury Bills are directly controllable by the Government. By defining the proportion which must be held by the Discount Houses, the Government limits the Houses' holdings of other assets and ensures its own short-term finance is met.

3. DEVELOPMENTS IN THE SECONDARY BANKING SECTOR

3.2.1. THE SECONDARY BANKING CRISIS 1973 – 1975

In 1975, a banking crisis developed, caused by general economic difficulties and misjudgements by some banks. Following Competition and Credit Control, competition among the banks increased. Interest rates were lowered to attract industrial borrowing. Much of the borrowing, however, was by speculators on rising land values. In 1973 came the oil price explosion. World-wide inflation and rising interest rates followed. The Government raised Minimum Lending Rate without reference to Treasury Bill rate, to prevent sterling draining abroad.

The clearing banks kept their rates lower than those prevailing elsewhere partly because of commitments already made, partly because of miscalculation of future events. Customers borrowed from the clearers at low rates and relent elsewhere at higher rates, a profit-making process known as arbitraging.

Most borrowing was for property but, in 1973, the boom began to collapse. As interest rates rose, property prices fell, so that speculators were left holding assets worth less than their debts to the banks. The biggest losers were the secondary banks, such as London and County Securities, Mercantile Credit, United Dominions Trust which lost £31 m. in the six months to December 1974, and First National Finance Corporation which lost £73m in the first half of 1975. The clearers were also involved.

The Bank of England mounted a 'lifeboat' operation to provide support for the banks most heavily in debt. Some secondary banks went into liquidation, e.g. London and County Securities, Triumph Investment Trust, Israel-British Bank. Others, such as Mercantile Credit, were taken over by successful bidders, or undertook major capital reconstruction (J. Vavasseur; Cedar Holdings,) in order to continue in business.

The secondary banking crisis led to concern about the prudential ratios and capital adequacy of the banks in the United Kingdom, a speech by the Governor of the Bank of England on this subject, and to a White Paper in 1976 which provided a basis for the Banking Act 1979.

3.3 THE BANKING ACT 1979

The Government White paper published on 3 August 1976 (The Licensing and Supervision of Deposit-Taking Institutions) took up the question, what is a bank? Though not providing an answer, it made a distinction between banks and licensed deposit-taking institutions. The White Paper proposed that financial institutions should fall into one of the following groups:

(a) Banks granted official recognition and entitled to be called 'banks.'
(b) Institutions granted a licence to take deposits but not to be called 'banks.'
(c) Institutions not licensed to take deposits and forbidden to conduct any banking business based on holding deposits.
(d) Building societies, trustee savings banks, the National Giro and Friendly Societies, all of which were covered by existing legislation.

Whether a bank came into category (a) or (b) depended on 'exacting criteria for such recognition (as a bank) covering such matters as (i) minimum capital and reserves, (ii) the type or range of banking services required to be provided, and (iii) the reputation or status needed'.

The Bank of England and the Treasury would determine these criteria. In order to come into category (b) and receive a license as a deposit taker, a company needed (i) capital and reserves of a minimal figure to be determined, but high enough to ensure security, low enough to encourage competition, (ii) honest, trustworthy and suitably qualified managers (iii) adequate liquidity and solvency (iv) continued adherence to these three conditions after a licence was granted.

Companies' balance sheets would be examined with special regard to the degree of risk of the various assets; the distribution of lending to different economic sectors; the matching of assets and liabilities in sterling and other currencies; loans to and from connected companies; provision for contingencies such as bad debts; and the level of past profits. Companies with head offices abroad would also have to obtain a license or recognition as a bank, but supervision would be by the country of origin.

Parts I and III and certain sections of Part IV of the Banking Act 1979 came into force on 1 October 1979.

Following the proposals of the White Paper, Part 1 of the Act set up a statutory framework for the authorization and supervision of deposit-taking institutions by the Bank of England. It established a two-tier system of authorization: for 'recognized banks' and 'licensed deposit-taking institutions.' To take deposits unless authorized by the Bank of England to do so constitues an offence under the Act. Deposit takers carrying on business on 1 October 1979, had a transitional period of six months in which to apply for authorization.

Part III of the Act provides for the control of advertisements for deposits. As a general rule, the use of banking names and descriptions is restricted to recognized banks. Part IV contains miscellaneous and general provisions. Part II of the Act mainly concerns the setting up of a Deposit Protection Scheme. Recognized banks and deposit takers must contribute to this scheme, which will compensate depositors for part of any losses if the contributing institutions ever failed. The clearing banks objected strongly to this part of the scheme on the grounds that the guarantee covered only 75% of depositors' money and on sums under £10,000. Even more important from the banks' point of view was that the institutions subscribing the largest amounts were those least likely to default.

The aims of the 1979 Act were (a) greater protection of depositors from institutions taking insufficient care of their clients' money; (b) greater clarity in the supervision of banks under existing rules such as minimum reserve asset ratios; special deposits, and directives on lending, (c) supervision of licensed deposit-taking institutions for the protection of depositors; and greater financial control generally; (d) harmonization with E.E.C. policies which favour stricter regulation of deposit-taking institutions. The gap between the Bank of England and the Department of Trade through which the fringe banks operated will be closed and the title bank allowed only to authorized operators, as is the law in the E.E.C. The Bank, as supervisor and regulator of the banking system now becomes an agent of the Treasury and its actions can be subject to appeal to the Treasury, and questions in Parliament. Other developments that can affect the future of commercial banks are (a) harmonization (b) nationalization (c) pricing (d) profitability (e) automation.

3.4 E.E.C. HARMONIZATION

A step towards *harmonization* with E.E.C. laws on *financial institutions* came in 1973. This was an establishment directive for *non-life insurance companies*. It required them to keep the same regulations and solvency standards in the E.E.C. country where they intended to set up new business as were imposed on national companies there. British insurers regarded this directive more as a hindrance than a help. And if invisible exports are any indication of financial growth, those of Britain to the E.E.C. are still at roughly the same level as they were 10 years ago (other than tourism, q.v.).

A draft directive on *bank harmonization* proposed in November 1977, went ahead in 1978. It aimed to get rid of the more obstructive inequalities of banking law between states, to make licensing mandatory for credit institutions and dependent on certain liquidity and solvency ratios being maintained. Company law, too, will undergo radical change as a result of the directive which lays down minimum disclosure and audit requirements. The U.K. Companies Act 1980 arose partly in response to this directive.

3.5 NATIONALIZATION

The second development was the defence mounted in 1977 by the banks against nationalization. The argument for nationalizing banks is (a) the power they wield through their ability to create credit and (b) the effects that this power has on individual and national well-being. The argument against nationalization is also about power. Is it better for bankers to control the business of banking, or the state? The Bank of England is nationalized. Why should not other banks and financial institutions such as insurance and building societies similarly come within the state orbit?

Some nationalized industries run as a kind of social welfare service; others as a commercial profit-making business. The *function* of nationalized industries in general, and specific groups in particular, would need to be very clearly defined before banks joined their ranks. If all financial institutions came under the hegemony of the state, then to be refused credit by one group could be the same as being refused credit by all. Competition gives the appearance, and sometimes the reality of choice. Monopoly, however beneficent, can become less so, and even positively harmful. The arguments for and against Bank nationalization can be summed up in columnar fashion so:

For	Against
1. Better industrial relations/greater worker efficiency.	1. This does not always follow nationalization.
2. Power of giving loans should be in government rather than private hands.	2. Practising bankers are better able to judge who should be given loans.
3. The above power should not necessarily be made on purely commercial criteria.	3. Lending based on non-commercial judgements could lead to banks' bankruptcy (or being bailed out by taxpayers).

For	*Against*
4. Money supply control should be directly in the control of the state.	4. Controls of all types can be levied against the banks, including fiscal penalties.
5. The banks are not competitive enough for bank customers.	5. There are public sector alternatives such as the National Giro and the National Savings Bank.
6. Control could be exerted over bank customers and their aims and policies.	6. German banks already do this by taking seats on company boards and by using shareholders' proxy votes lodged with them.
7. The profits from 'invisibles' should be available to all.	7. Who is 'all'?
8. Promotion in public-sector industries is open to all.	8. So it is in the banks (but women can be rightly sceptical about getting to the top in banking *or* in public sector industries).

3.6 BANK CHARGES FOR MONEY TRANSMISSION SERVICES

In May 1967 there was a Report by the Prices and Incomes Board on bank charges. In 1978, a new type of Prices Board, the Price Commission, again reported on bank charges, but this time specifically on those levied for money transmission services, more generally known as current accounts.

The Prices and Incomes Report of 1967 emphasized that during periods of high interest rates, banks made what could be classed as monopoly profits. Worse: the profits were not due to any additional productivity or hard work by the banks or their staffs. It was merely an 'endowment' effect created by the Government's monetary policy for which the banks were in no way responsible yet which gave them, unlike less fortunate groups, higher rewards. This report led ultimately to some stiffening of controls on banks. In June 1969, the interest paid to banks on their Special Deposits was halved until the banks brought their advances down to a specified level. In October 1973, interest was paid only on Special Deposits relating to *time deposits* of the banks.

The climate was very different when the Price Commission made their report. They decided that current account charges were not too dear for the services provided. The clearers used a 'notional interest allowance' which varied between 4 − 5% to offset current account charges. The 4 − 5% represented 'part of the value to the bank of the balance maintained on the account'. As a result, around 70% of all current accounts received free banking.

The Price Commission wanted a new system. The banks could relate their notional interest more to current market rates, or current account customers could be paid interest on their balances. The Big Four banks used varying tariffs for 'free' banking and notional interest rates. They ranged from a minimum credit balance of £50 (Midland and Natwest) to £150 average at Lloyds, and from 4 – 5% notional interest with 9 – 10p per debit entry. The Co-op Bank merely asked that customers remained in credit for free banking.

Around 15m people had current accounts. They cost the banks about £800m to service while charges on them recouped about £200m. The Price Commission also reported, surprisingly, that the banks should not bear the cost of holding and distributing cash to their branches from the branches of the Bank of England. This money earned nothing. Neither did it count as part of the reserve asset ratio. Yet in total the sum came to £750m and was in effect, an interest-free loan by the banks to the Government. The Commission thought 'that the provision of notes to the public at large should be a national expense, as many of those who use notes are not themselves customers of the bank.'

3.7 PROFITABILITY

1. *High Interest rates*: 'endowment' effect: the gain from lending money at high rates which has cost them nothing.
2. *Low interest rates* may attract large volume of business
3. If interest rates low without many borrowers, banks try to improve profits by widening margins: the difference between what they charge for lending and what they pay for borrowing

Prices naturally play a large part in the profitability of firms. With banks, prices can largely be interpreted as interest rates. The higher the price margin over the cost of their lending, the bigger the profits that banks can make. This principle is well illustrated by the following figures. Paying an average 8.2% for their money, in 1977 banks made £134 million out of their money transmission services. Had the interest rates been lower at 6.15%, the profit would have turned into a loss of over £60m. Banks are trying to reduce the cost of their retail operations by automation and computerization where possible. They are also trying to increase their wholesale banking activities.

However, the effort to achieve maximum profitability is only one of a bank's aims. There is also the need for sufficient liquidity to meet claims when they become due. This dichotomy of purpose is difficult to resolve. The more liquid a bank's assets, the less profitable are they to hold. Cash, the most liquid, is the least profitable of all.

Yet future controls may insist on a higher cash ratio. Since the secondary bank crisis, the authorities have looked much more closely at banks' overall liquidity. Other factors leading to a re-appraisal of liquidity positions have been the inefficacy of moral suasion and 'corset' controls and the greater emphasis on monetary policy. The Banking Act strengthened supervision. It did not deal with the question of the appropriate liquidity ratios for different types of banks and claims.

The Bank of England's discussion paper, The Measurement of Liquidity

(1980) set out a new system of liquidity requirements. The present system of monitoring did not apply to the overseas branches of U.K. banks or to the sterling business of the U.K. branches of overseas banks. Under the proposed system, the sterling business of overseas banks operating in the U.K., would be included.

The system put forward by the Bank was an 'integrated' test of liquidity. This moved away from the idea of a fixed proportion of assets to liabilities. It favoured a time-based asset ratio. The sooner that a bank had to repay borrowed money, the higher should be the bank's liquidity. The range might be 100% for less than a month's borrowing down to only 5% for borrowing that had to be repaid after a year.

In order to achieve this 'integrated' test, the Bank had devised a measure of liquidity which distinguished between maturity-uncertain liabilities and maturity-certain laibilities. The former included sight deposits, money at call, bank overdrafts. The gross total of these liabilities should have a liquidity requirement of 25%. Maturity-certain liabilities such as fixed-term deposits should have a scaled-down liquidity ratio.

The 'integrated' test could replace the $12\frac{1}{2}$ % reserve asset ratio. Furthermore, 40% of the liquid assets should be primary liquid assets i.e. cash or assets which in all circumstances were a ready source of cash. If such changes were implemented, what would be their effects? They are likely to be as follows:

(1) Overseas branches of U.K. banks, where liquidity costs were likely to be easier, would gain.

(2) U.K. branches of overseas banks would lose the advantages they may have enjoyed through being outside the present liquidity monitoring arrangements.

(3) Clearing banks and others with large retail banking bases would gain by the inclusion of cash in the definition of primary liquid assets.

(4) The $12\frac{1}{2}$ % reserve asset ratio includes money at call with certain groups of brokers and gilt-edged jobbers. Primary liquidity excludes such money. Gilt edged jobbers could thus find themselves unable to raise funds on the same favourable terms as they formerly did.

Banks may now have to decide whether to go for 'higher' or 'better' custom. Only around 55% of the adult U.K. population has a current bank account compared with 90% of adults in Canada, France, Germany, Holland and the U.S.A. This is far from saturation point. Banks could (1) woo more adults (2) go 'up market', giving a better range of services: investment, trustee, insurance advice and so on and/or (3) increase automated services possibly at the expense of alternative (2). In any event, they cannot achieve maximum profitability, so they declared to the Wilson Committee, while fiscal and regulatory advantages are given to other groups.

3.8 AUTOMATION

Automation is increasing in the banks as elsewhere. This can be seen particularly in the handling of cash. Cash handling is a very costly operation in relation to the low value of the commodity. And costliness increases with volume. Supermarkets need coin in greater amounts than formerly. So too do public houses and transport service industries. This coin has to be sorted and repackaged by banks. A surplus cannot be returned to the Mint yet a deficit of coin means further ordering (for banks do not want unprocessed coin from another bank,) and the volume of coin in circulation increases. The Bank of Scotland was one of the first banks to use cash in rolls. Prepared coin like this saves 25% on storage space. Unlike the plastic bags now commonly in use for parcelling coin, it is secure and pilfer-proof. The denomination breakdown (£2 in silver, £1 in 2p, 50 in 1p and 25 in $\frac{1}{2}$ p) is so practical that some big departmental stores have purchased their own equipment for the delivery of coin in this way.

In addition to the use of rolled coin, some bigger banks use machines for counting notes, worn, damage or repaired. These operate at a speed of 100 notes counted in 5 seconds. Computerization is increasing: Natwest opened a fully computerized Money Centre in Threadneedle Street in 1978. Foreign exchange and euro-currency operations take place here in 40 different currencies and with 34 dealing positions in one dealing room. New Zealand banks are operating a group computerized system to reduce expenses, while the Japanese are already trying out Electronic Funds Transfer Systems in 13 of their banks. Credit cards and cash cards are being more commonly used (though not to the same extent as in America, where a cash customer could be viewed askance because it is assumed he has no credit rating).

3.9 THE WILSON COMMITTEE

Twenty years after the Radcliffe Committee reported on the Working of the Monetary System, a Committee under the chairmanship of Sir Harold Wilson was set up in January 1977 to review the functioning of financial institutions.

Its terms of reference were:

"To enquire into the role and functioning, at home and abroad, of financial institutions in the U.K., and their value to the economy; to review in particular the provision of funds for industry and trade; to consider what changes are required in the existing arrangements for the supervision of these institutions, including the possible extension of the public sector, and to make recommendations."

The Committee's first task was to consider the provision of funds for trade and industry. Their report on this subject had three main themes; *the availability of finance for investment,* defects in the system; the growth of wholesale deposits and terms of lending. On the first the Committee felt that the channelling of funds by financial institutions to meet the needs of industry had been adequate. The main problem had been an unwillingness to borrow. Therefore, the Wilson Committee decided that a shortage of finance was not the main deterrent to industrial investment. It was an insufficient return on borrowed funds, due to 'low productivity, low profitability, low demand, and problems caused by government policies. . .'.

The second theme of the first part of the Report was that there were *defects in the system*. Thus, the clearing banks were criticized for lending too much to property and financial sectors. The banks argued that it was industry's own lack of demand that was at fault. Companies were criticized for having too low a gearing to which the companies concerned replied that 'A high gearing ratio makes a company more vulnerable to fluctuations in its profits, reduces its credit worthiness with lenders, and may reduce its share rating thereby making equity capital more expensive.' The Japanese banks in London agreed with the view that U.K. companies were too low geared, and this was one of the reasons why their lending to U.K. companies was so low.

Another defect was what the Wilson Committee called the 'temporal gap'. Firms had difficulty in getting long-term loans of 15 – 20 years. Clearing banks preferred a 5 – 7 year period or to lend on overdraft, while Finance for Industry's normal lending period was for 10 – 15 years. In the 1950s and 1960s, companies issued debentures for long-term loans, but lenders are now unwilling to lend on fixed terms for long periods because of inflation, and companies do not like borrowing long-term at high fixed interest rates. A floating rate bond was suggested as an answer to this problem, but only blue chip companies would have the credit rating for a successful issue of this type, and they had no need of such loans.

The difficulty of small firms in raising finance was discussed by the Committee and suggestions made for official loan guarantees similar to the U.S.A. small business administration scheme. The Confederation of British Industry proposed 'a more explicit subsidy element to help very small, or starting, firms with small loans'. This subsidy element should take the form of a contribution towards interest rates. On the wholesale deposits, the banks showed how these had increased and how any expansion of term lending would be imprudent. They described how their business had changed since Radcliffe and showed that they were losing their market share of the deposit-taking and lending business to other institutions. This loss was not due to any diminution in efficiency by the banks themselves, but to the system of controls and regulations which only they suffered. Other deposit takers were not hindered by such penalties. On the contrary, they received greater freedom, subsidies, incentives and/or fiscal advantages.

Examples of such discrimination included tax relief on insurance policies, pension funds and mortgages for home ownership. Building societies were allowed to deduct a composite rate of tax from their depositors; National Savings did not have to keep a $12\frac{1}{2}$ % asset ratio nor the same proportion of capital and reserves as did the clearing banks. And no saving institution had to keep $1\frac{1}{2}$ % of their deposits as non-interest bearing balances at the Bank of England.

The clearers criticized the supplementary deposit scheme because it was levied against the banks and interfered with their ability to lend to commercial customers. The banks also defended themselves against the charge that they used less sophisticated appraisal techniques for lending than did the Americans, by saying that a high proportion of their lending was to small companies and companies of long standing. Furthermore, 40% of their lending was now also in the form of American-style term loans.

The banks concluded 278 pages of evidence by arguing for (a) a stance of 'fiscal neutrality' by the Authorities so that only the borrower should get beneficial finance (such as tax relief loans), not the institutions providing the loans (such as building societies). (b) Improvements in the techniques of monetary policy, and in the facilities for channelling term finance to industry.

In March 1980 the discussion document (Green Paper Cnd. 7858) on Monetary Control proposed that the banks' requirement to keep $1\frac{1}{2}$ % of their eligible liabilities at the Bank of England should be reviewed, and that supplementary special deposits (SSD) should be discontinued. The latter event took place in June 1980. In January 1981, the reserve asset ratio of $12\frac{1}{2}$ % which had been in force for 10 years was reduced to 10% but special deposits would continue to be used to drain off excess liquidity from the system.

TYPICAL QUESTION

Outline the functions of the London discount market today

SUGGESTED ANSWER

The discount market is a market for short-term money. The institutions operating in this market are discount houses, merchant banks, clearing banks and the Bank of England acting as lender of last resort.

The discount market's function has always been to draw in short-term funds and lend them out profitably to private and public sectors. The system works by the Houses borrowing short-term funds (call money) from the banks. The Houses use the borrowed funds to 'discount' Bills of Exchange or other short-term paper into liquid cash. They charge a fee (or discount) for doing so. The discount can be regarded as interest charged on the amount advanced until the maturity date of the bill.

Formerly the discount houses financed world trade by accepting and discounting Bills of Exchange for traders all over the world. The decline in the use of the Bill of Exchange coincided with a growth in government expenditure, and the discount houses dealt more heavily in Treasury Bills. They thus switched from financing short term trade to financing the short term needs of the Government.

Today the discount market still trades in commercial bills for internal and external trade. They deal in Treasury Bills; Government securities (bonds) with a life under 5 years; local authority securities and certificates of deposit. These latter are taken up by the Houses when first issued by the banks. Others are later discounted by the market.

They underwrite the Treasury Bill tender each week, and because they get last resort facilities from the Bank of England, they help smooth out the daily fluctuations in the supply of money. They provide banks with reserve assets and commercial customers with instant liquidity for market investments.

ADDITIONAL QUESTIONS

1. Outline the British Government's proposals for the licensing and supervision of deposit-taking institutions, as published in its White Paper of August, 1976.

2. Classify the different types of commercial bank which operate in Britain, giving brief details of their main functions and activities.

3. Write brief notes on central bank discount rates.

4. What are the main functions of the Bank of England? Have these functions changed since the secondary banking crisis of 1973 – 1975?

5. Compare and contrast the techniques used by the Bank of England in implementing monetary policy with those used by the central bank of another country with which you are familiar.

4 The Central Bank

4.1 INTRODUCTION

All developed and most developing countries have a central bank. Whether the central bank consists of several institutions each responsible for a particular area as in America; or in one institution with several branches as in Nigeria; or in one institution covering the whole country as in Britain, its functions are nearly identical everywhere.

Central banks act for the government in controlling the credit system, the money supply and the note issue; they act as the government's bank and represent it in international institutions; they accept deposits from and make loans to the commercial banks and/or money markets; influence interest rates and arrange transfers of money and bullion with central banks in other countries.

4.2 THE BANK OF ENGLAND

The Bank of England carrries out the functions described above but has a few unique to itself as well, e.g. as lender of last resort to the discount houses and as an informal regulator of City codes and practices.

The Bank is a nationalized corporation. In theory, it has complete independance over its internal affairs. The Bank of England Act 1946 lays down, however, that "The Treasury may from time to time give such directives to the Bank as, after consultation with the Governor of the Bank, they think is necessary in the public interest".

Similarly, the Bank has power under the 1946 Act to "request information from and make recommendations to bankers", and can, with Treasury authority, issue directives to ensure that such requests are obeyed. In practice, the Treasury has not exerted its power over the Bank, nor the Bank over other banks. Requests usually suffice.

The Bank is run by a Court of Directors consisting of a Governor, Deputy Governor, both appointed for 5-year terms; 4 executive directors and 12 part-time directors, all appointed for 4 years.

The appointments are made by the Prime Minister on the recommendation of the Chancellor of the Exchequer. The part-time directors are industrialists, bankers, civil servants and trade unionists. They are not involved in policy decisions. This is a safeguard to avoid any conflict of interest.

The Treasury makes policy decisions, aided technically by the Court of Directors and the Bank's various departments. The division of the Bank into Issue and Banking Departments is retained only for accounting purposes. Ten departments of the Bank now cover all aspects of the Bank's work.

These ten departments are (1) the Cashier's Department, which deals with the transactions by which the Bank finances the government and carries out monetary policy; (2) the Printing works which employs 2,000 people to print and scrutiny 2,000 million banknotes a year; (3) the Accountant's Department which keeps the registers of gilt-edged securities; (4) the Exchange Control department which administers exchange control for the Treasury; (5) the Overseas department which gives advice on overseas financial development to the government and the Bank; (6) the Economic Intelligence department which collects bank statistics and analyses and advises on the domestic economy; and lastly (7—10) four small departments: the Audit, Secretary's, Establishments and Management Services which aid the internal administration of the Bank.

4.3 FUNCTIONS OF THE BANK OF ENGLAND

The Bank of England's functions can be grouped by its (a) banking (b) regulatory and (c) monetary policy roles. Alternatively, the Bank's functions can be thought of as (d) domestic and (e) external.

In its *banking* role, the Bank of England as central bank acts for (a) a small number of private customers, including its own staff; (b) other banks: the clearing banks use their balances at the Bank of England to settle their indebtedness to one another; the discount houses use their accounts in order to borrow from the bank; (c) overseas central banks and monetary institutions; and (d) the central government, by the Bank's management of the Exchequer Account, the National Loans Fund and in its role as issuer of notes.

The Bank has a *regulatory* role in (a) representing the views of the City of London and ensuring conformity of the financial institutions therein, with City codes and practices and (b) in supervising the development of banks by seeking information from the non-clearers on such items as the maturity patterns of sterling deposits and claims; associations with associated companies; provision for bad debts and depreciation of investment portfolios; and standby facilities with banks and other financial institutions. Until the Banking Act 1979, the Bank of England held annual discussions with each clearing bank about its profitability, capital adequacy and liquidity. After that date it will issue guidelines on the prudential ratios to be observed by banks, and which will be backed by statute.

The Bank's *monetary policy role* covers (a) the National Debt. The Bank raises money for the government and repays its debt; (b) the Foreign exchange market by which the Bank controls the flow of external finance, and stabilizes, within limits, the exchange rate it thinks desirable (or possible). Finally, the Bank's monetary role covers (c) the control of the money supply through decisions such as the quantity and quality of assets of the banks to their liabilities; and through instruments such as special deposits, minimum lending rate; open market operations; supplementary deposits, directives or voluntary restrictions.

Grouping the Bank of England's functions into (e) external and (f) domestic gives the following features.

4.3.1 EXTERNAL FUNCTIONS OF THE BANK OF ENGLAND

4.3.1.1 *Management of the Exchange Equalization Account*

The Exchange Equalization Account was set up in 1932. The gold held by the Issue Department of the Bank of England was transferred to it in 1939. Since then, the Account has been the depositary for the nation's gold and foreign exchange reserves and Special Drawing Rights issued by the International Monetary Fund.

The Bank uses the Account to stablize the exchange rate. An exchange rate is the price of one currency in terms of another. Since 1972, the price of the pound in dollar terms has fluctuated with demand and supply. If the demand for dollars goes up, the value of the dollar rises (the exchange rate of the pound falls). The Bank enters the market as a buyer of pounds (seller of dollars). This depresses the dollar rate. The dollar reserves in the Account will fall. If dollars are plentiful in the market, the value of the £ in dollar terms will rise. The Bank sells pounds (buys dollars) to keep down the parity of the £. The dollar reserves in the Account will rise.

If the Bank wants the exchange rate to be completely 'free' to reflect true demand and supply forces, it does not intervene. The result is a freely floating pound, technically known as a 'clean' float; when the Bank intervenes to stabilize a floating rate, this is known as a 'dirty' float.

Under the terms of the National Loans Fund Act 1968, the Exchange Equalization Account draws sterling from the National Loans Fund to pay for gold and foreign currency. The sale proceeds go back to the National Loans Fund. Sterling balances held by the Exchange Equalization Account are also lent to the National Loans Fund as interest-free 'Ways and Means' advances or invested in 'tap' Treasury Bills.

(a) Operation of the Exchange Equalization Account

The Account does not normally operate in the forward market. When it did so in 1967, just before the November devaluation, it lost over £350m. In 1977, by contrast, the inflow of funds boosted Britain's reserves to $10,130m, the highest figure on record. Forward operations were undertaken by the Bank to prevent the exchange rate moving too high too quickly.

(b) Administration of Foreign Exchange Control

The Exchange Control Act of 1947 gave the Treasury wide powers of control over the exchange of foreign currencies into sterling and vice versa. The Treasury delegated most of these powers to the Bank of England which, in turn, delegated many small decisions to banks, stockbrokers, solicitors, etc. Dealings in foreign currencies were allowed only by authorized banks; investment currency dealings could be undertaken by authorized depositaries.

(c) Relations with other monetary authorities
Although the role of sterling in international payments is no longer so important as it once was, the Bank of England still acts as banker for one hundred overseas banks and monetary institutions. It holds working balances for clearing international indebtedness among these banks. For some, formerly in the sterling area, it invests in Treasury bills or other instruments, and it provides investment advice for longer-term deposits.

The Bank of England is a member of the central bank institution, the Bank for International Settlements in Basle, and represents the government at the I.M.F., the I.B.D.R., the I.D.A. and I.F.C.

4.3.1.2 *Domestic functions of the Bank of England*

(a) As the government's banker
It keeps the Exchequer Account and provides overdrafts in the name of Ways and Means Advances. All government balances are shown under the heading 'public deposits' in the Bank of England return. It borrows for the government, short-term – by the weekly sale of Treasury Bills to the money market; long-term – by issuing bonds and stocks on the capital market. It keeps the register of stockholders and is responsible for payment of dividends. Through its dealings as outlined above, the Bank of England can influence the money supply. Finally, as the government's banker, it gives advice to the government.

(b) As the bankers' bank
It provides normal banking services except overdrafts and loans. The cash reserves of the banks are shown collectively in the Bank return as 'bankers' deposits'. The banks use these balances to settle any debts to each other which arise after the clearing; to augment their supply of coin and notes, and to pay government debts. 'Open market operations' (the selling or buying of securities by the Bank to the market) transfers deposits from Bankers Deposits to Public Deposits or vice versa, so influencing the asset ratios of the banks and their money-creating powers.

(c) As the banker of the discount houses
The discount houses have deposits at the Bank (included in 'bankers' deposits'). Unlike the banks, however, they can obtain loans from the Bank against first-class security. The Bank will buy Treasury Bills from them at market rates or, (to pursue a contractionary monetary policy), at any penal rate it chooses. The rate at which the Bank lends to the discount houses has a strong and rapid effect on other short-term rates, but as lender of last resort

to the discount houses, the Bank enables the asset structure of the commercial banks to be less liquid than it would otherwise have to be.

(d) As the banker for the acceptance houses
Some acceptance houses, for historical reasons, bank with the Bank of England. So too, do a few other customers, including the Bank's employees. These deposits are of no economic significance.

(e) As a bank of issue
The Bank of England is the only bank in the U.K. with the right to issue notes in England and Wales. Scottish and Irish banks issue their own notes, but these are backed by Bank of England notes kept in the vaults. The note issue is backed by government securities and a tiny fraction of gold. When notes are backed by other paper this is known as a fiduciary issue.

(f) Control of the money supply
One of the functions of the Bank of England as a central bank, is to control the money supply. The money supply is the amount of money used in the economic system at any one time. It comprises simply, notes and coins in circulation and current accounts, the latter being a medium through which indebtedness can be cleared. A broader definition (M3) comprises the above totals (M1) with private sector deposit accounts at the banks and discount houses; and public sector deposits. M3 sterling is the same less U.K. residents' deposits in currencies other than sterling (Table 4.1).

Control of the money supply comes through the rules and understandings that link the Bank of England with the banking system. When the government wishes to reduce the money supply, the amount of reserves held by banks in relation to their liabilities, is raised. They have to keep more of their assets in liquid form. They cannot expand lending. This leads to a slowing down or contraction on the growth of deposits and ultimately a slowing down or contraction in the supply of money.

Banks were required to keep a minimum $12\frac{1}{2}$ % of their 'eligible liabilities' in 'reserve assets' but 10% from 5 January 1981.

Eligible liabilities
The components of each bank's 'eligible liabilities' are
(i) All sterling deposits of an original maturity of two years or under, from U.K. residents (other than banks) and from overseas residents (other than overseas offices — see (iv) below) and all funds due to customers or third parties which are temporarily held on suspense accounts (other than credits in course of transmission — see (vi) below)

The scheme is based on deposits; notes issued by the Scottish and Northern Ireland banks do not count as eligible liabilities. Suspense accounts representing the bank's own internal funds, e.g profit and loss accounts, reserves, provisions for tax, etc. are excluded.

Table 4.1 U.K. Money stock — amounts outstanding at 16 January 1980 (£m unadjusted).

1 Notes and coin in circulation with the public	2 U.K. private sector sterling sight deposits non-interest-bearing*	3 U.K. private sector sterling sight deposits interest-bearing	4 Money stock M 1	5 U.K. private sector sterling time deposits	6 U.K. public sector sterling deposits	7 Money stock sterling	8 U.K. residents' deposits in other currencies	9 Money stock M 3.
9,319	14,379	3,798	27,496	27,353	1,169	56,018	4,857	60,875

* After deducting 60% of transit items.
M 1 = columns 1 + 2 + 3; Sterling M 3 = M 1 + columns 5 + 6; M 3 = sterling M 3 + column 8.
Including U.K. residents' holdings of certificates of deposit.

(ii) All sterling deposits of whatever term from banks in the U.K. less any sterling claims on such banks.

(iii) All sterling certificates of deposit issued of whatever term less any holdings of such certificates.

(iv) The bank's net deposit liability, if any, in sterling to its overseas offices. An overseas office is defined here as a head office, a parent company or a branch overseas, or a wholly-owned overseas banking subsidiary of the U.K. bank or its parent.

(v) The bank's net liability, if any, in currencies other than sterling
less

(vi) 60% of the net value of transit items in the bank's balance sheet.

This adjustment is necessary to avoid over or under-statement of the banking system's total eligible liabilities. The value of a cheque, for example, which has been credited to the payee's account at one bank, but not yet debited to the drawer's account at another bank will, if both accounts are in credit, appear in both banks' reported deposits without increasing the sterling resources of the banking system as a whole.

Reserve assets
These comprise

(i) Balances at the head office or branches of the Bank of England* (other than special deposits.) Notes and coin held in banks' tills do not count as reserve assets, nor do Bank of England notes and coin held as cover for notes issued by the Scottish and Northern Ireland banks in excess of their authorized i.e. fiduciary issues.

(ii) British government and Northern Ireland government Treasury bills.

(iii) Money at call with the London money market.

(iv) British government stocks and nationalized industries' stocks guaranteed by H.M. Government, with one year or less to final maturity.

(v) Local authority bills eligible for re-discount at the Bank of England. These are eligible for re-discount if they have an original term of maturity of less than six months and meet certain requirements concerning publication and notice. A complete list of such bills is displayed in the Discount Office of the Bank.

(vi) Commercial bills eligible for re-discount at the Bank of England, up to a maximum of 2% of total eligible liabilities.

(vii) Company tax reserve certificates, *originally part of the Reserve assets were discarded in 1977,* because they gave too high an interest to companies compared with other 'savings'.

---

* Balances at Bank of England agreed at $1\frac{1}{2}$ % of deposits.
+ This amounts to about 4% of a bank's liabilities.

Money supply and the aims of monetary policy
By controlling the money supply, the government hopes to achieve certain aims or economic objectives. These objectives, outlined in paragraphs 69 – 71 of the Radcliffe Report on the Working of the Monetary System 1959, are (a) a high and stable level of employment (b) a stable level of prices (c) economic growth (d) strengthening of exchange reserves implying (e) a stable exchange rate and a balance of payments surplus, which would enable aid to be given to less developed countries.

The difficulty of achieving all aims simultaneously
Some of these aims were achieved in the sixties. Others proved mutually exclusive. The Phillips curve indicates a relationship (or 'trade-off' between unemployment and wage increases: the higher the level of unemployment, the lower the rate of wage increase. This may have been true when Professor Phillips set out his ideas in *'Economica'* in 1958. In 1970, however, unemployment and wages rose together, a situation far more in keeping with the Wages Fund theory than the Phillips curve.

Efforts to reduce unemployment even by methods disapproved by the E.E.C. (such as the Temporary Employment Subsidy) proved unavailing. Unemployment in the U.K. rose in August 1977 to 1,635,950 or 6.9%. Though wage earnings to June 1977 increased by 10% inflation increased still more: to 17.7% for the 12 months to June 1977. This was the biggest annual recorded fall in average real disposable income for over a century. Efforts to increase employment have been followed by inflation. Efforts to control inflation have been followed by higher unemployment. By January 1980, the retail price index was at 248.8 (January 1974 = 100), with unemployment at 1,338,800. In both cases, the trend was rising. So too was the level of average earnings. They rose by 19.2% between November 1978 and November 1979.

Similarly, efforts to keep the exchange rate down (as happened in the U.K. in 1977 when huge inflows of sterling came into the country) pushes the money supply up. The money supply cannot be controlled if the authorities are at the same time trying to control the exchange rate. This is why Keynesians prefer exchange rate control with less ability to control the money supply, while Monetarists favour freer exchange rates and tighter money supply.

Management of government debt
This function may be seen as part of the Bank of England's role as banker to the Government. The management of government debt may also conflict with other objectives, e.g. there may be a large maturity of government debt at a time when a deflationary policy is required by the Government. The Bank of England then tries gradually to 'fund' (i.e. lengthen the maturity date of) the debt. This is part of its effort to maintain an orderly money market by smoothing out fluctuations in Government payments and receipts.

The Government may wish to reduce the servicing charges on its National

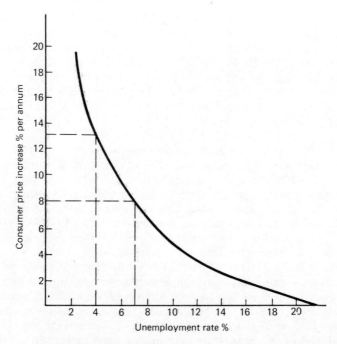

Figure 4.1 The 'trade-off' between price stability and unemployment (Phillips Curve). This *hypothetical* diagram shows a trade-off between inflation at 13% and unemployment at 4% or between inflation at 8% and unemployment at 7%. To get an 'acceptable' level of inflation may mean an 'unacceptable' level of unemployment — if the trade-off theory is accepted — for it implies that a particular level of unemployment means a particular rate of wage increase, therefore low unemployment and low inflation rates would not be consistent. A choice must be made between acceptable/possible combinations of inflation and unemployment.

Debt. These rise steeply during periods of high interest rates. Reduction in interest rates could, however, stimulate the demand for capital. This makes control of the money supply more difficult. The Bank of England, like most central banks, therefore uses several techniques to control either the money supply or interest rates. These techniques are discussed under the general heading of *Monetary Policy* in Chapter 10. They can be summarized here as: control over the quantity and quality of assets which banks must hold against their liabilities; interest rates; open market operations; requests and directives; and, in the U.K., special deposits and supplementary deposits (colloquially referred to as the 'corset') as well as 'targets', the aim of which is to keep control over the money supply by specifying a maximum permitted percentage expansion rate over a given period.

TYPICAL QUESTION

(a) Define the term 'eligible liabilities', as used in the Bank of England's publication on Competition and Credit Control.

(b) Using the balance sheet and information given below, list the bank's eligible reserve assets and calculate the bank's reserve asset ratio.

Smallbank Limited

	£m		£m
Capital	30	Cash in tills	60
		Balance at Bank of England	30
Reserves	60	Treasury bills	50
		Commercial bills	50
Current accounts	600	British Government Securities	
		(of which £20m have less	
Deposit accounts	500	than one year to maturity)	200
		Money at call with London	
		discount market	40
(note: Eligible liabilities		Other call money	60
are £1,000m)		Advances	600
		Investments in subsidiaries	30
		Special deposits	40
		Premises	30
	1,190		1,190

SUGGESTED ANSWER

Eligible liabilities are defined as the sterling deposit liabilities of the banking system as a whole excluding deposits having an original maturity of over two years plus any sterling resources obtained by switching foreign currencies into sterling. Inter-bank transactions and sterling certificates of deposit (both held and issued) will be taken into the calculation of individual banks' liabilities on a net basis, irrespective of term. Adjustments will be made in respect of transit items.

In the example given, the reserve assets are Balance at the Bank of England, £30m + Treasury Bills, £50m + 2% of eligible liabilities in commercial bills, i.e. 2% of £1,000 = £20m + British Government Securities with less than one year to maturity, £20m + call money to the discount market, £40m. This makes a total of reserve assets of £160m. The reserve ratio is thus 16%:

$$\frac{£160}{£1,000} = \frac{16}{100} = 16\%$$

62   THEORY AND PRACTICE OF MONEY

It should be noted, however, that 'other call money' could be ranked as a reserve asset if it is placed with certain other firms carrying on a similar type of business to that of the London Discount Market Association, such as discount brokers and the money trading departments of certain banks, money brokers concerned with the overnight finance of the gilt-edged market, jobbers on the London Stock Exchange provided the funds are secured against Government stocks or Government guaranteed stocks or certain other specified public sector or foreign Government stocks.

ADDITIONAL QUESTIONS

1. What are the main functions of the Bank of England? Have these functions changed since the secondary banking crisis of 1973 — 1975?

2. What functions are usually carried out by a central bank?

3. Outline the special characteristics that in Britain distinguish the banks from other financial institutions.

4. Write brief notes on the Bank of England as 'lender of last resort'.

5. Why does a country need a central bank?

5 Other Financial Institutions: Non-Bank Financial Intermediaries

There are many financial institutions which are not ranked as 'banks', or whose liabilities are not classed as 'money'. It may need a semantic turn of mind to see the difference between a deposit in a building society and one in a bank. Yet there is a difference. The depositor cannot directly transfer assets in a building society to somebody else. The owner of assets held in pension funds, investment trusts, or stock exchange investments cannot use them against purchases of goods. The assets must first be changed into money by borrowing against the security of the assets; or selling them for liquid cash; or for a cheque drawn by the holders of the assets, payable to the asset owner.

In other words, the liabilities of non-bank financial institutions, unlike the liabilities of the banks, do not perform one of the functions of money: a medium of exchange. They act as a store of value, and as a unit of account. They are therefore classed as quasi-money — nearly money, but not quite. The institutions holding this quasi-money are classed as *non-bank financial intermediaries*.

Barter is an exchange of goods for goods. It takes place only when there is a *double coincidence of wants*: each side wanting what the other has at exactly the same time. The invention of money allows two separate transactions to take place: the sale of one good, the purchase of another. The development of financial intermediaries goes still further. It splits borrowing and lending into 2 different processes.

Banks borrow in exchange for their own debt (liabilities) and separately lend money in exchange for a borrower's debt (assets) i.e. a bank takes deposits and offers short-term advances. Other financial intermediaries specialize in different types of borrowing and lending. Building Societies take deposits and lend to home buyers against a mortgage. Finance companies take deposits and finance consumer durables or other goods. Insurance funds take deposits on policies and buy securities. Savings banks take deposits and acquire government debt.

To study the banking institutions and not the other financial intermediaries would give a false picture of the economy and its liquidity. Firstly, their deposits are very large; secondly, they are an additional source of credit; thirdly, some, particularly building society deposits, can be quickly substituted for money. Building society deposits have two further effects. They influence housing demand, and the construction industry, for 80 – 90% of all mortgages come from the building societies, with the rest from local authorities, insurance companies, banks and loans by employers to employees.

5.1 FINANCE COMPANIES

These go under many names: houses, trusts or corporations. They specialize in instalment credit, lending money mainly for consumer durables. Sometimes longer loans will be made for company finance.

Finance houses had eligible liabilities in 1980 of around £500m. This was small compared with the £30,000m of the London clearing banks, but important in the provision of credit. Before 1971, the houses were subject to Orders which regulated the amount of down payments and length of life of a loan. Eight changes of these conditions took place during the eight years between 1961 and 1969 to control their expansion during a period of bank restriction. Under Competition and Credit Control 1971, finance houses became, like the banks, subject to asset ratio control. If they had total deposits from the public of over £5m they had to observe a reserve asset ratio of 10%. The largest houses which had become banks, had to observe the banks' $12\frac{1}{2}$ % ratio. Calls for Special Deposits can be at a higher rate than for the banks, if the Bank of England so decides.

Many industrial companies use the services of finance houses. They like the fixed time period and fixed interest rates, the latter being of great importance during times of financial instability. Between 1971 and 1978, Minimum Lending Rate changed 67 times compared with 14 times in the six previous years. Such changes can cause serious cash flow problems, whereas borrowers who are on fixed rates for a medium term, know in advance the extent of their commitment. Other advantages of finance house instalment credit include standard documentation, no legal fees, and no charge over a borrower's asset, though security is taken on the equipment financed.

As well as providing instalment credit for consumers and industry, finance houses are now moving into leasing. This is an expanding activity because of tax concessions. For customers who prefer a variable interest rate, this can be arranged. It is related to the *Finance House Base Rate* which is calculated in the following way: A leading firm of money brokers takes the weekly average of the interbank three month rate at 11.00 am each day of the week. The F.H.A. averages the last 8 weekly figures, rounding the result up to the nearest half point. This figure is announced on the last business day of each month as the Finance House Base Rate effective from the first day of the following month. Other institutions outside the F.H.A. use this Base Rate.

5.2 INSURANCE FUNDS

The word insurance is generally used to cover all types of savings against life's vicissitudes. Life insurance companies manage over £15,000m deposits and there are many other branches of insurance such as marine, fire, aviation, motor, which bring in large sums as 'invisible' exports. They are a powerful force in the financial markets, with the life funds largely invested in the gilt edged sector. This is the traditional outlet for long-term funds.

5.3 PENSION FUNDS

Pension Funds have grown along with legislation to ensure that retirement should not mean penury. Employers, the state and trade unions run statutory and voluntary schemes. From the private sector alone, pension funds amount to some £15,000m, all long-term and stable. £10,582m represented the market value for funded schemes in the public sector with £5000m accounted for by local authority funds.

Increases in income lead to increases in savings. Whether this saving is voluntary or compulsory depends on the type of pension scheme, but most pension fund managers try to find the highest and safest return for the money deposited with them. This aim is complicated by two factors (a) the large percentage of U.K. equities owned by *institutions* — around 70% and growing by 2% a year. This causes some inflexibility in investment opportunities, and (b) the growing social awareness of investors which leads them to be concerned how pension and other institutional funds are being used.

5.4 THE CORPORATION OF LLOYDS AND LLOYDS REGISTER OF SHIPPING

The Corporation of Lloyds provides a competitive international market for all types of insurance. The 8000 elected members have a premium business amounting to over £1000m, 50% earned in North America, the rest divided equally between home and overseas. The public do not deal directly with the underwriters, but with the 270 Lloyds brokerage firms, who are free, however, to place their clients' business anywhere they see fit.

Separate but historically associated with the Corporation is Lloyds Register of Shipping. This is a classification society which publishes a register of ships, rules for their construction, and surveys them. It operates a research laboratory, inspection services for industrial plants and offshore engineering projects.

5.5 BUILDING SOCIETIES

Building societies perform two functions in modern society: (a) providing finance for home ownership and (b) acting as a remunerative haven for small savings. Investors can have various types of account, some at higher rates for fixed terms or regular saving. Interest rates vary with the general movement in Minimum Lending Rate; both for borrowers and depositors, but the Societies try to avoid frequent changes of rates. People who borrow for a period of twenty years or more do not want their rates altered continually upwards. . . . . on the other hand savers will not deposit funds in the building societies if more competitive rates are obtainable elsewhere. Hence, there is usually a time lag in adjusting mortgage and deposit rates to market interest rates, and occasionally, rationing of mortgage advances.

The importance of building societies to the economy is that they provide almost the whole of private sector home ownership funds. They channel savings into long-term advances and so release bank deposits for the financing of shorter-term investment projects. In this way, building societies fill an important niche in the financial markets as suppliers of capital. The banking institutions are, however, becoming increasingly concerned about the competition for savings from the building societies, and particularly by the societies' preferential treatment from the Inland Revenue. Banks would like to enter the housing market, possibly on the same terms.

5.6 UNIT TRUSTS AND INVESTMENT TRUSTS

A unit trust is a pool of money belonging to many subscribers. They invest their money, indirectly, in a wide range of stock market securities by dividing the invested fund of shares into equal units of a prescribed amount. The units belong to the investors in proportion to the amount subscribed by them. The aim of the unit trust movement is to enable the small investor to have an interest in a large number of securities under experienced supervision.

The unit trust is not a limited company. It has no directors but a management company who buy and sell the shares and collect the dividends. They charge a fee for their services, deducted from the dividends collected. When the unit trust movement started, the power of investment was usually restricted to certain stocks with a percentage in each stock. They were known as 'fixed trusts'. This is no longer the case. The management companies who invest the funds have far more flexibility within rules laid down by the Department of Trade and Industry.

Every Fund has a trustee, usually a bank or insurance company which holds the stocks and shares on behalf of the unit holder. The trustees have the right to appoint managers, and most of the documentation comes under their eyes, if not their supervision. The trustee is bound by the Prevention of Fraud Act, particularly in regard to advertising for funds for the trust.

An investment trust differs from a unit trust in that it is an ordinary registered company. It invests share and loan capital almost entirely in marketable investments. Like any other registered company, there are directors, who buy and sell shares as the business of the company. The investment trust company holds the shares purchased in its own name, unlike the unit trust where the shares are held in the name of the trustees.

Both groups have grown rapidly, particularly in the last decade, and contribute greatly to the funds in the capital market.

SUMMARY

Non-bank financial intermediaries (N.B.F.I.S) sell a financial service to one group of people; take the money for this service and then sell another financial service to another group of people. The financial services sold, e.g. insurance, cannot usually be provided by the individuals themselves. The money raised by the sale of financial services is on-lent to another group, e.g. companies. Banks act as intermediaries too, but they do more than transmit funds; they create them. They issue primary securities. N.B.F.I.s issue indirect or secondary securities. Secondary claims lead to the purchase of other claims. Primary claims lead to the direct purchase of goods and services.

Financial intermediaries create claims or liabilities against themselves which are more liquid than the assets they hold, and which the ultimate lender finds more acceptable. N.B.F.I.s can operate successfully with liabilities more liquid than their assets because they work within known degrees of probability and on a very large scale. They provide the community with purchasing power and extra transmission mechanisms between ultimate borrowers and lenders. Their role is very important from the viewpoint of overall monetary control. This is why there are restrictions on consumer credit from time to time; and why building societies and pension funds are not shielded from the movement of interest rates, although tax concessions are permitted to them to encourage home ownership and community thrift.

QUESTIONS ON SYLLABUS

In the A.I.B. examinations of recent years there have been few questions set on the subjects covered in this chapter 5, but the new Financial Studies Diploma of the Institute of Bankers includes in the syllabus, *the role of the Stock Exchange* (see Chapter 6) *and other financial institutions*.

TYPICAL QUESTION

Discuss how far a country's money stock comprises:
   (a) liabilities of its central bank;
   (b) liabilities of its commercial banks.
Does it usually comprise the liabilities of other financial institutions and if not, why not?

SUGGESTED ANSWER

Different countries use different definitions for their money stock (supply). A general definition covers those assets which the public use to fulfil the functions of money (medium of exchange; unit of account; store of value; standard for deferred payments). Such assets comprise the liabilities of the central and commercial banks. In some countries (not the U.K.) the liabilities of other financial institutions may be included in the money stock.

The liabilities of the commercial banks used by the public as money in the U.K. consist of private sector sight deposits (M1). For the wider definition of the money supply (M3) the following are added to M1: private sector time deposits, public sector sight and time deposits and deposits of U.K. residents in currencies other than sterling. Other countries use roughly similar definitions depending on the sophistication of their financial institutions.

Liabilities of the central Banks used by the public as money are notes issued by the Banks and held by the public. Coin is a negligible part of the money supply in the U.K. and other industrialized countries. It can usually be regarded as a liability of the Government: its purchase by a central Bank creates an inpayment to the relevant Government department.

The reason why the liabilities of financial institutions are not included in a country's money stock definition, is that those liabilities are not considered to fulfil all the functions of money.

ADDITIONAL QUESTIONS

1. Do Building Societies create credit? Give reasons for your answer.
2. What problems face investment managers (pension funds, trade union funds, union trusts, etc.) in the investment of their funds? Describe possible solutions, their advantages and disadvantages.

SUGGESTED ANSWER TO QUESTION 1

As building societies accounted for 48% of the £69.639m personal sector liquid assets held in major financial institutions in 1978, and were still growing by 1980, the following brief answer is given to Question 1.

Building societies are playing an increasing role in the money and gilt edged markets. Do they create credit? Credit involves borrowing by one person or group, lending by another. But there is a difference between the transfer of credit and the creation of credit. Banks create credit because their loans make new deposits in the banking system. These deposits enable further loans to be made.

Building societies transfer credit from savers to borrowers. The credit is restricted to the purchase of homes. Bank credit however, is interchangeable with money for all purposes. Building society credit acts in a strictly limited sense as a medium of exchange and payments but functions better as a store of value (for house purchasers, not always depositors) and as a medium of deferred payments. The building societies act as intermediaries in the transfer of credit from savers to borrowers. They do not create credit but the boundary between creation and transfer is ill-defined and building societies must be regarded as a very important source of liquidity in the economy.

6 The Stock Exchange

A stock exchange is a financial market where stocks and shares can be bought and sold. The London Stock Exchange, by value of turnover, is one of the three largest exchanges in the world. It is governed by a Council of 36 Members. Twelve of these are elected every year by ballot from among the members. The Council regulates the procedures of the Stock Exchange and permission from the Council must be obtained before the shares of any company can be dealt in on the Stock Exchange.

When a private business wants cash for expansion, this cannot always be raised from private resources, profits or reserves, and the amount may be too large or too long-term for banks to provide. The business may then choose to go 'public'. It can offer shares or loan capital in the business through a Stock Exchange listing. If successful in its application for a listing, it becomes a company owned by a group of shareholders. A listing is only granted if a company fulfils certain conditions and publishes full and true particulars. Thereafter, the shares of the company are quoted on the Stock Exchange and dealings in the shares can take place in the open market.

The issue of shares by a company going 'public' is a common way of raising capital. There are three main methods. The new issue may be made by *prospectus*. This is a direct offer to the public with the announcement and particulars of the company and its history in a prospectus or newspaper. The issue may be made by *placing*. Here the company places a proportion of the issue with a certain number of investors who have already expressed an interest in the company. Some part of the issue, however, must always be kept for the general public. A new issue may also be made by an *offer for sale*. Here an issuing house buys the shares from the company and then offers them to the public. In effect, the issuing house is underwriting the issue.

British funds are first issued by the Bank of England, usually by way of a newspaper advertisement. Later purchases and sales go through the Stock Exchange, or for smaller holdings, through the Post Office Register. Raising capital for both the private and public sector would be much more difficult if there were no way by which holders of the various securities could convert them into cash.

Commercial companies and nationalised industries can raise money from individual savers and from institutions such as pension funds, insurance companies and trade unions. The savers can place money in the investments they choose. The nominal value of those investments may change. It can move up or down in line with market sentiment and the profitability, or otherwise, of the company and with the performance of the economy.

Buying and selling of quoted securities on the Stock Exchange takes place through jobbers and brokers. Jobbers are the wholesalers in the market. As principals, they buy and sell on their own account with brokers or other jobbers; never with the public direct. Brokers are not principals, but agents. They are the link between jobbers and clients. Without revealing whether they are buying or selling, the broker approaches a jobber dealing in the stock for which the broker has an order. The jobber quotes two prices: the lower the price at which he is prepared to buy, the higher at which he will sell. The difference makes the jobber's 'turn' or profit. Different jobbers may well quote different buying and selling prices for the same stock. The price they ask, or offer, depends on the amount they hold of the stock, and the view they take of its current and future demand.

Investors who buy new issues are called stags. New issues are popular with investors. If the issue is oversubscribed, some form of rationing will have to take place. Stags who subscribe over or under a given sum will receive a certain proportion of the shares or there may be a ballot.

Investors, contracting to buy at today's prices, and hoping that the price will go up by the time they must pay for the contract, are called bulls. Sometimes bulls will buy options, which for a price, gives them the right to buy a share at today's price up to any time within the next three months. Sellers who hope for a downward turn in prices by the time they have to deliver the shares, are called bears. Being a bull or a bear can result in large gains or losses. The bear position is potentially the most dangerous, for whereas shares cannot sink below a price of zero, they can soar, in theory, to any height, and the seller must still deliver.

When a bargain is struck, whether for the shares or for an option on them, a contract note will be sent to the client. If he is selling, he signs a transfer form and forwards his share certificate. Payment for shares has to be made soon after the end of the Account, a 14-day period except during public holidays when the Account covers 21 days. A buyer of shares gets a certificate proving ownership some time after the bargain is struck.

Transactions in government stocks are on a daily cash basis. No capital gains tax is paid on sales of Government stock held for more than one year, and overseas holders can get their dividends paid gross. Small savers in government stock are better served through the Post Office Register than through the Stock Exchange as the commission charged by the Post Office is minimal. However, the Register does not carry the full range of Government stocks and, unlike the broker who carries out bargains immediately, it may take several days, or longer, for orders to be carried out through the Register.

Brokers charge a commission of 1.5% plus V.A.T on purchases and sales. There is also stamp duty on purchases of non-Government securities. These charges can often turn a small gain into a loss. But then brokers do not, rightly, view their function as encouragement of the small saver. They are vital cogs in the mechanism of the Stock Exchange, an institution which encourages investment, but also allows speculation to take place. Speculation is the activity of forecasting the psychology of the market, or as Keynes put it so well, a place 'where we devote our intelligences to anticipating what average opinion expects average opinion to be'.

The Stock Exchange is often quoted as an example of the perfect market in economics, where there is freedom of entry, an homogenous product, large numbers of buyers and sellers, and perfect knowledge/communication. The latter is a condition not easily attainable anywhere with the result that stock market prices can be very volatile.

Keynes gave several reasons for this volatility:

(a) The divorce of ownership of shares from company management so that shareholders, generally, are ill-informed about the companies they invest in.

(b) The tendency for only 'fools and philanthropists' to invest for the long term.

(c) The sensitivity of stock market prices to sudden changes of mass psychology.

(d) The exaggerated importance given to day-to-day fluctuations in profitability which turn out to be of an ephemeral nature.

(e) The confidence in security prices of those who lend money.

(f) The importance of expectation in determining values.

Volatility of price can be an advantage to the short-term operator on the Stock Exchange. Without big swings in share prices, there would be little short-term advantage in taking risks. The institutions tend to be more cautious in their choice of investment and to spread their funds over a wide range of shares. The existence of a Stock Exchange enables them to find such a range, both in this country and abroad.

Other advantages of a Stock Exchange to an economy can be summed up as follows:

(a) Large organization (insurance companies, pension and trade union funds, etc.) can buy stocks and shares and earn interest on funds not immediately required.

(b) The prices quoted on the Stock Exchange assist the assessment of certain taxes such as capital gains and transfer tax.

(c) The movements in quoted prices give an indication of the level of economic activity. A rise in the price of a company's share reflects confidence (sometimes misplaced) in that company; a rise in gilt-edged, usually indicates a sign of increasing strength in the economy.

(d) Liquidity can be exchanged between those who prefer financial assets to cash. . .and vice versa.

(e) Capital becomes easier to raise for business because of (d) above.

(f) Government and local authority stocks can be bought and sold on the Stock Exchange. So can those of foreign governments and international monetary institutions. This helps the authorities in raising finance.

6.1 TRADED OPTIONS

On 21 April 1978, the London Stock Exchange began providing a market in traded options. The difference between traded options and the conventional kind is that the former are marketable; the latter are not. The conventional option is a contract between two parties which gives one the right to buy, the other the right to sell stock, at a mutually agreed price within a certain time limit. Traded options give greater flexibility. A clearing corporation enables buyer and seller to act independently of each other. The European Options Exchange in Amsterdam offers traded options in European and American shares. London specializes in British shares.

6.2 INTRODUCTION TO INVESTMENT

Having given a brief outline of the Stock Exchange and the methods by which it operates, we now come to the sensitive area of investment — sensitive because if the practice of investment principles always resulted in gain, who would choose to lose?

There are no 100% certainties in investment. One can buy shares in a company with an impeccable earnings record, excellent management, and before the next company report is out, find the shares have halved in value owing to some unforeseeable calamity at home or abroad; buy oil shares just before the wells are expropriated, destroyed or run dry; coffee plantation shares minutes before a frost freezes the whole crop; shares in a vineyard weeks before a worriesome weevil winkles out every drop of wine.

On the other hand, a person knowing absolutely nothing can make a 'killing' by luck alone: investors who bought an Australian mining share some years ago were informed by their broker a few days later that a new drilling had revealed millions of high-grade ore. The share price tripled overnight. The holders sold — just in time before it was discovered that the figures for the drilling results, wired from Australia, had left out a vital decimal point. The missing 'damned dots' to use Randolph Churchill's memorable phrase, had inflated both the mineral wealth and the share price.

Between these extremes of good and ill fortune, however, some principles of investment can be used to achieve specific aims: to protect savings from inflation; to increase income or capital or make provision for dependants, or charities.

6.2.1 FINANCIAL INVESTMENT

In speaking of investment in this context, we are referring to personal or *financial* investment: claims to wealth in the form of bonds, mortgages, stocks and shares. The buying and selling of such claims is called personal or financial investment to distinguish it from *real investment* in which capital goods are produced for the production of consumption goods and further capital goods.

6.3 STOCK EXCHANGE PROCEDURE

The procedure has already been outlined. Brokers act for clients in buying and selling shares to and from jobbers who hold the stock. The bargain having been made, a contract is sent to the client with commission and other charges, and the date of the bargain and payment (due at end of Account). Most shares are *registered securities*. Title holders are registered in the Company books by Transfer deed, and a share certificate is issued to the holder. *Bearer securities* are usually issued in the form of bearer bonds and are physically passed from seller to buyer.

Interest or dividend payments may be collected by presentation of a coupon from a block attached to the bearer security. The disadvantage of bearer securities is that, as there is no register of ownership, any loss means the forfeiture of capital and income. Under the Exchange Control Act 1947, bearer securities had to be lodged with an authorized depositary.

6.4 FOREIGN SECURITIES

The London Stock Exchange deals in many types of foreign bonds. 'Americans' are among the most popular, accounting for probably 60% of U.K. portfolio investment overseas. The front of the American share certificate shows the name of the shareholder. The reverse side is used for transferring title. When this is completed, the certificate goes to the company's transfer agent. A fresh certificate is then issued to the new owner. American securities owned by U.K. citizens are usually registered in 'recognized marking names'. These are the names of individuals and institutions who deal in American and other foreign shares and who have undertaken to pay the owners thereof, dividends at the rate of exchange fixed by the Stock Exchange.

Sums of less than £5,000 are better invested in appropriate unit trusts than directly in American or other foreign shares. U.S. share purchases and sales require virtually cash payment. Commissions are very much higher than those for comparative U.K. shares. The U.K. broker has to deal through an overseas broker who also gets commission.

Almost all U.S. stockbrokers have a London office. There are 13 Japanese firms, as well as Australian and Canadian ones. Dutch and German banks cover many European shares. Foreign-based brokers in London often — but not always — have a better knowledge of their home markets and their commission charges are less than those of U.K. brokers for foreign stock.

Buying seats on overseas exchanges avoids the need for paying foreign commission, but foreign firms are not allowed to buy New York Stock Exchange seats. U.K. brokers tend to set up offices in the West coast of the U.S.A. They offer institutional clients in depth research on a small number of companies in that area. This avoids competition with New York broking firms working on the same kind of data, nationwide.

6.5 NEW ISSUES

The Stock Exchange does not issue new shares. This is done by merchant and other banks, or, for gilt-edged stocks, by the Bank of England. The existence of the Stock Exchange however, facilitates the raising of such capital by new issues. Without a market for 'secondhand' shares, which the Stock Exchange is, how could 'new' shares be later sold?

6.6. NON-MARKETABLE CLAIMS

Non-marketable claims do not go through the Stock Exchange but other outlets such as Post Offices, finance houses, insurance and building society offices. Included in these non-marketable 'investments' (savings is often a more appropriate word) are deposits in Savings and Trustee Banks; Savings and Premium Bonds; National Savings, Save-As-You-Earn (SAYE) and Retirement Certificates; deposits in Building Societies, Finance Houses and Insurance companies. All, except the last, are highly liquid; money can be withdrawn within one day to a month. All, except Premium Bonds, Save-As-You-Earn and Retirement Certificates pay interest at a rate fixed at the outset or which varies with fluctuations in Bank or other pivotal rates. In all (except equity-linked insurance schemes), the *nominal* value of the initial capital is maintained.

Premium Bonds are more like a lottery with cash prizes for the lucky ticket holders. The SAYE and Retirement Certificates are inflation-proofed. They pay no interest, but SAYE gives a bonus if the Certificates are held for 7 years rather than the contractual five. Certificates which are tax-free at the end of the saving period are suitable for high taxpayers.

Building Society deposits give savers liquidity, interest, and mortgage facilities for house purchase. This still remains the biggest and best investment most people will ever make, certainly in their younger years. It provides among other things, security as well as collateral for later investment/expenditure. Tax relief is allowed on the interest paid on mortgages where the borrowing is for under £25,000.

Insurance, like home ownership, has favourable tax reliefs, and acts as a safety net for life's hazards. Returns for policies over 10—30 years differ enormously. It is wise to look at a company's past records before taking out any long-term commitment. Some companies head the 'league table' of good profit records for their insured clients, year after year. Magazines like *Planned Savings* publish a comparative profits survey, past performance record of many types of fixed interest investments including insurance companies. They also give the 'Top Ten' surrender values on whole life and endowment policies, a very useful survey, for a policy prematurely surrendered may not give the saver the money he has paid in. Equity-linked insurance can result in an even worse return, for there is no guarantee that even over 10 years, the equities with which the insurance is linked, will have risen enough to make the investment worth-while. The return depends on the expertise of the trust and insurance fund managers.

For shorter terms, income and growth bonds are better than the conventional endowment (10) year policies. They are issued for terms of 3—10 years. A fixed rate of return is guaranteed, paid out as a regular income once or twice a year (income bonds) or altogether in a lump sum at the end of the bond's life (growth bonds). 'Property' and 'managed' bonds are also issued by insurance companies and others. In these bonds, the value of the bond fluctuates because it is linked to a fund of investments. It can go up or down, unlike the income and growth bonds. Other bonds cater for a variety of tax- and non-tax-payers' needs. Examples are single premium endowment bonds and hybrid-type endowments with annuities.

Other organizations, such as Finance for Industry, take deposits for a fixed period of time for a fixed rate. So do local authorities. The Loans Bureau supply a list of the local authorities wanting money and the time length of the desired loan. This type of local authority loan is not marketable, though very safe. Early encashment may be difficult. *Public issues* of local authority stocks can be bought and sold on the Stock Exchange. Their prices go up and down in the same way and usually in the same direction as Government stocks. (The Saturday issue of the *Financial Times* gives a full list of the prices of corporation stocks dealt in the preceding week.) The income received from the stocks is related to the market price of the stock and its interest rate (sometimes called 'coupon'). The return is known as a flat or *running yield*. *Redemption yield* takes in the total value of the yield from purchase to maturity plus or minus any capital gain or loss at that date. The result is divided by the number of years held, to give a percentage per annum return on the purchase price of the stock.

The yield on shares used to be higher than that of gilt-edged (up to about 1960) to offset the supposed 'riskiness' of equities, compared with government stock. Gilts now have to give a higher return than ordinary shares in order to compensate for double figure inflation. The difference between the lower return on the *Financial Times* ordinary share index and the gilt-edged $2\frac{1}{2}$ % Consols today has become known as the 'reverse yield gap'.

A stock issued at £100 (its nominal or par value) which is currently priced at £110, will give a capital loss at maturity date and hence will cause the redemption yield to be lower than the running yield. High-rate taxpayers often buy shares or stock before the dividend or interest is due, wait for the price to rise as it usually does before the dividend date, and then sell 'cum div', i.e. with the dividend passing to the buyer. In this way they make a capital gain which is less severely taxed than is investment income, into which the dividends would be classed by the Inland Revenue. 'Yearlings' (one year gilt-edged) are often bought and sold in this way, but the investor who tries to make too regular a market in 'yearlings' (at £1,000 a time!) may be classed as a 'trader' in which case the profit will be treated as income and subject to the investor's highest tax rate.

Fixed interest stocks and shares such as local authorities, government bonds and preference shares, suit the person who is interested only in income and not too worried about price fluctuations in the value of the stock held. Local authorities give a higher yield than similar-dated gilts. This compensates for the fact that all capital gains on gilts held for more than one year are tax-free. Irish government stocks also yield more than comparable British ones. They do not have the capital gain advantage, but are better for non-tax payers because, unlike interest on British government bonds other than War Loan, they are paid gross. A similar concession is allowed for buyers of U.K. government stock from the Post Office Register at Bootle. Like all stocks, these prices will vary with market sentiment and economic conditions.

Convertibles have the merits of fixed interest with the opportunity of converting to the ordinary shares before a given date. Debentures are another form of fixed interest stock. So are preference shares. The former are classed as loans to the company. If it is wound up, the debentures will rank before the preference shares in any ultimate payout.

Gearing alters the rewards accruing to ordinary share holders. When a company is *highly geared*, it has a *high proportion* of fixed interest shares or other prior charges which must receive their allotted percentage first. Thus, ordinary shareholders do exceptionally well in highly geared companies in good times. In bad times, there will be little profit left over for ordinary shareholders after the prior charges have been met. The following simple example shows the effect of gearing on equity earnings.

Example
Company X issues £1m capital
divided into 500,000 Preference Shares of £1 @ 5%
        and 500,000 Ordinary Shares @ £1
In a good year, the profits for distribution are £100,000.
The 500,000 Preference shareholders get 5% on their holdings:
$$\frac{5 \times 500,000}{100} = \underline{£25,000}$$
This leaves £100,000—£25,000 for the
Ordinary shareholders = $\underline{£75,000}$
    i.e. a dividend of $\underline{15\%}$

In a bad year, the profits for distribution are only £30,000.
The 500,000 Preference shareholders get their £25,000 leaving only £5,000 to be shared among the 500,000 Ordinary shareholders: a dividend of 1%. Such is the effect of *gearing*.

6.7 TECHNICAL ANALYSIS

This is the name given to forecasting techniques which depend on past patterns of share price behaviour patterns. Extrapolations are made from them to predict future movements. Technical analysis depends more on visual patterns, and less (sometimes not at all) on *fundamental analysis* such as a share's intrinsic worth, its price earnings ratio or dividend potential. Chart analysis (a form of technical analysis) plots share price movements to establish a trend and predict one. Three types of chart are in general use (a) line, (b) bar (c) point and figure.

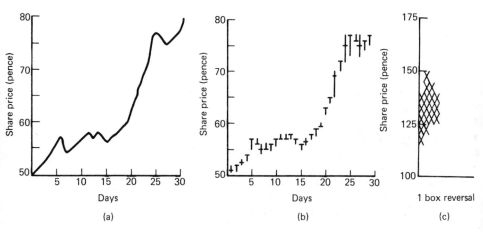

Figure 6.1   (a) Daily line chart for 30 days.
             (b) Daily bar chart for 30 days.
             (c) Point and figure chart plotting the following price
             recordings: 120, 125, 127, 129, 132, 140, 125, 141, 152, 130, 131,
             141, 145, 140, 130.

In *line charts*, entries are made of the closing prices of shares over a period of time and a line drawn connecting them. The vertical axis shows the price, the time period is on the horizontal axis. Line charts are commonly used to record highs and lows over a short period, say a month. *Bar charts* are similar to line charts. They also record the high and low points for the day (or other period) but the closing price is marked with a bar. *Point and figure charts* try to show a compressed picture of significant price changes. Prices are marked on the vertical scale. The horizontal scale is used to show reversals from a previous trend. The analyst chooses the scale. A trend can be more easily seen from a 5p than a 1p scale. Thus from a list of prices, 120, 125, 127, 129, 132, 140, 125, the following marks would be shown on a point and figure chart. X would be placed against 120, the start of the series. Then an x would be marked against 125 (5p up the scale). No x would be marked for 127 (not a price change of 5p). Similarly with 129: this too, has not crossed into new 5p territory. But 132 does, and gets an x. Two marks are made for 140 as it has crossed two 5p points. The next figure 125 shows a *reversal*. It therefore goes into the next column. Rises of 5p continue to be marked with an x and any reversal goes into the next column (Figure 6.1). Some variants do not record reversals of less than 15p (three box reversal). Rises are marked with an x and falls with o's. The month numbers 1—12 may be used instead of an x or o for the first transaction of the month to highlight any sudden bout of activity. Patterns are sought in point and figure markings: trend lines or channel patterns. From the many variants, analysts make their predictions of what shares to buy/sell/hold.

6.8 PRINCIPLES OF INVESTMENT

From all the savings and investment media available, what kind should be recommended to clients? This is an exercise that constantly taxes the brains of investment advisers. They, and their clients, record varying (and even contradictory) degrees of success. Two basic principles operate in investment as in taxation or even management: to know what you want, and how best to get it. The first is a personal or psychological problem: the second a technical one, and easier to solve than the first.

6.8.1 INDIVIDUAL INVESTMENT

Typical investment aims of a single investor, (as distinct from a group manager of funds) are the provision of capital or income; the protection of savings from inflation: to make provision for retirement, house purchase, dependants or charity. One objective may have to be given up for another of greater priority. Thus, an older person can get a higher income during her lifetime but only by giving up the capital she might have passed on to her heirs.

A knowledge of tax law is vital. It is no use trying to get the highest yield if this brings an investor out of a low tax bracket into a high one, whereas a capital gain could be almost tax-free.

Property was at one time, a rewarding and socially useful investment. Residential letting in the U.K., except by local authorities or for/by rich landlord and tenant, is now virtually extinct. Look only at *commercial property*. The big Funds: pension, insurance, trade unions, take no interest in providing rented accommodation. They are currently nibbling, (and some even swallowing) *agricultural land*.

6.8.2 GROUP INVESTMENT

The management of funds collected from a large number of members is group investment. One of the dilemmas facing managers of such large funds is how do they reconcile the aim of maximum growth from their investments with the channelling of money into sectors of which their subscribers may disapprove? The best solution is to divide the funds between a group of managers, and for each manager to make decisions in the light of *his/her knowledge* and *conscience*, even if members of the fund disapprove.

Investment decisions based on economic/financial criteria are made easier today by the many excellent publications which analyse company reports and provide evaluations of future company profitability. Further help in judging the merits of different securities can be based on the following principles (a) the yield on the security, (b) the possibility of redemption, (c) 'cover' for the income, (d) the degree of risk in the share, (e) the likelihood of capital growth, (f) market conditions and risks outside the company's control, (g) the investor's tax position, (h) the management of the company, (i) the structure of the company, e.g. gearing; liquidity; asset values; cash flow; price/earnings ratio. The latter represents the number of years' purchase of current year profits and is found by dividing the earnings per share figure into the share price.

6.9 SUMMARY AND READING LIST

This chapter will aid the student in answering some of the questions in the Investment paper, (Stage 2) and the paper for direct entry to the Financial Studies Diploma of the Institute of Bankers. For wider study, there are many excellent books (*Investment Analysis*: Michael Firth, Harper and Row) and a succinct appraisal for students: *Theory and Practice of Investment* by T.G. Goff (Heinemann, 1980). There are also the highly readable introductory books recommended in the Institute's reading list.

Even more essential, in my view, are the city pages of newspapers such as *The Daily Telegraph* and the *New Evening Standard*. *The Daily Mail* has a very readable city page with a 'Money' inset on Wednesdays. *The Financial Times* is a 'must' at least on Saturdays. On that day too, *The Times* answers readers' tax problems and covers aspects of family finance. *The Economist* provides authoritative economic comment; the *British Economy Survey* publishes a succinct termly appraisal of different sectors of the British economy while the *Investors Chronicle* has sections on company reports, finance and investment. *Which* covers consumer affairs. *Time* and *Fortune* are useful for the American business scene. *Planned Savings* assesses U.K. savings media. *Money Management* goes a little wider. The *Investment Trust Year Book* gives data on investment trusts. *The Bankers' Magazine* occasionally publishes a portfolio problem and answer while the booklets of Julian Gibbs Associates give guidelines on lump sum investment, taxation and inflation. Radio and T.V. also should not be ignored by the aspiring student of investment.

QUESTIONS ON SYLLABUS

Questions on Investment have been set in the Institute of Bankers' examinations since 1979. They tend to be of two types: those requiring (a) knowledge of stock market terms and the provisions of the Company Acts, and (b) the evaluation of portfolios for clients with differing financial objectives. To answer the first type of question, the student must be able to memorize and appraise. Answering the second type of question needs knowledge of current taxation as well as investment principles.

TYPICAL QUESTION (type 'a')

(Three of these have to be answered from five. 20 marks per question.)
Explain what is meant by each of the following terms:
(a) put through
(b) best terms
(c) floating rate
(d) new time.

SUGGESTED ANSWER

(a) This is a deal between two parties or by an investor acting in two capacities which is 'put through' a jobber to establish a proper market price for the transaction. Jobbers are expected to watch these deals to ensure that a false market is not created in them.
(b) 'Best terms' is a phrase used by jobbers for unshared commission rates on bargains over £7,000. The phrase should be distinguished from the order to brokers to buy or sell 'at best' which means the lowest or highest price respectively that can be obtained from a particular share transaction.
(c) A 'floating rate' is one which is not fixed at the date of issue but tied to an interest rate such as Treasury Bill rate or LIBOR. Prices of these floating rate stocks (such as Treasury Variable 1983) tend to be more stable than those of fixed interest stocks. (Note that 'floating rate' can also refer to currency movements but is obviously not meant in this connection here.)
(d) 'New time' refers to the last two days of an account when deals can be done for settlement in the next account.

TYPICAL QUESTION (type 'b')

(One has to be answered from two. 40 marks per question.)
A married customer, aged 30, with three children aged 3, 5 and 8, seeks your advice on the investment of £20,000 he has inherited on the death of his mother. He has a steady job with a salary of £6,000 per annum, but neither he nor his wife has other sources of income. He is not averse to risk, but would not wish to take more risk than is necessary to try to maintain the real value of his capital. He would also like to supplement his income. He owns his house subject to a mortgage, the balance of which is about £10,000, and says he is

thinking of paying this off. He has been asked to invest some money in the private company for which he works.

(a) Detail the advice you would give this customer concerning the investment of the inherited sum, and suggest a suitable portfolio structure (you are not required to suggest individual holdings.)

(b) State the advice you would give him in connection with the proposals (i) to pay off the mortgage and (ii) to invest in the shares of his employer.

(c) If your customer wished to give £1,000 to each of his children, how would you suggest these sums were invested?

(d) Your customer says he has heard about index-linked investment. He asks you (i) to explain what this means; (ii) to describe briefly the available index-linked investment; (iii) to advise him on whether any of them is suitable for his circumstances, and (iv) to let him know whether any of them would be suitable for the investment of £300, which his mother has left to her unmarried sister aged 62. What answers would you give?

SUGGESTED ANSWER

(a) A married man of this age with a wife and three young children needs a fairly large cushion of liquidity: not less than 20% which should be invested in building society share accounts (none to 7 days notice of withdrawal) and term shares (3 months withdrawal). Bank time deposits may give as good a return, taxable but paid gross, depending on the level of interest rates at a given time though returns fluctuate more frequently. About 40% of the remaining capital should be invested for the medium term and another 40% for the longer term with some flexibility so that there can be encashment without penalty. Suitable investments would thus be building society term shares (1 – 5 years); guaranteed income bonds which are issued by insurance companies from time to time and offer high rates because the companies have a tax position which allows them to invest in Government securities free of tax. Such issues are limited. The rate is guaranteed for the period of the bond (3 – 5 years). National Savings Certificates (19th issue) yield 5% tax free the first year and 10.33% tax free over five years with a limit of £5,000 per person. An investment in unit trusts or a managed fund may be good for the long term but much depends on the nature of the managements and the underlying investments. With falling interest rates gilts and local authority, mortgages should provide some capital growth over the long term. Lifetime income bonds which are in effect a form of annuity might be acceptable, but few younger men, except the self employed, like to tie up their capital for the rest of their lives, even for a pension with tax advantages.

(b) The customer should not pay off the mortgage as he would then lose the tax relief granted on the interest payments. Furthermore his capital available for investment would be greatly depleted by the payment of the outstanding mortgage. Investing in the shares of his employer does not appear to be a good idea. Presumably they would not be very marketable, though it should be remembered that private companies do go public and one would have to know much more about this private company employer before coming to an irrevocable decision.

(c) A single premium endowment policy is likely to be the best choice here.

(d) Index-linked investments are investments whose returns are linked to the Retail Price Index, thus giving some cover against inflation. For a 62 year old unmarried woman, the best index-linked investment is likely to be the Retirement issue of National Savings Certificates (granny bonds) or the Save As You Earn (third issue.)

ADDITIONAL QUESTIONS

1. How is each of the following calculated and what is its significance to the investor? (a) Liquidity ratio; (b) Asset value; (c) Dividend cover; (d) P/E ratio.

2. Customer B is a married woman, aged about 45, who tells you that she has just inherited a legacy of £25,000 from the estate of a relative, but does not want her husband to know of it. She asks you to suggest investments which are free of all taxes so that there is no obligation on him to include reference to them in his tax returns.

3. (a) Differentiate between the flat yield and the redemption yield on a gilt-edged stock.
Calculate, roughly, the gross redemption yield of the following stock (ignoring accrued interest and expenses): Treasury 12% 1983 at a price of 110.
If this security stood at a price below par, what would be the effects on the redemption calculation and yield?
    (b) A customer asks you to purchase a gilt-edged security 'specially ex-dividend'. What do you understand by 'specially ex-dividend', and for what reason would the customer want to deal in this way? Does this facility extend to all gilt-edged securities?

4. A married customer, who is a small investor, asks you for advice on an overall strategy for his savings. What would you suggest as his priorities, and why?

7 The London Money Markets

In a stock exchange, people buy and sell securities, exchanging financial assets for cash. In a money market, people exchange money claims for money debts. These vary greatly as do the institutions which deal in this 'paper.'

7.1 THE PRIMARY MONEY MARKET (OR DISCOUNT MARKET)

The primary money market developed during the 19th century to finance world trade. Today, the market's primary functions are:
  (a) To make a market in bills.
  (b) To act as a pool of liquidity for banks.
  (c) To finance the government's short-term debt.
  (d) To finance short-term trade debt.

The *institutions* in the primary market are the Bank of England, the deposit banks, the discount houses and merchant banks. The *instruments* are Treasury and commercial bills; short-dated 'gilts' and local authority bills. Certificates of deposit, though part of the secondary market, are now also issued by the clearing banks.

The Bank of England acts in the money market as lender of last resort to the discount houses. Without this 'back-up' facility, discount houses would not be able to underwrite the weekly issue of Treasury bills, and would have to alter their operations in the market.

The Deposit Banks lend money at interest to the discount houses. With this borrowed money, the discount houses buy commercial and other *bills* from traders, Government, institutions and local authorities. They also buy short-dated *bonds*. The money lent by the banks earns interest for the banks and is also highly liquid.

Merchant banks, by providing acceptance credit, complete the primary market which deals in the issue of 'paper' to the first purchaser.

7.2 TYPES OF MONEY MARKET CLAIMS AND DEBTS

A *Bill*, one of the oldest type of credit instruments, is defined by the Bills of Exchange Act 1882, as
  an unconditional order in writing
  addressed by one person to another

signed by the person giving it
requiring the person to whom it is addressed
to pay
on demand or at a fixed or determinable future time
a sum certain in money
to or to the order of a specified person
or to bearer.

Discount Houses trade in the bills, and other paper. Sometimes they hold them to maturity. Sometimes they sell them in conveniently dated batches to the banks. They hope for a profit from either operation, but if interest rates rise, as happened in 1972—3 and in 1976—7, their assets depreciate. Losses ensue. If interest rates fall, as happened during the earlier part of 1977, the discount houses make large gains. The discount houses use the following formula for discounting bills:

$$\text{Discount} = \text{Principal} \times \frac{\text{Rate}}{100} \times \frac{\text{Number of Days}}{365}$$

Example
A Bill of Exchange for £100,000 with 90 days to maturity is discounted at $9\frac{1}{2}$ % per annum.

$$\text{Discount} = £100,000 \times \frac{9\frac{1}{2}}{100} \times \frac{90}{365} = £2,342.47$$

Settlement	£100,000
less	2,342.47
Net Amount:	97,657.53

$$\textit{True Yield} \text{ Formula for a Bill} = \frac{\text{Rate of Discount} \times \text{Principal}}{\text{Net Amount}}$$

In the example above, this gives the *true yield* as follows:

$$\frac{9\frac{1}{2} \times 100,000}{97,657.53} = 9.728\% \text{ per annum.}$$

As well as buying commercial bills, the Houses also buy short-dated *Government bonds* and *Treasury Bills*. The former are known as 'gilts'. Short-dated gilts run to 5 years before maturity; 5—15 years are medium: over 15 years are long. Undated gilts are not redeemable. They include $2\frac{1}{2}$ % Consolidated Fund stock (Consols) and War Loan $3\frac{1}{2}$ %. Such undated stock is bought for income. The nominal value of Government stock is £100, but the market price alters with changes in economic conditions and stock market sentiment. This affects the yields or income on any given stock at a particular time.

A new floating rate 4—year Government stock (£400m) was issued in 1977, partly as an aid to the marketability of short-term Government debt; partly to test the market for this kind of security. The Government finds it harder to sell securities when interest rates are expected to rise. The interest on this Treasury 1981 stock was linked to the average weekly Treasury bill rate over the period plus $\frac{1}{2}$ %. It was therefore more akin to a continuous 7—day instrument (but with interest paid half yearly.) Other variable stock has since been issued.

These 'floaters' as they are called, have also been issued by local authorities. It is too early to judge the success of these new instruments. Investors need a high margin over 7 – day money to compensate for the rate volatility of the 'floaters'.

Treasury Bills were the inspiration of Walter Bagehot. He recommended their introduction in these words: "The English Treasury has the finest credit in the world, and it must learn to use it to the best advantage. A security resembling as nearly as possible a commercial bill of exchange, that is, a bill issued under a discount and falling due at certain intervals, would probably be received with favour by the money marker and would command good terms."

The Treasury Bills Act was passed in 1877 and Treasury bills first appeared in March of that year. They are bearer securities charged on the Consolidated Fund. The Government through the Bank of England, issues them in denominations of £5000 to £1m in weekly 'auctions'. The Bank announces the total amount of bills for the market and invites tenders. Bidders offer to take up bills at a specified price and in denominations of their own choosing on a day in the following week. Bills are allocated to the highest bidders (the institutions offering the highest tender). The minimum tender is £50,000 and the weekly total on offer is between £300m—£600m. The amount depends on the Government's need for residual short-term finance, and tends to fall in the tax-gathering season.

The 11 members of the London Discount Market Association used to put in a syndicated bid (a single price) for all the Treasury Bills issued by the Government each week. This system ended after Competition and Credit Control 1971. The Houses continue to cover (i.e. underwrite) the tender, but they bid against each other and 'outside' institutions such as brokers, insurance companies and foreign banks. London clearing banks are entitled to tender, but do not usually do so except on behalf of clients. When the highest bidders have received the full allocation of bills, lower tenders are met, and so on until all the bills have been sold at varying prices. The rate of interest is the discount on the bill. Assume this to be a nominal £100. The bill runs for 91 days: approximately three months. Then if the buyer pays £97 and gets £100 in three month's time he is getting rather more than 3% over three months: approximately 12% per year. This figure is known as the discount rate. The average rate for all the bills discounted at the weekly tender is known as the Treasury bill rate. Because the government cannot control the daily fluctuations in the Government's cash position, and because the day when bills will be taken up remains with the purchaser, temporary cash surpluses and shortages will emerge in spite of the Treasury bill tender. Tap bills are then bought or sold by the Bank. Tap bills are new bills created in the Bank of England's portfolio and offered to Government departments or agencies or foreign central banks who have a temporary surplus of funds. Examples of such institutions are the Exchange Equalization Account and the National Insurance Fund. Special deposits received from the commercial banks are also sometimes used to buy tap bills. The rate of discount for tap bills is fixed by the Treasury and not made public, and the bills may be of any maturity.

7.3 THE SECONDARY OR PARALLEL MARKET

The secondary market embraces three major markets and two minor ones. The major markets cover transactions in sterling Certificates of Deposit, the inter-bank and local authority markets. The minor markets are the finance house and inter-company markets, both of which have declined in importance since the 'fringe' banking crisis.

The secondary market developed in the 1950s and 1960s. Severe credit restrictions on the clearing banks encouraged other financial institutions, not so restricted, to create new types of lending and borrowing alongside the primary market. Since 1971, the clearing banks and discount houses have participated actively in this secondary market.

7.3.1 NEGOTIABLE STERLING CERTIFICATES OF DEPOSIT

These were launched in October, 1968, following the very successful introduction into London by the First National City Bank of New York, of dollar certificates of deposit in 1966. Dollar C.D.s are issued in units of $1000 with a minimum of $25,000 for 1 month—5 yrs. Sterling C.D.s are negotiable bearer securities issued by banks in amounts from £50,000 to £500,000 for period of three months to five years. The advantages to issuing banks of C.D.s are (a) They are a useful way of raising large sums of money at a fixed rate of interest for a fixed period as funds cannot be withdrawn before maturity. By contrast, it might be difficult for a bank to refuse early repayment on a fixed term deposit to a customer who unexpectedly needed his funds. (b) The sums deposited are large which reduces costs. (c) Margins can be competitive. This suits depositors who are sophisticated enough to switch funds to where the returns are highest. Raising deposit rates would have only a very slight effect on the number of depositors who would switch accounts; and enormously increase costs to the banks. (d) The redemption date is known. This helps in planning the use of funds.

Advantages of C.D.s to holders are (a) there is a competitive fixed maturity yield. (b) Liquidity is assured in case of need, at market prices. (c) The Certificates lend themselves to more flexible techniques such as 'forward' transactions. (d) There is anonymity between ultimate lender and borrower: an advantage for some. (e) Tax is not withheld on transfer or maturity. (f)The depositor has the opportunity of capital gain if rates move in his favour.

A C.D. issued by a bank is a liability for the bank; a purchase, an asset. Holdings of C.D.s can be deducted against C.D.s issued so that adjustments in liquidity ratios could easily be made (until the Supplementary Deposits

Scheme in December 1973) by sales and purchases of C.D.s. After 1971, when the clearing banks entered the market, the C.D.s showed phenomenal growth. The number issued by all banks rose from £1.86bn in 1971 to £4.61bn in 1973. By January 1980, these liabilities were at £3648m.

7.3.1.1 *The market in C.D.s*

(a) Primary
This includes the clearing and merchant banks, some overseas banks in London and most of the American banks in London. Primary C.D.s are normally issued for fixed periods of 3 months to 5 years unless a specific maturity date is required by the depositor.

(b) Secondary
This market comprises those houses who do not themselves issue paper, but run dealing books. They quote buying and selling prices in all periods for paper from their own portfolios. Some banks deal in both the primary and secondary markets.
Sterling
C.D.s are dealt in on a discount-to-yield basis on the following formula

Short-term maturities up to one year

$$\text{Proceeds} = \text{Principal} \times \frac{36{,}500 + \text{issue rate} \times \text{tenor in days}}{36{,}500 + \text{quoted yield} \times \text{days to run}}$$

Medium-term maturities over 1 year

The Proceeds are calculated by the repeated discounting of the proceeds of maturity + successive annual interest payments.

Example
A £500,000 C.D.s issued at 12% for three years is bought at $11\frac{1}{2}$% with 2 years 150 days to run to maturity

Amount at maturity	= £500,000
+ 1 year's accrued interest =	60,000
	560,000

Discount for 3rd year

$$560{,}000 \qquad + 1 + \frac{11.5}{100} + 1 \text{ year's accrued interest.}$$

= £502,242.152
  60,000.00
  _____
  562,242.152

Discount for 2nd year

$562,242.152 + 1 + \frac{11.5}{100} + 1$ years accrued interest

$= £504,253.051$

$\underline{ 60,000}$

$ 564,253.051$

Discount for 150 days of 1st year

$564,253.051 + 1 + \frac{11.5}{100} \times \frac{150}{365}$

$= £538,789.70$

Settlement Amount
(*Example provided by Clive Discount Company.*)

7.3 LOCAL AUTHORITY MARKET
From 1945 until 1954, local authorities were allowed to borrow only from the Public Works Loans Board, which received its resources from the Exchequer. In 1955, the P.W.L.B. became virtually a lender of last resort to the local authorities, and was allowed to lend to them only if they could not meet their requirements through the open market. The bigger authorities (those with a rate call of £5m) have since become a formidable force in the financial markets issuing long-term bonds of, e.g. £10m (Stockport 1977). In addition to issuing bonds in their own name under the Local Government Act 1972, and the Stocks And Bonds Regulations 1974, the local authorities borrow short-term by way of bills. These bills are usually issued by tender in anticipation of revenue. They are very popular with institutions, including the discount houses, when Treasury Bills are in short supply. If they have a maturity of less than six months and meet certain requirements concerning publication and notice, local authority bills count as reserve assets for the banks.

7.3.3 THE INTER-BANK MARKET
This is very much smaller than the local authority market and serves to even out the peaks and troughs of the banks' cash flow. A bank with surplus cash lends it to another at a higher rate of interest than could be earned in the discount market. This flow of funds becomes dangerous when the money is on-lent perhaps several times, ending up in an organization that not even by its friends could be called bank. The market appeared threatened after 1971 when reserve asset ratios were introduced. The inducement to gain higher interest rates by lending to non-statistical banks, common before 1971, was now offset by the fact that such non-bank lending could not count as a reserve

asset. However, the need for short-term liquidity is often very strong, particularly by merchant and overseas banks who may have arranged a deal and need urgently to finance it. This need keeps the market alive and thriving in spite of the risk. The inter-bank market thus helps to even out the flow of payments and receipts between banks; to indicate the future trend of interest rates through the three month inter-bank offered rate (LIBOR) and to provide profitable (unsecured) transactions for the clearing banks. The market totals about £9 bn.

7.3.4 THE INTER-COMPANY MARKET is one where, as in the inter-bank and local authority markets, lenders and borrowers are usually put in touch with one another by brokers. Companies with spare funds lend them to banks which on-lend them to other companies in need of funds. In this market, interest rates are high, for the loans are unsecured, and credit rating could be better. Dealers in the market are gradually evolving a system whereby business is limited to the large companies and to minimum sums of £50,000.

7.3.5 THE FINANCE HOUSE MARKET

7.3.5.1 *Structure*
Finance houses specialize in the granting of a range of instalment credit facilities. Hire purchase, conditional sale and instalment loans are the main ones. There are around 800 finance houses. Most of these are small and provide a service to consumers within a limited geographical area. The main finance houses comprise the 40 members of the Finance Houses Association. These write over 80% of the business of all finance houses. In 1979, F.H.A. members extended new credit as follows:

	£m	%
Advances to business customers (excluding leasing)	2,087	43.1
Leasing facilities (cost of new assets acquired)	1,055	21.8
Advances to consumers	1,699	35.1
Total	4,841	100.0

Outstandings to members at the end of 1979 were £5,989m.

7.3.5.2 *Funding*
Deposits are obtained from the public and from banks. Two main methods are used: the money market and advertising. The former brings in large amounts; the latter attracts the small saver. Finance houses issue commercial bills, C.D.s and other instruments which are discounted in the money market.

Since 1971, finance houses with deposits in excess of £5m have been required to maintain a 10% reserve asset ratio. Those with banking status are subject to the same requirements as banks, i.e. $12\frac{1}{2}$ % reserve assets plus special deposits as required by the Bank of England from time to time.

7.3.5.3 *Lending*

Since 1952, instalment credit has been regulated by terms controls. These are imposed by the government to regulate the demand for consumer credit. Under these controls, a minimum deposit (down payment) is usually specified and a maximum repayment period for all hire purchase transactions. In 1980, the minimum down payment was $33\frac{1}{3}$ % deposit on a new car with a repayment period not exceeding 24 months. The Bank also asks finance houses, together with other lenders, not to grant loans or other facilities on easier terms than those available on hire purchase.

7.3.5.4 *Leasing*

About 50 finance houses are members of the Equipment Leasing Association. This is a growing industry. The increase in the volume of leasing business in 1979 was over 30% and member companies owned equipment costing £5,030m compared with the 1978 figure of £3,407m.

Leasing is a system of separating use from ownership. A mortgage or hire purchase contract gives, from the start of the contract, the ownership of the asset or the opportunity to acquire it, to the user. The contract is a method of financing the purchase of the asset. Under a lease, title does not pass but remains with the lessor. A lease enables the lessee to use capital equipment by making payments out of revenue. The lessee pays specified rentals over a given period for the use of a specific asset. Such payments differ from hiring in that the asset is chosen from a manufacturer or vendor of such assets by the lessee. In lending/hiring, the assets are usually bought by the hiring firm before any lender appears.

Finance houses were pioneers of leasing in the mid-nineteenth century. They leased railway wagons to colliery owners to move coal from the pits to the factories. The facility later became hire purchase when the colliery owners wished to buy the wagons at the end of the lease. In the early 1960s, finance houses re-introduced leasing facilities, first on office equipment and then on all types of commercial vehicles, industrial machinery, ships and aircraft. Of the £1,802m total of assets bought in 1979, the major finance houses wrote 58%.

The main advantage for industrial companies and consumers in dealing with a finance house, is certainty. The rate of interest and the repayment period are usually fixed. The repayments are therefore known in cash terms from the outset. The finance house takes the risk of interest rate changes. The borrower can plan his expenditure in this area with certainty. For industrial borrowers who prefer the flexibility of variable rate terms, these can be made available. The Finance House Base rate is a good indicator of changes in the cost of money in the money market (see Chapter 9; Interest Rates).

7.4 SUPERVISION OF THE STERLING MONEY MARKETS

Both the primary and secondary markets, described above, are *domestic* money markets, dealing in *sterling* instruments. Participants in the secondary market include banks, local authorities, building societies and various other financial and commercial groups.

Although the secondary market is made up of different groups, these distinctions are based mainly on the different interest rates for borrowers and on instruments within that market. Essentially, however, it is a unitary *unsecured sterling* money market, unlike the primary market which is a *secured* one.

The Bank has regular daily contact with the *primary market* as well as weekly meetings attended by the chairman and deputy chairman of the Discount Market Association. Thus, primary market operations and proposals for new instruments to be traded therein are always under the scrutiny of the Bank.

In the secondary market, some shortcomings in market practice were revealed by a working party set up by the Bank in 1974. It was suggested that a Sterling Brokers Association should be established and a code of practice drafted to govern transactions in the market. Meanwhile, however, the Bank, (as it has done for many years) enters the market in bank bills and, to a lesser extent, in trade bills, to sample the paper in circulation. Any which fail to reach the highest quality are discounted at less than the prime rate. In this way, the Bank demonstrates, not as forcibly, perhaps as some would wish, the standards which participants in the secondary market are expected to maintain.

7.5 OTHER FINANCIAL MARKETS

In addition to the Stock Exchange which provides a market in securities, and the primary and secondary markets which provide a market for money debts and claims, there are two further financial markets operating in London which are among the largest of their kind in the world: (a) The Euro-currency Market and (b) The Foreign Exchange Market. A brief outline of London's Commodity Markets is also given.

7.5.1 THE EURO—CURRENCY MARKET

A Euro-currency is any currency operating for loan and repayment outside the country of origin. Euro-dollars are deposits of US dollars with commercial banks outside the U.S. Euro-sterling are deposits of sterling with commercial banks outside the U.K. The Bank for International Settlements gives a somewhat lengthier definition of Euro-dollars as those that have been acquired 'by a bank outside the U.S. and used directly or after conversion into another currency for lending to a non-bank customer, perhaps after one or more re-deposits from one bank to another'. The Euro-currency market is short-term, consisting of deposits lent out through a system of bank credits.

Euro-dollars look no different from ordinary dollars. Those that are drawn from a Euro-currency deposit in London are exactly the same as the dollars used in the U.S. The major difference from a banking point of view is that they are free from the direct controls of the U.S. Federal Reserve Board. This freedom from control by the central banks of origin applies to all Euro-currencies and is at once a source of their strength and their weakness.

7.5.1.1 Origins of the market

Several factors led to the development in the late 1950s of the Euro-currency market. They can be summarized as follows:

(i) The acquisition of dollars by Russian agencies after World War 2. They on-lent the funds at short-term to a west European bank, who might relend the dollars, and so on.

(ii) U.K. exchange controls prevented the financing of foreign trade in sterling. Fears of sterling devaluations, and the resultant flow of funds out of sterling into deutschmarks, caused the Treasury to impose restrictions on sterling loans. Banks circumvented these by borrowing in dollars.

(iii) The U.S. balance of payments deficits caused large holdings of dollar deposits in central banks abroad. These dollars eventually passed into non-resident hands.

(iv) By Regulation Q, U.S. banks were forbidden to bid up interest rates. This meant that dollar deposits could earn more abroad than at home and borrowers obtain lower rates than the prime rate of a U.S. bank. The Interest Equalisation Tax 1963 also made New York a very unattractive market for foreign borrowers.

(v) The oil revenues and further restrictions in some domestic capital markets gave a further boost to the Euro-dollar market in the 1970s.

7.5.1.2 Operators in the market

The main operators in the market are wealthy individuals, multinational corporations, overseas-based companies and commercial banks who exchange local currencies into dollars, and similar large institutions which have or need different currencies. An Association of International bond dealers (A.I.B.D.) was set up voluntarily by market participants as a self-regulatory agency in 1969. It deals, as the name suggests, in the long-term Euro-bond market, and by 1980 had 563 members.

7.5.1.3 The Euro-bond market

The Eurobond market comprises the long-term end of the Euro-currency market. A Euro-bond is a bearer security denominated in a Euro-currency. It is an international debt obligation issed in return for investors' funds. The borrower can be a resident of the domestic market of the currency of issue or of any foreign market. The bond may be denominated in any currency. It need not be that of the lender nor of the borrower. The bond is underwritten and distributed by an international syndicate of banks and investment institutions.

Neither the bond nor the currency in which it is denominated, is controlled in any way. There are no registration requirements, and interest is paid gross without the deduction of any tax. Coupons are attached to the bonds. These are cut off and presented on or after the specified payment date to any of the paying agent banks which are listed on the reverse side of the coupon.

The issuers of Euro-bonds (i.e. the borrowers) include U.K. nationalized industries and local authorities; the European Investment Bank; continental governments and municipalities and multinational corporations. The Third World, too, has borrowed in the Eurobond market where loans can be a cheaper and more flexible way of raising funds than other sources.

Dealing procedures

Almost all public issues of Euro-bonds are listed on a recognized stock exchange. The majority of dealings in existing bonds, however, takes place over the counter (OTC) between dealers by telephone or telex. Most dealings are on a net basis, which means dealing costs are incorporated into the price quoted. Participants in the market normally act as principals. They are therefore free to deal with anyone. The investor may find as many as 20 market makers. The price quoted will show a spread of about $\frac{1}{2}$ % between buying and selling in amounts of $100,000 to $1m. U.S. dollars are the most marketable securities with dealing costs around $\frac{1}{2}$ % for transactions up to $50,000 and lower thereafter.

Types of bond

Euro-bonds may be fixed rate, floating rate or convertible. Fixed rate bonds have an interest rate which is fixed at the time of issue. Interest is paid annually and the bonds are dealt in plus or minus accrued interest based on a 360-day year and a 30-day month. Interest on floating rate bonds (see below) is based on calendar months.

Floating rate bonds have an interest rate which is usually fixed every six months at a set margin over the six months London Inter-Bank Offer rate (LIBOR) for the specified Euro-currency deposit (published daily in the financial press). A minimum interest rate is often stipulated so that, if LIBOR plus the set margin should fall below it, the stipulated rate will be paid.

Convertibles, when issued, normally carry a rate of interest higher than the dividends on the related shares. The rate of exchange is fixed at the time of issue so that currency movements can increase (or lower) the value of the bonds.

When a Euro-bond is issued, the interest (or coupon) rate represents the annual rate of return over the life of the bond. Thereafter the length to maturity lessens, and market conditions (demand/supply/interest rate trends) may change. The price of the bond will then change to reflect these conditions.

About 50% of all bonds are quoted in U.S. dollars. The deutschmark comes next in popularity, but all the major currencies of the world are dealt in, and there are also currency cocktails such as the European unit of account and Special Drawing Rights.

Financial centres

London remains the largest centre with a 34% share of the Euro-bond market but as London cannot hold Euro-sterling, Paris has become the main market for this currency. Other centres have developed in Amsterdam, Frankfurt and Zurich. In eastern markets, Singapore is the main centre. There are also markets in the Bahamas, Bahrain, Hong Kong, Panama and the Cayman Islands. Since the first issue of Euro-bonds in 1963, over $90bn equivalent has been raised in Euro-bond issues.

Many suggestions have been put forward for the control of the Euro-currency market, or for some kind of reserve requirement. However these ideas have been given up, because as the market developed out of a desire to be rid of controls, it is possible that the same kind of ingenuity would circumvent newer controls. Meanwhile the danger of an international financial crisis in this market has not been ruled out.

7.5.2 THE FOREIGN EXCHANGE MARKET

The foreign exchange market appears to have no physical entity. If you asked where you could find such a place, you would probably be directed to a bank. Alternatively, you could find yourself at one of those small shops with the sign CHANGE-WECHSEL in many languages over the doors, which operate in some cities and frontier points. There is no composite market place where trading in foreign currencies takes place.

In London, as in other financial centres, the foreign exchange market centres round the *operators*. These are British and foreign commercial banks and a few intermediaries. The Bank of England, acting for the Treasury, authorized the banks to carry out transactions under the Exchange Control Act 1947; they were then known as 'authorized' banks. The intermediaries (defined in E.C.1. para 4), mainly stockbrokers and solicitors, are 'authorized depositaries'. They are allowed limited dealings only, usually in connection with stock exchange securities. A few travel agents got limited permissions under the Act. The Customs and Excise have duties and powers also, mainly to see that movements of currency, as well as goods, do not infringe the law.

The telephone, telex and teleprinter are the *mechanisms* by which the market works. Through them come immediate knowledge of prices in financial centres overseas. Demand and supply normally fix the price for one currency against another, but national governments rarely allow these forces free play. They regard the price of their currency as too important to be dominated by market forces. Some governments restrict or forbid the export of capital. Goods, too, may not be bought overseas unless enough foreign currency has been earned to pay for the imports. This prevents balance of payments deficits, but at what cost? Barter often has to be resorted to and one city firm thrives on this trade. As well as such restrictions by national governments, international monetary agreements can prevent the free price movement of currencies. So it was under the Bretton Woods Agreement from 1944—1971.

Even within such constraints, tourists, traders, investors and multinational corporations constantly exchange currencies. If the English sell to the Japanese the earned yen cannot be spent in Britain. It must be changed into sterling. If a German visits Britain, he needs sterling to spend. In Spain, he requires pesetas. The processing of monetary transactions like these, form the basis of the world's foreign exchange markets.

Rates for different currencies vary from day to day and hour to hour, depending on economic and political conditions in the countries concerned, their internal interest and inflation rates, and the effect these factors have on the demand for a particular currency by traders, tourists, multinationals and, inevitably, the ubiquitous 'speculator'. Commercial banks, merchant banks and Central Banks are also active in the market, buying and selling currencies.

The foreign exchange market enables money to be changed from one currency to another; companies to get short-term trade credit; firms to minimize foreign exchange risks.

The market is another theoretically 'perfect' one. Market dealers can switch in and out of currencies whenever there is a temporary non-alignment. To take, for clarity, an extravagant example, assume there are three currencies A,B,C. 1A = 1B = 1C. Demand for C by A pushes up the rate: 2A = 1C = 1B, B meanwhile is still at 1B = 1A. It obviously now pays B to change into C and change C into A. In this way B gets double the rate: 1B = 2A instead of the current market price of 1B = 1A. Eventually an equilibrium will be found. In this way the 'perfect' price results. In fact, interest rates and payments positions affect exchange rates. Speculation heightens observed tendencies.

On the stock exchange and in commodity markets, future dealing can take place at agreed current prices. This system also works in the foreign exchange *forward* market. Exchange contracts are made to minimize deviations from the present or 'spot' price. In the spot market, currencies are bought and sold for immediate delivery; in the forward market for one, three or 12 months ahead, but the exchange rate is agreed now.

If a car importer contracts to take delivery of 5000 foreign cars and to pay at the end of 3 months a price fixed in deutschmarks, yen or francs, and Britain devalues (lowers the foreign exchange value of) her currency during that period, the importer will have to give up more pounds for the cars. Buying 'forward' francs, etc. covers him against loss.

In spite of the declining importance of sterling as a trading and reserve currency, the London foreign exchange market still retains its pre-eminence. It has many advantages such as the variety of ancillary markets and the range of financial intermediaries and instruments. In addition to the market's integrity and efficiency, there is the geographical time zone advantage, whereby London is able to trade with northern hemisphere countries during at least part of their working day.

7.5.3 COMMODITY MARKETS

Commodity Markets earn 'invisibles' and for this reason have been included in financial markets.

Originally, a commodity market was a place where producers met users of the commodity. Through an auction, they agreed on a current selling price. Today, the markets remain. The commodities have, apparently, vanished. Of all the transactions taking place in the London commodity markets, 98% never result in physical delivery of the traded commodity. The same situation exists in similar markets in other centres.

London boasts the corn and freight markets of the Corn and Baltic exchanges, the Mark Lane produce markets, the Metal Exchange, the Wool Exchange, the Smithfield meat market (largely domestic), the Hatton Garden diamond market and markets for fur, gold and fish. All these commodity markets are *geared* to physical delivery of produce or metals, yet they are more akin to a great financial market which deals not in goods but in paper promises, saying delivery will be made or taken at a specific date. Exchanging these contracts are producers who sell and business men who buy raw materials; and speculators who do neither.

Around 600 commodity trading firms operate in London, earning £100m in 'invisible' exports (services) each year. The Americans have more futures markets but trade is mostly in domestic items. In the American markets, there are limits on price rises and falls, beyond which trading stops for the whole day. This may be good ethics but bad economics, for more 'perfect' markets are then used, where such restrictions do not exist, or not to the same degree. London gains from this and also by its time position: dealing with Japan and the Far East in the morning, the U.S.A., Canada and Latin America in the afternoon, with western and eastern European trade throughout the day.

Raw materials are traded on long-term agreements between producer and consumer. Commodity markets fix prices for the rest. This has an effect similar to gearing in shares, where profits and losses are magnified for equity holders, the smaller their total percentage holding of the company share capital. A very small change in demand for a commodity enormously exaggerates its price. In 1973/4, a large increase in demand for commodities: zinc, copper, sugar, cocoa, grains, soya beans, coincided with a reduction in supply due to crop failures, production difficulties or shipping delays. Prices soared. Currency problems did not help. How this affects producer and consumer countries can be seen in their terms of trade and balance of payments figures.

Manufacturers, like other users of the market, must take a view of future prices. There is often a large time lag in demand for a crop and its eventual production. They 'hedge'. Such hedging increases trading volume, and lessens so it is argued, price volatility.

Hedging irons out differences between 'spot' and future prices. A spot price is that quoted for current shipment. Futures are similar to stock 'call' options: a contract to deliver (or take delivery of) a commodity at a price fixed at the time of the contract. In the nineteenth century, the time span of the contract was about three months. Today it can be up to 15 months. If a cotton merchant buys 300 bales of cotton from a grower, from that time forward the risks of all price fluctuations until the cotton is sold, are his. He must therefore guard against loss. He does this by selling 300 cotton futures. If prices fall, the loss on the value of the physical cotton is offset by the profit from the futures. If prices rise, the loss on the futures is offset by the profit on the sale of his cotton.

Commodity markets work. Do they help primary producers who, until the oil price explosion, were amongst the poorest countries in the world, and some of whom (the non-oil producers) are now even poorer? Do they help stabilize prices? Answers vary. But there is no disputing that commodity markets (a) contribute to a country's invisible exports (b) through their trade in futures, they ease the financial risks caused by price fluctuations, and so encourage international commodity trading.

It should be noted too, that trade through central buying and selling agencies, (an alternative trading mechanism), often has to be supplemented by skilful resource to the capitalistic commodity markets. Even in the E.E.C., the effort to help farmers *and* consumers achieve an acceptable price for agricultural products has led to butter and beef mountains and wine lakes, as well as the Lomé Convention to try and stabilize prices for primary producers overseas.

Commodity markets like those in London, and other key centres in the world are likely to continue until a viable and acceptable alternative can be found. Protagonists proclaim that it never will.

TYPICAL QUESTION

From what sources does the London discount market obtain its funds? What purpose does lending to the market serve in the affairs of each of the sources?

SUGGESTED ANSWER

The London discount market comprises the 11 discount houses which are members of the London Discount Market Association. They deal in bills and similar short-dated securities. They finance these activities by borrowing money at short notice (a) directly from the Bank of England and the commercial banks and (b) indirectly from the secondary or parallel markets, which have developed in the last decades.

The Bank of England provides the discount houses with funds by the issue of Treasury Bills and short-dated gilts and in its capacity as lender of last resort. The members of the Discount Market Association keep loan accounts at the Bank of England which give a right to borrow from the Bank at rates the Bank chooses.

Before Competition and Credit Control, the clearing banks were the major source of funds to the Discount Houses. Such lending counted as a liquid asset. After 1971, money at call became a reserve asset for all banks. Non-clearing banks therefore switched large amounts of short-term funds to the discount houses.

The discount houses and the Bank of England are part of the traditional London money market. But the secondary or parallel markets which have developed in the last decades also cause some seepage of funds into the discount houses. These secondary markets comprise overseas banks, finance houses, companies with excess liquidity, the inter-bank and local authority markets, the Euro-currency market and the market in certificates of deposits. Though the discount houses have some dealings in all these markets, the principal one in which they engage is that of sterling certificates of deposit. This market expanded rapidly in 1971 from £1.86 million issued by October 1971 to nearly three times that figure in 1972. By 1978 (February) the value of C.D.s issued was £4804m.

Why discount houses borrow funds and from whom, is perhaps easier to understand than why money is lent to the houses. What purpose does such lending serve to the sources of those funds? The banks need money at call as part of their reserve asset ratio. In addition, the discount market provides a source of liquidity more profitable than cash. The discount houses use the money borrowed from the banks to obtain marketable paper: commercial and local authority bills. These can be traded at a profit back to the banks, and if they are discountable at the Bank of England, they further count as reserve assets.

The Bank of England lends to the discount houses because in the issue and buying and selling of Treasury Bills to the market, the authorities have a powerful aid to the control of the money stock and a tool of monetary management. The Bank further lends at last resort to the discount houses because this lending gives it some influence over interest rates and last resort facilities add strength to the money market. Other groups lend to the London discount market because in this way they get safe, liquid and profitable assets for their surplus funds.

ADDITIONAL QUESTIONS

1. Describe the so-called 'parallel' sterling money markets in London.

2. What are the main services offered by British merchant banks? Why are they able to offer these services without the support of a network of branches?

3. Write short notes on the sterling interbank market.

4. Write short notes on sterling C.D.s.

5. Write short notes on negotiable certificates of deposit.

8 The Value of Money

8.1 DEFINITION

Value, in an economic sense, has two meanings. Firstly, there is value in exchange: how much one thing will exchange for another. In modern societies, goods and services do not exchange for other goods. They are exchanged against money. Money measures their value by price. The price can be settled in the market place or by central planners. It does not matter. The consumer decides how much utility a particular good or service has for him. He pays the price himself, or gets aid to do so, or goes without.

The second meaning of value arises from the fact that money itself has a price. The price is called interest. Like the price of other goods, interest depends on the supply and demand for the commodity in question, in this case, money. Interest is discussed in Chapter 9.

In this chapter, we are concerned with the first meaning of value: the value of money in exchange for other goods, that is with the general price level; and what causes that level to change.

8.2 A SINGLE PRICE CHANGE

Prices of individual goods vary from time to time because of changes in the conditions of demand and supply.

Figure 8.1 (a) shows a normal demand and supply curve for sugar. All the points on the demand curve show how much sugar will be demanded at a particular price. All the points on the supply curve show how much sugar will be supplied at a particular price. Only at one point, P_1, do buyers and sellers agree.

At this *equilibrium price*, P_1, demand and supply match. At all points below P_1 on the demand curve, potential customers cannot be satisfied, for not enough sugar is being supplied at the price they are willing to pay. At all points above P_1 on the supply curve, potential suppliers cannot be satisfied, for there are not enough buyers willing to pay the price.

If the supply of sugar increases due to new production techniques (b), more people will be satisfied, for the new supply curve S_2 now brings the price within their reach P_2. Conversely, with a decrease in supply: the price rises; the demand contracts. Changes in the conditions of demand and supply for a good thus cause changes in its price.

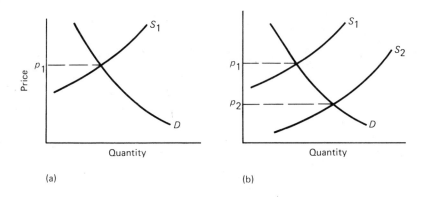

Figure 8.1

8.3 CHANGES IN THE PRICE OF MANY GOODS

But what happens if the price not merely of sugar rises, but of many other goods and services; indeed, of nearly everything? When there is a general rise in the price level, the process is known as *inflation*. Inflation means a fall in the value of money. The consumer gets fewer goods for his money than he previously did. The exchange value of his money has fallen. The price level can be taken from one or more sources, but for purposes of comparison the index of retail prices is usually used. This is a 'cost of living' index. It is made up of prices from a typical 'basket' of goods and services. The 'basket' is altered from time to time so as to keep up with the changing patterns of expenditure. In January 1974, the index of retail prices in the U.K. stood at 100. By March 1980, it had risen to 248.8. When all prices fall, the process is known as deflation. The consumer can buy more goods with the same amount of money than he could before. The exchange value of his money has risen.

8.4 ECONOMIC EFFECTS OF CHANGES IN THE VALUE OF MONEY

Changes in the value of money have important effects on the economy. During inflation they can be summed up as follows:

8.4.1 EFFECT ON THE EFFICIENCY OF MONEY

8.4.1.1 *As a medium of exchange*

During inflation, money becomes less efficient as a medium of exchange. More is spent and more quickly. Consumers attempt to beat rising prices by buying in advance. The velocity of circulation rises.

8.4.1.2 *As a store of value*
Less is saved and invested, more consumed. Productivity falls.

8.4.1.3 *As a unit of account*
Planning, forecasting and costing become difficult, sometimes hazardous, for individuals and governments. If there is a serious decline in the value of money, a new unit of account may be introduced.

8.4.1.4 *As a standard of deferred payments*
Creditors lose. Debtors gain by repaying loans in depreciating money. Higher interest rates may be introduced to offset this loss.

8.4.2 EFFECT ON THE DISTRIBUTION OF NATIONAL INCOME
Changes in the general price level alter the distribution of the National Income in an arbitrary manner.

8.4.2.1 *Creditors and debtors*
In a period of inflation, repayment of loans costs less in real terms. Holders of fixed interest securities lose, as do people with fixed incomes not adjusted to changes in the cost of living.

8.4.2.2 *Entrepreneurs*
Entrepreneurs gain in the early stages of inflation from the time interval between purchases of raw material and the sale of finished goods. Demand is high and fixed costs such as interest, rents and salaries are slow to rise. Stock appreciates in value, but replacement costs can offset this gain.

8.4.2.3 *Wage earners*
Wage earners in strong trade unions gain while those without industrial 'muscle' tend to lose. The skilled tend to gain at the expense of the unskilled.

8.4.3 EFFECT ON THE SIZE OF THE NATIONAL INCOME
In the early stages of inflation, increased prices and profits stimulate production. If there are spare resources, output increases. But as these spare resources are used up, stocks are run down and bottlenecks appear. Wages and other costs rise without any corresponding increase in output. Hyper-inflation may set in when confidence in the value of money is lost.

8.4.4 EFFECT ON THE BALANCE OF PAYMENTS
Unless prices abroad are rising faster than those in the home country, inflation causes an adverse balance of payments and/or pressure on the exchange rate.

8.4.4.1 *Import expenditure rises*

Imports and prices of raw materials rise because of higher output and increased demand. More is spent on imported finished goods, too. They are cheaper than the home products, and wage earners have more money to spend.

8.4.4.2 *Foreign currency earnings fall*

There is an increase in sales of imported goods. Export earnings fall because the price of exports is too high to compete in overseas markets.

These are the effects of inflation on an economy. Deflation shows opposite trends, e.g. an increase in unemployment. However, a new and ugly hybrid of both inflation and deflation is now appearing in many countries: *slumpflation* or *stagflation*. This is a situation where high prices are combined with low productivity, low investment and high unemployment.

8.5. CAUSES OF CHANGES IN THE PRICE LEVEL — SOME EARLY THEORIES

8.5.1 THE LABOUR THEORY OF VALUE

What causes changes in the average price level? Various answers have been given to this question. Early economists ignored money altogether. To have value, a good had to have use. Then its exchange value depended on the labour involved in producing or acquiring the good. They ignored demand. Thus in a hunting community, "If. . .it usually costs twice the labour to kill a beaver which it does to kill a deer, one beaver should naturally exchange for or be worth two deer. It is natural that what is usually the produce of one day's or one hour's labour should be worth double of what is usually the produce of one half day's or one half hour's labour." (Wealth of Nations.)

8.5.2. OBJECTIONS TO THE LABOUR THEORY OF VALUE

Objections to the labour theory are (a) the difficulty of measuring the amount of labour in a product or process; (b) the assumption that longer means better. The third objection to the labour theory of value was that factors other than labour were ignored.

8.5.3 THE COST OF PRODUCTION THEORY OF VALUE

J.S. Mill propounded a theory of value which included factors other than labour. The price of a commodity was determined by *supply* and that meant the cost of *all* factors of production. Like other early economists, Mill also took no account of demand. "The cost of production together with ordinary profits may be called the necessary price or value of all things made by labour or capital." Hence his theory was essentially a short-run analysis.

8.6. CAUSES OF CHANGES IN THE PRICE LEVEL: CURRENT THEORIES

When prices are high or rising, more attention is given to inflation; to deflation when prices are falling. Current theories on changes in the price level concentrate on inflation. These theories can be summed up as those which focus on the demand for and supply of goods; and those which focus on the demand for and supply of money. Cost-push and demand-pull inflation cover the former. Keynesian and monetarist theories cover the latter.

8.7 COST-PUSH INFLATION

Some economists aver that inflation is caused by increases in the cost of production, mainly wages and raw materials. They argue that an increase in the money supply is the result, not the cause of inflation. But neither increased costs nor increased money supply tell the whole story. The annual rate of increase in consumer prices in the U.K. during the period 1968—1973 of 7% was only a fraction under Japan's increase of 7.1% in consumer prices during the same period. Yet Japan's money supply increased by 23% compared with the U.K.'s increase of 8.8%. Why then, was there not a higher inflation rate for Japan? The clue to the disparity lies in output. Japan's output increased by 9.7% compared with the U.K.'s output increase of 2.5%. Japan's money supply increase was matched by an increase in output.

Sometimes, however, output cannot rise. The economy may be inflexible, or already fully employed. If wages then rise above the level of national productivity, this will push up unit costs. Part at least of this increase will be passed on to the consumer in higher prices. The alternative to higher prices is likely to be higher unemployment. U.K. experience confirms this.

A rise in consumer prices tends in the long run, to move in line with the growth in unit wage costs. The latter increase reflects the difference between the growth of per capita earnings and the growth of per capita output. The short-run relationship between unit wage costs and prices, however, may vary for different reasons. There may be lags in the response of prices to changes in money earnings, or productivity. External factors may be at work so that large changes take place in the terms of trade.

Firms can avoid passing higher wages on in higher prices if they absorb them in lower profits. In the U.K., profits as a ratio of net output (both excluding depreciation and stock appreciation) fell to about 10% to 12% in 1974—1976. In 1977—78, they recovered to around 15% as activity increased. This figure still contrasts with the 20% profit ratio of net output in the late 1960's and early 1970's. The cushion for absorbing pay rises, though varying from industry to industry and firm to firm, is now fairly small. If wages rise faster than productivity and prices are unchanged, the share of profits falls, and profits are one source of funds for investment.

Firms respond to wage increases by raising prices, cutting expenditure, or both. Increased living standards are only possible (without borrowing) if productivity improves. The average output per worker in the U.K. for the 10 years to 1973 grew by over $3\frac{1}{2}$ % per year. If that trend had continued to 1978, the output per worker would have risen by 15%. From 1974—1979, output grew less than half as fast as it did over the previous 20 years, and about a third as fast as in other industrialized countries.

How is cost inflation to be controlled? Higher import prices cannot easily be altered by domestic measures. Price controls tend to restrict the supply of goods or divert them to other markets. Incomes policies on wages cannot be imposed, or continue, in a democracy without some form of public or trade union consent.

8.8 IMPORT CONTROLS

One solution is import controls. A group of Cambridge economists suggest that insufficient output causes inflation. Unemployment results from lack of export demand, and public sector deficits result in balance of payments problems. Thus, unemployment and inflation are the inevitable consequences of the U.K. not having introduced import controls. If money income claims (especially wages, taxes, import prices) exceed the total real income available, inflation results. Incomes policies merely add to the problem. They erode differentials for skilled work. This erosion leads to further money claims to restore the balance. But it is underproduction that is the major cause of inflation. Such underproduction makes it impossible to meet demands by workers and government. Import prices and money claims of wages and taxes therefore rise. So too, do domestic prices. To cure this inflation a fall in unemployment is needed, but unemployment is caused mainly by lack of export demand. So, according to the Cambridge economists, there is only one cure, namely import controls.

But if machines replace labour-intensive industries, what guarantee is there that import controls will cure unemployment? Import controls certainly restrict freedom of choice. They can also harm primary producers in the Third World and encourage the inefficient domestic producer to be even more inefficient with even less risk.

8.9 DEMAND-PULL INFLATION

This type of inflation is said to occur when total demand for goods and services exceeds the total supply. Demand-pull inflation can be seen most clearly during periods of war. There is not enough production of those goods and services which consumers want. Excessive spending in relation to the goods available drives prices up. If price controls are introduced, a 'black' market develops in which those who can pay the highest price can get the goods. The alternative to price controls is rationing, which shares out the available goods on a basis thought to be equitable. Similar situations of demand-pull inflation arise when governments concentrate on the production of those goods and services which may be 'necessary' but cannot be consumed. Workers, e.g. in the defence industries, receive incomes that compete with others for the fewer consumable goods available. Prices are again driven up.

Suggested cures for demand-pull inflation are changes in production to match consumers' needs. This is difficult, politically, to implement. A 'hidden' form of rationing may develop with queues or waiting lists for the available goods and services. Innovative societies could develop alternative goods or sources of supply. These alternatives would only be permitted if they did not use factors of production required by the government for its own output. Other policy measures include altering the tax structure and the control or 'freezing' of wages. The latter is only possible as a short-run objective and usually leads to an acceleration in wage rates as the freeze ends and the thaw begins.

8.10 MONEY — SUPPLY AND DEMAND

Monetarists ascribe inflation to one cause only, namely an increase in the money supply. Keynesians declare that the latter leads to the former only through changes in interest rates. These changes are influenced much more by the demand for money than its supply. Further, such changes only indirectly influence prices. Though equilibrium between the demand for and supply of money would eventually be reached through the mechanism of interest rates, the pace is too slow. The economy would suffer too drastically in the meantime. Fiscal policy is the correct short-run remedy. Keynesians are therefore said to be 'fiscalists'.

8.10.1 DEMAND FOR MONEY

Money is held ('demanded') for 3 motives:

(a) Precaution. The need for a fund for emergencies.

(b) Transactions. The need for money for the normal expenses of daily life.

(c) Speculation. The need for money to take advantage of changes in the value of the various financial assets that can be held instead of money.

The precautions and transactions funds are affected by national and personal income levels, and by spending and income patterns. A person who is paid monthly, 'holds' more money than one who is paid weekly. The inhabitants of a country with a high level of national income hold more money than those in a poor country.

Speculation is a different matter. Increased government spending results in people having more money than they require for their immediate needs. If they spend the excess, it will be on a narrow range of financial assets (bonds). Buying drives up the price of those assets and lowers interest rates. Because of the fall in interest rates, and higher business expectations, more capital investment is likely to take place. Economic activity will be stimulated. These movements will continue until interest rates establish the equilibrium prices between the demand for and supply of money, and until the augmented money supply bears the same relation to national income as it did before the increase.

Thus, according to the Keynesians, it is the demand for money which is important, particularly the speculative demand. An increase in money supply may or may not be spent. If, and only if, it is spent, it will drive up bond prices, drive down interest rates and so affect investment and employment.

8.10.2 THE VALUE OF MONEY — SUPPLY

There was a movement away from Keynesian economics in the latter part of the 1970's. Fiscal measures seemed to work better in controlling deflation. The work of Milton Friedman in America also led to more attention being given to the relationship of changes in the supply of money and changes in its value. One of the most well-known expositions of this relationship is contained in the quantity theory.

8.11 THE SUPPLY OF MONEY — THE QUANTITY THEORY

The idea that the quantity of money in an economy determines the price level, has been held by many economists. They include Locke, Hume, Ricardo and John Stuart Mill. Irving Fisher (1867—1947) popularized this 'quantity theory' by his famous equation of exchange $MV = PT$.

The theory starts by looking at the quantity or stock of money in the community. Let us say that this is £10,000. If the total value of all sales is £50,000, this means that the quantity of money has been used five times to get a total purchasing power of £50,000.

To the money stock, Fisher gave the term, M. To the number of times the money stock was used for sales, he gave the term, V, for velocity. MV equalled the total value of all sales, including financial transactions such as the purchase of bonds, bills and shares. This totality MV can be looked at from another viewpoint: the number of transactions and the average price of each. To the former, Fisher gave the term, T: to the latter, the term, P. Then PT equalled the total value of all sales. Thus the equation of exchange was written $MV = PT$ (money value of sales = money value of purchases).

The difficulty about Fisher's equation was, in practical terms, T, because T included financial transactions. For economic policy measures, economic output was more useful. Further, M, V and T were defined as indices, using the same base year. P expressed the prices of transactions measured in base year prices. This meant that it was statistically difficult to get an accurate measure of T.

As a result, a new version of the theory of exchange was formulated. It relates the stock of money to the flow of income. It is called the 'Cambridge' equation because Marshall, Keynes and other Cambridge economists used it.

The Cambridge equation takes the form of the quantity of national output and the average price of the 'final' prices which makes it up. Final price means the end price after all intermediate transactions have been eliminated. Thus, the final price of a loaf of bread ignores the intermediate values of wheat/flour etc., and takes in only the final price of bread in the market. Purely financial transactions such as share purchases are excluded from the Cambridge equation.

The average of the prices of goods and services which make up the total output is termed p (to distinguish it from the P of Fisher's equation). The national output is the total value of goods and stocks produced in one year. Though normally quoted in money terms, national output is given in this equation, a numerical value denoted by the term, R. We then get $R \times p$: the actual quantity of final goods and services (R) multiplied by their average price (p). Thus $R \times p$ is another way of expressing national output in money terms (national income = expenditure = output). If the total value of national output, $p \times R$, is divided by the quantity of money used to purchase R, we get the number of times the money stock 'changed hands', i.e. its velocity. This is termed the income velocity of circulation and is given the letters Vy. The Cambridge version of the quantity theory is expressed thus: M (money stock) $\times$ Vy (income velocity of circulation) $= R$ (the quantity of final goods and services) $\times$ p (their average price). The Cambridge equation tells us that national income equals the quantity of money multiplied by the income velocity of money. With a net national expenditure at market prices of £100,000 and the quantity of money at £50,000, the income velocity of circulation will be 2.

In both versions, if V and T are constant (Fisher equation) or Vy and R are constant (Cambridge equation), then any change in M must lead to a corresponding change in P or p. The quantity theory is, or should be, as much concerned with the velocity of money in the economy as with its quantity. The Cambridge equation however led to an interest in the factors affecting national income/output and the demand for money.

The demand for money for transactions by all households and firms depends on the size and frequency of their income-receipts/payments and on the number of firms. The last two are expected to remain constant. Thus, there is a short-term relationship between the transactions demand for money (desired cash balances) and the level of national income. This relationship can be expressed as $M = k(p \times R)$ where k = the fraction of national income ($p \times R$) that the desired level of money balances (M) represents. Thus, if national income were £100,000m and $k = \frac{1}{2}$, households and firms want to hold cash balances of £50,000m. This balance is the amount they find convenient at this level of national income. If the quantity of money in the country is £50,000m, national income is in equilibrium. National income = £100,000; £50,000 is the amount people want to hold as cash balances, which equals k (national income) which equals £50,000 which equals the money stock. Thus, demand for money (cash balances) equals the supply of money equals a fixed proportion (k) of the national income. Now assume that the money supply increases from £50,000 to £75,000. People will find that they hold cash balances that are higher than they need at current income levels. They will therefore spend some of their cash. In doing so, they increase the cash balances of others by the same amount. If k is constant at $\frac{1}{2}$, a new equlibrium can only be achieved by a rise in national income to £150,000. The desired cash balances are then back to their former relationship of $\frac{1}{2}$ of national income.

An increase in prices will always follow an increase in M if: (a) The national income in quantitative terms (R) is constant; and (b) the desired cash balance/national income ratio (k) is also constant.

Condition (a) is always likely to be fulfilled for the total output R cannot easily be increased in the short term. If unemployment is particularly severe, R could rise in response to an increase in M; otherwise the latter situation (with k constant) must lead to an increase in p.

Condition (b) above is not always valid. During periods of price stability, k remains relatively constant. But expectations of future inflationary trends can cause people to hold less cash balances and increase their current spending. With money supply and output unchanged, k would fall and p would therefore rise. Thus, if people decided to reduce their money balances from $\frac{1}{2}$ to $\frac{1}{4}$ of national income and money supply remained constant at £50,000, national income would rise from £100,000 to £200,000. With R unchanged, this would mean a rise in p of 100%. Such a price increase would influence people to hold smaller ratios of cash balances to national income, e.g. $\dfrac{\text{National Income}}{\frac{1}{4}}$ to $\dfrac{\text{N.I.}}{\frac{1}{8}}$ to $\dfrac{\text{N.I.}}{\frac{1}{20}}$ etc. Velocity would increase, and prices rise higher and higher. Expectations therefore play an important part in changes in the value of money.

Keynes did not agree that money was held only for transactions. People and firms also held money for speculative reasons. Thus, in his view, the total balances that firms and households wished to hold rested not only on current income levels, but also on the level of interest rates.

The quantity theory in one or other of its forms, is still held by many economists. It is useful in that it seeks to show the relationship between changes in the supply of money and changes in its value.

8.11.1 A SUMMARY

The quantity theory states that, in a simple economy, there is a relationship between the quantity of money and its value. If the supply of goods is fixed and the supply of money is increased, one of two things will happen. Money will change hands more slowly (the velocity of circulation will fall) or the price of goods will rise. Monetarists postulate the latter because, unlike the Keynesians, they believe velocity to be fairly stable.

8.12 KEYNESIAN AND MONETARIST THEORIES

8.12.1 THE MONETARIST VIEW

The old quantity theorists have today given way to the Monetarist or Chicago school. The latter term derives from the work of Professor Friedman of the University of Chicago who is the leading exponent of Monetarist ideas.

Today's monetarists, like the old quantity theorists similarly view the quantity of money as the main determinant of the price level. But they see it also as the short-run determinant of economic activity. Like the old quantity theorists, the new monetarists assume that velocity is fairly stable. Hence, a change in the money supply will change aggregate spending and the Gross National Product (which is national income less an allowance for capital consumption). This link between a change in the money supply, aggregate spending and G.N.P. can be seen thus. If the Government increases the money supply by, e.g. buying securities on the open market, the public will hold more cash and less other assets (government securities.)

Having already sufficient cash for their needs based on the current G.N.P., the public now spends the extra liquidity on real goods and services, driving up the G.N.P. During a recession, this increased spending absorbs unemployed resources. But, if the economy is already fully employed, the G.N.P. increase wil be due to higher prices. G.N.P. will keep rising until it bears the same relationship to the augmented money supply as it did before the Government's open market operations. Changes in the money supply thus have a direct effect on the price level. Though the effect on the price level is direct, it is not immediate. There may be a time lag of as much as two years before changes in the supply of money show up in the price level. Such changes were observed by Hume in 1752, and by Jevons in 1863 when he was speaking about currency increases.

Because the monetarist cause of inflation is excessive growth of the money supply, the solution to inflation is simple, in theory at least. It is control of the money supply, and thus of government spending. Some monetarists suggest index-linking to protect the capital of the saver when inflation erodes the purchasing power of money. The object of index linking, also known as inflation-proofing, is to adjust monetary values by the extent to which the general index of retail prices has risen. It can be applied to wages and other incomes.

Such an adjustment maintains money's original purchasing power. Some people think such indexation consolidates rather than cures inflation. Two index-linked schemes in the U.K. are

(a) National Savings Certificates: Retirement Issue, available only to older people. They can be bought in £10 units up to a maximum of 300 units (£3,000). After one year, their value increases monthly in line with the Retail Price Index.

(b) Save-As-You-Earn contractual savings scheme for savings of £4—£20 a month. Savings must be continued monthly for 5 years. After 5 years repayment is made revalued in line with the monthly Retail Price Index. A bonus is payable, if withdrawal is postponed for 1—2 years.

8.12.2 THE KEYNESIAN VIEW

Keynesians do not accept the link between money supply and G.N.P. Neither do they agree that velocity is stable in the short or long run. Their emphasis leans on the demand to hold money in preference to holding other assets.

If open market operations increase the supply of money, G.N.P. may, or may not, change. The public have extra cash. The monetarists believe this extra cash will be spent on real assets. The Keynesians believe that the holders of the extra cash may keep holding it. If they keep holding it, there will be no alteration at all in G.N.P. If the public do spend the money, their surplus cash will be used to buy financial assets (securities). Security prices rise, interest rates fall. Credit becomes easier. The lower rate induces some entrepreneurs to borrow and to buy real goods and services. G.N.P. goes up. Hence, the Keynesians see changes in the money supply affecting aggregate spending and G.N.P. only indirectly, through interest rates and the availability of credit.

The Keynesian solution to high unemployment and low investment is increased Government spending. This stimulates investment and has a multiplier effect leading to greater output and employment. Though Keynesian remedies have, in the past, proved successful in reducing unemployment, they do not appear so efficacious as a method of reducing the price level.

Both theories have this in common: they look to Government to control inflation: Keynesians suggest the use of the budget (fiscal policy) as a stabilizer; the Monetarists suggest monetary policy to control money supply—but as the Government is the biggest spender, it is the Government that must save the most. In both theories, it would appear that there must be a trade-off between inflation and unemployment. The more one falls, the more the other rises.

A variation on Keynesians ideas was suggested by some Cambridge economists in 1974. Their thesis was (a) that Budget deficits and surpluses have little impact on the level of production. The multiplier was near to unity owing to import withdrawals. (b) Exchange rate changes have little impact on the balance of payments on current account because the respective elasticities of demand for exports/imports did not alter much. This implied that the Budget influenced the balance of payments and the exchange rate influenced the level of domestic production. Government should therefore regulate the balance of payments by fiscal policy, and domestic production and employment by exchange rates. These ideas were not taken up, doubtless because the oil price changes had such an impact on the balance of payments. Perhaps the only answer to slumpflation is greater output per man-hour. This could mean, in the U.K., reducing the extremely long hours worked in many manual industries, increasing basic pay and abolishing overtime. Shift systems or work sharing could operate where flexibility was required. The present system in the U.K. is reminiscent of the German about 40 years ago when extremely long hours were worked for very little increase in production.

Such a change to higher basic rates, shorter hours, shared work, greater per capita output, would however require a radical change of views, often deeply entrenched, by management, unions, the employed and unemployed workers.

8.13 SUPPLY OF AND DEMAND FOR CREDIT

So far we have discussed the supply of and demand for money, and their relationship to the value of money. When we speak of the supply and demand for credit, from the borrower's point of view we are speaking of the same thing as the supply of money. The lender sees the situation differently. He is altering his assets from very liquid ones to less liquid ones, converting cash into credit instruments. He exchanges one kind of asset (money) for another type. He makes a loan against perhaps risky collateral. He is acting as a broker, a transmitter of funds often created elsewhere. He relinquishes money deposited with him for assets which unlike the original deposits lodged with him, cannot now be used as a medium of exchange. There are some further limitations on credit not applicable to money.

If I borrow from a finance house company to buy a car, they have extended me credit, but it is specific credit for a car, not for generalized spending. If I buy stock and I do not have to pay for it for 3—6 months, I have been given credit, but only for the stock. I cannot use this type of credit as a medium of exchange for something else. When I buy a house through a building society, or buy a consumer durable through instalment finance, I am receiving credit that may extend from 3—25 years. To the borrower, credit is purchasing power that differs little, if at all, from money. But the supply of credit, unlike the supply of money, depends on there being enough savers to make the transmission possible.

The immediate suppliers of credit are financial institutions. They act as intermediaries between the groups who supply savings at one rate of interest and the groups who borrow it at the higher rates charged by the intermediaries. The difference provides the intermediaries with their profit. Governments may place controls on hire purchase agreements but, even without such restrictions, there can be changes in the supply of credit. We then hear of a mortgage 'famine' because the financial intermediaries, in this case the building societies, have taken in an insufficient flow of funds to transmit them to potential borrowers. Again, the collateral of the borrower may not be good enough for him to get funds for the amounts he requires. Credit will then also not be forthcoming.

The supply of credit is determined primarily by savers. That supply is, naturally, affected by government policy, by interest rates and the range of alternative savings/investments. Let us assume government bonds (gilts) have a sufficiently attractive interest rate to cause people to switch their savings from banks or building societies, to a new issue of government stock.

An old issue will not do, because this will be merely transferring funds from one bank depositor to another, the owner of the stock. As a result of this switching to new government stock, by depositors, the banks suffer a fall in deposits. The money supply will fall. If money is withdrawn from the building society for the purchase of the gilts, the societies will have to reduce their lending on houses. People who wish to sell houses may have to reduce their prices as mortgages will be hard to obtain. The deflationary effect of this switch from funds in banks or building societies to the government (for stock) can be offset if the government passes on the money received in the form of increased public sector spending.

Banks are financial intermediaries. They are called bank financial intermediaries compared with building societies and similar institutions who are called non-bank financial intermediaries. But banks do more than transmit savings. Because their deposits are money, and the banks keep only fractional reserves, their loans create new deposits and thus new money. The only restriction on bank lending other than profitability, prudence and government directives, is that they must, in the U.K., keep the required reserve asset ratio. Every bank loan creates another deposit in the system. Credit advances by non-bank financial intermediaries do not. However, suppliers of credit such as the NBFIs do add to the general purchasing power of the community by passing on liquidity and receiving in exchange less liquid assets. In this way, NBFIs have an impact on GNP, and in some countries, their liabilities are included in the money supply for this reason.

Keynesian analysis is a credit analysis concerned with financial assets of all kinds, the availability of credit, interest rate changes and the reaction of borrowers/lenders to those changes. It is also concerned with the role of financial institutions as transmitters of funds.

Monetarists ignore credit. It is money alone that counts, and its effects, which are always direct, upon G.N.P. This difference can be seen in the following illustration. A lender makes a loan to a business firm, e.g. by way of a debenture. The monetarist will argue that there has been no change in the money supply because while the borrower has more, the lender has less. The firm has money and will spend it. This spending is offset by the lender's inability to spend the sum he has lent. But the Keynesian analysis is that there is more likely to be an increase in spending. The firm will certainly spend the money which, while it was with the lender, was merely an idle balance. Though money supply remains unaltered, velocity will increase.

Most governments play for safety, and though they may appear to take a monetarist stance, they will generally make sure that credit policy follows in the same direction of monetary policy.

8.14 DEFLATION

Deflation means a situation in which prices are falling. The value of money rises. More goods and services can be bought with the same amount of money. Such a deflationary situation may result from increased productivity.

If money incomes rise less than the productivity, then the supply of goods would exceed demand and prices fall. However, in practice, when prices fall, producers tend to lower their output, and retailers to carry less stock. Demand falls for labour, and there is a fall in money incomes. The reduced expenditure leads through unsold goods and unwanted stocks to a reduction in output, rising unemployment and falling prices.

The cause of the decreased demand may arise internally because of decreased Government expenditure; reduced consumption; reduced private investment. It may come from external factors such as a fall in exports due to changes in exchange rates/patterns of expenditure/or quotas and other controls.

Expectations of deflation, like those of inflation, tend to feed upon themselves, and make the feared event become inevitable. The decrease in demand will continue until some event or series of events alters expectations, and begins the impetus to recovery. The government itself may take steps to reflate. Alternatively, stocks and equipment may be so run down that they have to be replaced. This stimulates the capital goods industries. The marginal efficiency of capital increases because interest rates fall to their lowest point. Investment picks up. Finally, export orders may improve because the external value of the domestic money (the exchange rate) has fallen; quotas have been lifted or there has been an increase of demand for the exported goods. Any or all of these factors can provide the psychological/physical impetus for change. The change might even be engineered by rumours of oil strikes, or new supplies of precious raw materials. Providing these rumours change the climate of opinion and radically alter business expectations, they will be almost as good, in the short-run, as the real thing.

8.15 INFLATION AND DEFLATION—A SUMMARY

Inflation means a fall in the value of money. It may be cost inflation: due to changes in the cost of factor prices (labour, raw materials) which in turn may be sparked off by other causes: rigidity in labour/employer practices; inelasticity of supply; exchange rate changes and alterations in the terms of trade.

It may be demand-pull inflation which usually arises from an increase in aggregate demand out of proportion to the increased production of goods. But what causes aggregate demand to rise is still a subject of debate: an increase in the money supply; a change in aspirations so that people desire different commodity goods and services and/or different amounts of them? Money supply increase is the favourite culprit today.

Deflation means a rise in the value of money. This disease of money is much more amenable to diagnosis and treatment. Keynes prescribed fiscal measures to deal with the symptoms many years ago, and no better remedy has yet been put forward. In developing countries, this means injections from outside to raise national income levels.

TYPICAL QUESTION

Discuss the view that restriction of the money supply is the only effective way to check inflation.

SUGGESTED ANSWER

Inflation means a situation in which there is an overall rise in the price level. It is often summed up in the phrase 'too much money chasing too few goods'. Some economists assert that inflation is caused by an expansion in the money supply. This quantity theory can be expressed by the equation $MV = PT$ where M is the quantity of money, V the velocity of circulation, P the price level and T the number of transactions.

Other theorists say that inflation is due to cost increases brought about by excessive wage demands or higher import prices. The solution to this 'cost-push' inflation is to control wages by an incomes policy, to restrict imports and/or freeze prices.

But, whatever the cause of inflation, the result will be the same: a disproportionate increase in the supply of money relative to the supply of goods. The supply of money means the total quantity of notes and coins in circulation plus bank deposits in the country at a given time.

Increasing the supply of goods to the level of the increased money supply is not possible in industrialized countries where money supply can increase by as much as 30% in a year while growth rates range from 3% to, at best, 9% per year. The solution, according to the quantity theorists is therefore to reduce the quantity of money. Because velocity and transactions are independent of M, so changes in M must have a direct effect on P.

The Monetarist school, which is an updated version of the quantity theory, states that reduction of the money supply can be achieved by less government spending. This will lead to a fall in employment, in national income and the price level. Monetarists often suggest indexation as a palliative while their remedial measures take effect.

Keynesian economists hold rather different views. They state that changes in the supply of money affect the price of money substitutes, i.e. other financial assets. An increase in money supply drives the prices of alternatives up, and their yields down. This fall in interest rates affects investment and, through the multiplier, total demand. Changes in the money supply thus affect investment, demand and national income indirectly through interest rates. Keynesian economists therefore recommend fiscal policy acting on disposable income as the best way of checking inflation.

Monetarists disagree. For them, money is a unique asset and people may use an excess of it for goods as much as securities, and so control of the money supply is essential.

There is possibly another remedy. Providing incomes and prices march roughly in line, the effects of inflation, internally, may not be so doom-laden as prophets predict. To some people, inflation is preferable to mass unemployment, and one does not lead inexorably to the other. Providing production is kept up or increased (by a reduction in company taxation or a switch from 'social' spending to 'investment' spending or the export trades), the solution to inflation might be found in exchange-rate adjustments. As the £ fell relative to other currencies, our goods should become more competitive overseas. The cost of imports would rise very steeply, causing people at home to buy, even at internally high prices, more British goods, and less foreign ones, or to forego both. More use would have to be made of indigenous products, less bought abroad, not by any import controls but through the mechanism of market forces. In this way inflation could be 'contained' by methods similar to a siege economy. Standards of living would drop but more equably than through mass unemployment.

Summing up all these various solutions to the problem of inflation one could say that whatever methods are used: fiscal policy or monetary policy or incomes policy or exchange rate mechanisms: they will all eventually lead to a reduction in the money supply, that is the quantity of money stock, and hence a reduction in the price level.

ADDITIONAL QUESTIONS

1. Analyse how changes in the value of money affect its ability to fulfil its functions.

2. 'The value of money does not depend upon its intrinsic value.' Discuss.

3. Analyse the likely economic effect of a significant *appreciation* in the value of money.

4. 'Keynesians are fiscalists.' Explain this statement. To what extent is it true?

9 Interest Rates

9.1 THE NATURE OF INTEREST

When someone borrows money, other than from generous relatives or friends, a price has to be paid for its use. That price is *interest*. From the viewpoint of the lender, interest is a reward for giving up the use of money. He has exchanged a claim on present resources for a claim on future ones; abstained from consumption today, hopefully for consumption tomorrow. His abstinence is compensated by a reward, namely interest.

The lender wants this compensation in case (a) he cannot use the money should he need it (b) he loses some or all of it and (c) there is a fall in the value of his money during the period of the loan. (The risk element is rewarded by *profit*; any fall in the value of money is rewarded by an element of *insurance*, neither of which is, strictly speaking, part of the interest rate).

9.2 INTEREST RATES IN A MONEYLESS SOCIETY

Interest rates can be computed even in a moneyless society. Yields or returns on different kinds of activity have to be balanced against one another. Choices have to be made between present and future satisfactions and the best selected in order to achieve maximum productivity or other desired objective.

A Robinson Crusoe on a desert island may use a hook and line to get 5 fish a day. His catch rises to 7 if he has a boat. He builds one. The job takes 20 days during which he fishes not at all. His non-consumption of fish is *saving*; the building of the boat is *investment* and, when completed, *capital*. The extra 2 fish he has caught by using the boat is the *return on capital*, i.e. *interest*. In 50 days, he will recoup the 100 fish he was unable to catch during the 20-day investment period. In one year (365 days), the boat will have repaid for itself about 7 times over: a rate of 700% per annum. There surely won't be many better investments on his desert island!

9.2.1 THE CLASSICAL THEORY OF INTEREST

This view of interest as a reward for the loan of capital is known as the *classical theory of interest*. (In some text books there are other names: the non-monetary, or real; or loanable funds theory.) It shows interest as the equilibrium price between the demand for and supply of capital.

The *demand for capital* comes from borrowers who wish to use it to make a profit. Entrepreneurs will not borrow otherwise. The price of the loan, interest, is balanced against the reward from using it, profit. If the result is positive, the entrepreneur goes ahead. This is analogous to the *marginal productivity* theory in economics. If an additional unit of output brings in a positive revenue (the profit from the unit is greater than its costs of production), production continues. It will stop at the point where marginal revenue (the addition to total revenue caused by the production of one more unit) equals the marginal cost.

Similarly with capital: it will be borrowed up to the point where the expected return on a unit of capital equals the additional cost (interest) of borrowing it. This effect is called (by Keynes) the *marginal efficiency of capital*. Classical theorists called it the marginal productivity of capital. It can be depicted graphically as follows:

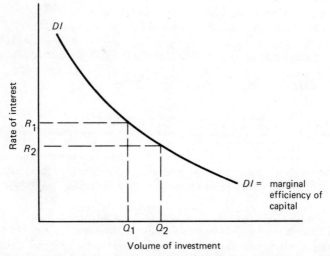

Figure 9.1   If the interest rate drops from R_1 to R_2, investment becomes more profitable and an increased quantity Q_2 will be undertaken.

The supply of capital comes from savers. The amount of saving in any society is determined by

(a) *Social influences*, e.g. the thriftiness of the inhabitants; the development of financial institutions.

(b) *The age of the population*, older people have usually accumulated more than young people.

(c) *Religious influences*, e.g. ascetism versus conspicuous consumption patterns.

(d) *The total income of the community*, rich countries have surpluses over basic needs. They can afford to save more. Saving cannot be done by those who have not enough to eat.

(e) *Distribution of income*, the rich put away more than the poor. There is a bigger margin when basic needs have been met, for saving (and investment).

(f) *The rate of interest* is thought to affect how much people save, but other considerations also affect savers: the safety of their capital and its ease of withdrawal. Nevertheless, a higher rate might induce more people to part with liquidity even at the cost of greater inconvenience.

These two forces of *demand for capital by borrowers* (entrepreneurs) and the *supply of savings* give a point of intersection, the rate of interest:

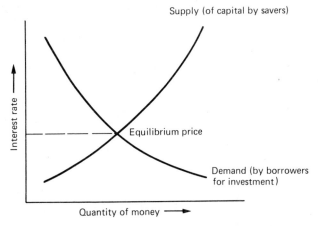

Figure 9.2   The classical (loanable funds) theory of interest.

9.2.2 THE KEYNESIAN (OR MONETARY) THEORY OF INTEREST

The supply of and demand for money capital coming into equilibrium via the interest rate, was challenged by Keynes in *The General Theory of Employment, Interest and Money*. He argued that the rate of interest was a *monetary* phenomenon, determined by monetary forces. The interest rate certainly *was* the equilibrium price between supply and demand. However, it was *not* the supply of and demand for *capital*, but money. The difference is that money is in the control of the authorities. The money stock depends on the banking system. Hence, the supply curve is inelastic. The holders of money do not, as do the suppliers of capital in the classical theory of interest, influence the supply.

Further, the demand for money is not for investment alone, as with the classical theory. This is only one aspect of the demand for money, which Keynes called the *speculative demand*. There are two further influences affecting the demand for money. People want money's liquidity to (a) finance current transactions, (b) have a pool of funds to meet unforeseen contingencies, *and* (c) for speculation; to take advantage of changes in investment returns.

People do not change their demand for money for *transactions* because of changes in interest rate. Demand for money as a *precautionary fund*, also does not alter much with changes in interest rates. But the *speculative* demand for money does change. Interest rate changes bring inverse changes in the prices of stocks and shares. People will switch their holdings of financial assets between holdings of stocks and holdings of liquid money.

9.2.3.1 *Liquidity Preference*
To induce people to alter their liquidity preference, a reward or price, i.e. interest, must be offered. The higher the interest rate, the greater the cost of holding money; the lower the interest rate, the lower the cost of holding money. There is thus a downward-sloping demand curve showing that the lower the rate of interest, the larger the amount of money demanded. By 'demanded' is meant held, rather than invested in interest-bearing securities. However, at one point, the demand for liquidity becomes perfectly elastic.

As the rate of interest falls, the prospect of further falls, diminishes. People believe the rate must go up in the future. They will not change their holding of money at this point, unless there is a very great increase in the supply of money and fall in interest rate. The elastic part of the demand curve is based entirely on past events and future expectations, and varies from country to country. It is known as the *'liquidity trap'*.

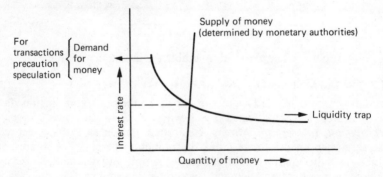

Figure 9.3

9.2.3 COMPARISON OF THE TWO THEORIES
The two theories, the classical and the Keynesian, are both supply and demand theories, with interest rates as the price bringing these forces into equilibrium. But the *classical theory* is a *long-term theory* while *Keynesian theory* is *short-term*.

The classical theory concentrates on the supply of *capital* as provided by *savers*; and demanded by *borrowers* (entrepreneurs); the Keynesian theory emphasizes the *demand for* the unique quality of money, its *liquidity*, and places little emphasis on the *supply* of money, this being in the hands of the monetary authorities.

9.3 MONEY MARKET INTEREST RATES

The two theories of interest explained above seek to show why interest rates alter over time. In any money market, however, there are many different rates, depending on the collateral of the borrower, the security and length of duration of the loan and its ease of withdrawal, as well as more technical considerations like the economic situation and the level of interest rates abroad.

The tax position of the lender/borrower and the costs of purchasing certain financial assets may similarly affect the net return to an investor. Generally, interest rates rise as the liquidity of an asset falls. Claims against governments and local authorities are 'safe' and thus highly liquid. But the higher and sooner the certainty of capital repayment, the lower the interest rate tends to be.

The most important rates quoted in the U.K. financial markets are (a) the *Bank of England's Minimum Lending Rate*, the minimum rate at which the central bank will discount or lend against the collateral of first class paper. Related to M.L.R. is (b) the *Treasury Bill rate* based on the average weekly tender rates of discount. (c) *Commercial banks' base rate* is the rate at which commercial banks base their loans to customers. It rises from 1% or 2% above base for the very 'best' industrial companies to over 4% for private individuals. There is a fairly wide margin between this rate and (d) the banks' *deposit rate* which is quoted for time and sight deposits. On this margin less costs, the banks make some of their profits. (e) *Finance House base rate* is always higher than the banks' base rate because of the higher risk in lending for instalment credit. (f) *local authorities* vary their *deposit rate*, depending on the length of time for which the deposit is made and interest rates elsewhere. (g) *Mortgage rates*, whether from local authorities or *Building Societies*, keep roughly parallel to Minimum Lending Rate, though trying always to offer sufficient reward to savers to enable the societies to continue giving mortgage advances to would-be house buyers. (h) *LIBOR* London-Inter-Bank-Offered Rate is the rate at which London banks lend to each other; it changes according to currency and length of loan. These are the main rates operating in financial markets, but there are others, including those for certificates of U.K. deposit.

9.4 U.S. INTEREST RATES

In the United States, the interbank (overnight) rate is known as the *Federal Funds rate*. U.S. member banks deposit their reserve requirements with the

Federal Reserve bank. No interest is paid on these reserves, so there is an incentive to banks to lend surpluses at very short notice at any available rate before settlement day at the end of the banking week. The Federal Reserve Bank alters reserve requirements and also intervenes directly in the market, so the Federal Funds rate is very volatile.

The Federal Funds Discount Rate is akin to the U.K. Bank Rate. It is administered by the Federal Reserve Bank and is the rate at which the Federal Reserve Bank will provide funds to member banks with reserve shortfalls, except at the end of the banking week when shortfall lending costs 2% more than the Federal Funds Discount rate.

The Federal Funds Target Rate is used to help the Federal Reserve Bank achieve monetary and economic objectives. The Federal Open Market Committee buy and sell securities for the Federal Reserve Bank in the New York money market to achieve a monthly target range. This interest rate is published 30 days afterwards as a guide to the market of the Bank's interest rate 'intentions'.

Treasury Bill rate is similar to the U.K. Treasury Bill rate, and the U.S. Prime rate is similar to U.K. base rate.

9.5 BOND PRICES AND YIELDS

Prices of securities vary with changes in interest rates. A £100 government bond paying 5% interest, will give £5 per year return (or dividend). If the interest rate in the market rises to 10%, nobody will buy a £100 security which yields only 5% i.e. £5 per year. The price will fall to £50. The annual return on the bond, now costing £50 instead of £100, will still be £5 per year. But £5 on £50 equals the current rate of interest of 10%. This is the *yield*: the percentage return on the purchase or market price of the bond.

To calculate the yield on a given stock, the following formula is used:

$$\frac{\text{Nominal or Par Value} \times \text{Rate of Dividend or Interest}}{\text{Purchase Price}}$$

Thus if £100 stock pays 12% fixed interest and costs £120 to buy, what is its yield?

$$\frac{\text{(Par Value)} \quad £100 \times 12 \quad \text{(Rate of Interest)}}{\text{(Purchase Price)} \quad £120} = 10\%$$

Yield calculated in this way is known as a *running yield*, the yield per year until maturity. At maturity stock is repaid at its nominal or par value. Any capital gain (or loss) is calculated on an annual basis and added to (or subtracted from) the running yield. The result is the *gross redemption yield*. After tax, it becomes a *net redemption yield*. A *yield curve* shows a graphical representation of yields on investments of different lengths.

9.5.1 THE TERM STRUCTURE OF INTEREST RATES

The yield curve summarizes the term structure of interest rates. From a given point in time, it shows how the yield of a financial claim changes. As the claim approaches its maturity (or redemption date) the risk element lessens. The yield curve flattens. It is usually upward sloping to begin with showing that interest rates rise with the time to maturity. Interest rates on short-term securities are normally low because the demand for them tends to be higher than for long-term claims. The term structure is a term-to-maturity structure of interest rates. It changes if conditions of demand and supply for the various financial assets change. Equally as important as actual rates are expectations of future bond prices and yields.

Keynes used this idea of yield expectations. He showed how people would switch their holdings of different kinds of financial assets according to their expectations of future interest rates. If the price of securities were high, (interest rates low), people would sell securities to get the high price before a fall came; their demand for money would rise. When security prices were low (interest rates high) their demand for speculative balances would fall.

In the classical theory of interest, equilibrium always came — eventually — between the supply and demand for funds. In Keynesian theory, interest rates were unable to ensure this equilibrium in the short run. Monetary measures would not therefore be able to smooth out disparities between saving and investment. Fluctuations in national income had to do the job. These could not be managed by the private sector alone. Public sector works would have to fill the gap between saving and investment. This meant fiscal measures. The Budget thus came to be used as a technique of increasing investment, output and employment.

For over twenty years, Keynesian demand management, as fiscal measures came to be known, proved successful in warding off unemployment. Then as inflation began to creep into western economies, so too did doubts about the Keynesian recipe. "We are all monetarists now," became the new 'in' phrase. The change from Keynesianism to monetarism was accelerated by changes in the value of money. All kinds of controls were tried to stimulate employment, reduce inflation. So far the U.K. has found no one solution that achieves both objectives together.

9.6 DISCOUNTING: AN ARITHMETICAL DIVERSION

Discounting is a process which estimates the value of a money claim due at some fixed future rate by reference to the current interest rate. When Discount Houses in the U.K. give a sum of money today for Treasury Bills maturing in three months they are using a *discount* rate, which is another way of looking at interest rates.

It is easy to see that if £100 is lent for 1 year at 5% the lender receives £105 at the end of the year. For longer periods of time, interest is added on to the preceding year's sum plus interest and so on for each successive year. The formula for compound interest is used for such calculations:

$$A = P\left(1 + \frac{r}{100}\right)^n$$

Where A = the Amount available after n years
r = the rate per cent
P = the Principal (original investment)
n = the number of years.

Example

How much will £250 invested at 15% amount to after 17 years?

$$A = 250\left[1 + \frac{15}{100}\right]^{17} = 250\,(1 + 0.15)^{17} = 250\,(1.15)^{17}$$

There are two methods for finding the answer to this calculation.

(i) using logarithms

$$
\begin{aligned}
\log A &= \log 250 + 17 \log 1.15 \\
&= 2.39794 + 17 \times 0.0606978 \\
&= 2.39794 + 1.0318633 \\
&= 3.4298033
\end{aligned}
$$

$\therefore \log A = 3.4298033$
$\therefore \quad A$ = antilog 3.4298033
       = 2,690.3159
       = 2,690.316 to 3D

Answer £2,690.316

(ii) using calculator

$A = 250 \times 1.15^{17} = 250 \times 10.76124 = 2,690.316$ *Answer* £2,690.316

Discounting gives the answer to such questions as how much should be given today with interest rate at 5%, for a claim to £100 in 1 year's time? The equation used for this type of question is

$$P = \frac{A}{\left[1 + \frac{r}{100}\right]^n}$$

Where r = the rate per cent
P = the amount to be given now for a claim to £A in n years' time

Example

How much should I receive now for giving up a claim to £500 in 2 years' time if interest is at 15%?

$$P = \frac{500}{\left[1 + \frac{15}{100}\right]^2} = \frac{500}{1.15^2} = \frac{500}{1.3225} = 378.07183$$

Answer £378.072

TYPICAL QUESTION

State the main effects of a rise in a country's interest rates on (a) its internal economy (b) its banking system (c) its external situation.

SUGGESTED ANSWER

(a) *The main effects of a rise in interest rates on a country's internal economy.* A fall in the volume of (i) consumption and (ii) investment by the private sector. Public sector investment is thought to be fairly insensitive to interest rate changes (inelastic demand) and is often accused of 'crowding out' the private sector. More important than interest rates themselves, are *expectations* of which way they are going, up or down.

When borrowing becomes dearer, firms will defer investment until a more 'profitable' time, when interest charges are lower. Governments may then introduce concessions to aid investment, with a possible misallocation of resources. Highly geared firms often go into liquidation during periods of very high rates, with side-effects on firms/banks who have lent them money.

This was seen in the property and 'secondary' banking firms who mushroomed in the low-interest period of 1970 and collapsed in the high-interest period some years later. 'Lifeboat' operations had to be undertaken by the Bank of England to help some companies and banks to survive. If confidence in a Government remains fairly high, in spite of a big public sector borrowing requirement, people will save in 'safe' havens when interest rates rise. Thus, there were large sales of Government debt in 1976 and even more in 1977 when interest rates soared to their highest ever, and them came tumbling down.

(b) *Banking system*

A rise in interest rates tends to increase bank deposits and reduce bank lending. The banks' fixed interest assets fall in value; so do those held as collateral. Profitability may increase however, in spite of a reduced volume of lending, if the margins between lending and borrowing are sufficiently wide.

A rise in interest rates means a fall in bond prices and can cause losses to Discount Houses and banks who hold them as part of their reserve requirements. (This was partly why the 1971 requirement for Discount Houses to hold 50% in public sector debt, was abandoned.)

(c) *External situation*

A high interest rate used to draw in international money. More important for an inflow of funds today are the country's growth rate, level of inflation and balance of payments.

If a country's money depreciates by 15% per year, then 15% interest is needed to keep the original value of the deposit without any increase in its purchasing power. Some countries/companies with large funds may be more concerned with the political stability of the country in which they place their funds. In this case, a rise in interest rates will cause an inflow of funds (U.K. 1977), and an increase in the reserves, with a rise in the exchange rate.

ADDITIONAL QUESTIONS

1. Outline the main reasons for the higher levels of interest rates in recent years.

2. If a bank, operating in a modern community, is free to determine its own interest rates on deposits and advances, what factors influence it in doing so? What particular considerations, if any, apply to U.K. banks?

3. 'The rate of interest is the rate at which the community as a whole discounts the future.' Explain this statement and comment on it.

4. Outline the structure of interest rates allowed on deposits and charged on advances by the clearing and other banks in London.

10 Monetary Policy

10.1 DEFINITION

Monetary policy may be defined as control through the banking system of the money supply, *directly* by a limit (target) on its growth; or *indirectly* by measures which affect the cost and availability of credit. Monetary policy is used to achieve certain ends. These ends vary over different time periods. They may be difficult, if not impossible to achieve together, e.g. a reduction in unemployment and a decrease in prices.

10.2 DEVELOPMENT OF MONETARY POLICY

In most countries, control of the banking system evolved from expendiency, not design. Central banks usually started life as fund raisers for kings or governments. From these origins, they developed as banks of issue, supplying the needs of commerce and industry. To guard against over-issue of notes by central banks (and others), bank credit then had to be regulated.

The bank crises in the U.S.A. in the early 20th century, like those in the U.K. in the 19th, gave a further direction to monetary policy. Governments now became concerned with the *financial stability* of banks and the *economic stability* of the country. In 1937, the Federal Reserve emphasized the change by defining economic stability: 'the maintenance of as full employment of labour and of productive capacity of the country as can comfortably be sustained.'

Some economists dislike full employment as an aim of monetary policy. Lionel Robbins in the U.K. thought its pursuit could lead to permanent inflation unless governments maintained 'high' employment at wage rates not increasing more rapidly than productivity. Dr.M.W. Holtrop of the Netherlands Central Bank saw full employment as an aim of *economic policy*.

Others were: maximization of wealth and growth; fair distribution of income; harmonious occupational ownership and some public ownership. By contrast, monetary policy had to be concerned with payments balances and stable prices. It was the *means* of achieving general economic ends.

10.3 DIFFERENCES BETWEEN MONETARY AND OTHER TYPES OF POLICY

Monetary policy is narrower than general economic policy. It uses the banking and monetary system to achieve certain ends. Economic policy sometimes does and sometimes does not use this system.

In practice, it is often difficult to distinguish precisely between different types of policies and their effects. If the Chancellor of the Exchequer restricts wage increases to 10% per year, this is not monetary but incomes policy. It may also be part of a general economic policy to combat inflation. The request to keep wages within a guide line of 10% is not aimed at the level of bank deposits (monetary policy) though it could affect them. The Chancellor may levy a tax on tobacco or wine. If there is an inelastic demand for these goods, he gets an increae in revenue. If there is an elastic demand for them, he gets reductions in imports. The tax is part of fiscal policy, but it could create a *balance of payments surplus,* which is often a monetary policy objective.

10.4 AIMS OF MONETARY POLICY

What then are, or should be, the aims of monetary policy: full employment; smooth funding of the national debt; a balance of payments surplus or ensuring that banks do not go bankrupt and that the issue of notes and coin matches the public's demand for them?

The Macmillan Report gave objectives in 1931 similar to those of the Radcliffe Report in 1959. Radcliffe wanted high and stable employment; reasonable stability of prices; steady economic growth, a contribution to overseas economic development, and a strengthening of foreign exchange reserves, implying a balance of payments surplus.

In the 1970s, monetary policy aimed for *targets*. A target was a ceiling for the growth of the money supply, however defined, over a given period. If the targets were reached, the ultimate aims of general economic policy, e.g. full employment, still had to be worked for. Fiscal or incomes or prices policies might then be tried in a policy 'mix' to achieve all the ultimate aims together. In 1979/80 the main aim of monetary policy was the control of the money supply and thereby the reduction of inflation, even if this meant the risk of higher unemployment and lower economic activity.

10.5 THE TECHNIQUES OF MONETARY POLICY

The *techniques* or *instruments* of monetary policy are any measures used to affect the money stock or the cost of credit. As in a monopoly situation, it is not possible to control both price *and* the *quantity* sold of a commodity, even when that commodity is money. High-interest rates usually cause less demand for money; control of the money stock by one variant or another, usually causes the price of money to rise. Nevertheless, Governments who try to please all, particularly at election times, do use a variety of monetary techniques on the money stock. They are discussed below:

10.6 TECHNIQUES OF MONEY SUPPLY CONTROL

10.6.1 RESERVE REQUIREMENTS

To exert control over the banking system, the monetary authorities must control, legally or informally, the type or quantity of reserves which banks hold to any given volume of deposits. This control also gives the authorities the power to control the money supply. Affecting the banks' reserves affects the banks' power to lend. If the banks' reserve asset ratio falls below $12\frac{1}{2}$ % of their eligible deposit liabilities, they must reduce those liabilities. This leads to a multiple reduction in the money supply.

One way of reducing the reserve assets is by *Open Market Operations*: the buying or selling of Government securities. This affects the banks' quantity of reserves held. It is a method of control available only in countries with a sophisticated money market and its efficacy is lessened where there is a large public debt. (U.K., Italy, Sweden.) Sales of government bonds are easiest when interest rates are high, but high-interest rates increase the cost of servicing public debt.

The Bank of England uses open market operations to influence the money supply. When the Bank *buys* securities from the public, the public gains cash in lieu. (Ex-holders of securities hand the cash/cheques to their banks.) When the Bank *sells* to the public, cheques are drawn on Bankers' Deposits to pay the Bank of England. Bankers' Deposits fall, and so does the banks' ability to create advances. Conversion of short-term borrowing by the Bank for longer-term debt, an operation known as 'funding' has the same effect. In France, Germany and the United States, the monetary authorities control the asset ratio directly, so that it is raised/lowered for different types of banks, different types of deposits and even different economic situations. This type of control is sometimes referred to as monetary base control (control of the sum of the balance-sheet liabilities of the central bank to the private sector.)

In the U.K., the Bank of England's influence on ratios is through its control on the supply of those claims, such as Treasury Bills, which count as reserve assets. If the banks' reserve asset ratio falls below the permitted minimum, it has to be made up. This means reducing the level of advances to customers, or acquiring other compensating assets. One technique for reducing reserve assets is the use of Special Deposits. Special Deposits were introduced in 1958 and first used in 1960. The Bank of England calls for a percentage of deposits from the banks. These 'Special Deposits' are 'frozen' in a special account at the Bank. They receive interest at Treasury Bill rate, but do not count as eligible liabilities. The effect is a transfer of balances from Bankers' Deposits at the Bank of England, which is part of a bank's reserve asset ratio, to Special Deposits, which is not. The asset ratio therefore falls, and banks must restore it by selling securities or reducing advances. The former drives down prices, and raises interest rates. The technique of Special Deposits therefore has to be used with some caution.

10.6.2 SUPPLEMENTARY SPECIAL DEPOSITS (THE 'CORSET')

In addition to operating on banks' reserve assets, the central bank can control the money supply by acting on *banks' liabilities*. The use of Supplementary Special Deposits was such a technique. Banks had to place with the Bank of England, Special Deposits in relation to the growth of their interest-bearing eligible liabilities (deposit accounts) above a certain level. If the average of a bank's interest-bearing liabilities in April, May, June, 1974 exceeded the average for October, November and December, 1973 when the scheme began, by more than 8 per cent, a non-interest-bearing Special Deposit was payable to the Bank. In April 1974, the Bank allowed the three monthly average of banks' interest bearing resources to rise above the previous 8% by a further $1\frac{1}{2}$ % a month before liability was incurred to make supplementary deposits.

Supplementary Deposits were known colloquially as the Bank of England's 'corset'. The rate on interest-bearing eligible liabilities (IBEL's) was progressive as follows:

Excess growth of interest-bearing eligible liabilities above specified level:	*Supplementary deposits required*
1% or less	5% of excess
1% to 3%	25% of excess
Over 3%	50% of excess

The purpose of this technique was to make it less profitable for banks to bid for deposits beyond certain level. It thus reduced the amount of credit available. Banks were not expected to increase their lending rates to circumvent these measures.

In November, 1974, the scheme was extended for a further six months but the penalties lessened:

3% or less	5% of excess
3% to 5%	25% of excess
Over 5%	50% of excess

By 1975 the demand for advances had fallen so much that the scheme was suspended. The authorities retained the right to bring it back if needed, and reactivated supplementary deposits in November 1976 and June 1978 but abandoned it in June 1980.

However, supplementary deposits have not proved very efficient. One method of circumventing them was by the use of acceptance credits. Instead of separately negotiating a number of bills of exchange, companies needing short-term trade finance could draw down a number of bills backed by a merchant bank's name, to an agreed total. The acceptance gave the bill the best discount rate and when it reached maturity, the company settled the debt or drew new bills to cover the face value of the maturing bill. Supplementary deposits had the unsatisfactory side-effect of increasing the volume of acceptance credit.

10.6.3 DIRECTIVES

The Bank of England can issue guidelines to the banks restricting the type of lending (qualitative controls) or the amounts of lending (quantitative controls). After 1971 (Competition and Credit Control), directives were not often used as an instrument of control, though the authorities retained the right to issue directives when they thought fit.

Directives were issued in August 1972 and September 1973 to restrict lending for property development and financial transactions. Later, in 1973, similar directives were issued. Hire purchase and credit controls did not escape. Credit card holders had their cash drawing facilities reduced and had to pay higher instalments on outstanding balances. However, to protect the finance of housing banks were not allowed to pay more than $9\frac{1}{2}$ % interest on deposits in amounts of under £10,000.

In 1974 and 1975 came further lending directives which restrained lending to persons; property companies; for purely financial transactions; or credit purchases on easier terms than hire purchase contracts, in order to ensure that 'the needs of manufacturing industry for finance or facilities for working capital are fully met.'

10.6.4 PUBLIC SECTOR BORROWING REQUIREMENT

The size of the public sector borrowing requirement, and the way it is financed, affects the money supply. An increase in taxation increases the Government's revenue, and lessens their need to borrow. Public deposits (i.e. the revenue of the Government) increase; Bankers' deposits at the Bank of England decrease. But if the borrowing requirement is financed by borrowing from U.K. banks, the money supply will increase. If the total revenue from taxation, etc. is less than total public expenditure, there is a public sector borrowing requirement. When this is financed by borrowing from U.K. residents or overseas, the money supply does not change. But if it is financed by the issue of Treasury Bills, this too will lead to an increase in money supply, but it will become a multiplied money supply for Treasury Bills are reserve assets, and so the increase in money supply could be up to eight times the initial value of the Treasury Bills issued.

10.6.5 INTEREST RATES

The original intention of Competition and Credit Control regarding interest rates, was that they should act as a market force between the supply of and demand for money. To this end, the Bank of England withdrew its support from the gilt-edged market and abolished Bank rate, so that Minimum Lending Rate should be market-determined. That has proved too difficult. So, too, has the effort to control money supply and interest rates. In May,

1978, the market-related formula for MLR was abandoned; in effect the market-determining Bank Rate was re-introduced, though the term MLR kept.

Minimum lending rate is one of the key interest rates. It is the minimum rate at which the Bank will lend to the Discount Market, either by discounting bills or lending against the security of those bills. It is calculated by adding $\frac{1}{2}$ % to the average Treasury Bill rate, and rounding the resultant figure up to the nearest $\frac{1}{4}$ % above.

Example

Treasury Bill rate	8.5909	
Plus $\frac{1}{2}$ %	.50	
	9.0909	
Rounded to nearest $\frac{1}{4}$ % above	9.25	= Minimum Lending Rate

By raising minimum lending rate, all interest rates in the market are nudged upwards. Interest rate changes are not highly efficient techniques of monetary policy. Low in 1970, they soared in 1973—74. The rapid rise led to the fringe banking crisis of 1973—1975. Property companies went into liquidation and several of the bigger secondary banks had to be rescued by the Bank of England's 'lifeboat'. Control of credit by price has unhealthy side-effects, including volatility of rates and high costs for social priority projects. Neither do low rates necessarily encourage investment. Investors cannot be forced to borrow if they see no profitable return. Hence, interest rate controls usually have to be supplemented by other techniques.

10.6.6 REQUESTS AND RECOMMENDATIONS

To the unitiated, these sound like polite notes from the Bank of England. Far from it. They may be couched in such a fashion, but requests and recommendations from the Bank have a mandatory force. This point was emphasized to the anti-cartel office of the E.E.C. in 1978 after a London-based foreign exchange dealer had complained of discrimination in the foreign exchange market.

'Such requests and recommendations' said the Bank in a memorandum to the E.E.C., "are in practice effectively mandatory, and no bank wishing to operate in the London market would refuse to comply. " The Bank explained how its control methods differed from those in Europe. "The general practice is to discuss matters with banks and to negotiate terms of rules and codes of conduct, and make or endorse recommendations based on these negotiations. Recommendations are rarely styled as such or made in any particular format." Lending guidance from the Bank was tantamount to a directive and obeyed accordingly. On the basis of information supplied by the banks, the Bank has interviews with and makes recommendations to "those banks, any aspect of whose general conduct and financial state is not in the Bank of England's opinion altogether satisfactory. After discussions these recommendations are put into effect."

Agreements among banking institutions were not, so the Bank declared to the E.E.C., a form of monopoly but the result of decisions reached by banks after consultations with and suggestions from the Bank of England. It was because of this effective system of control that London's foreign exchange and Euro-currency market, the most important in Europe, had not suffered the tremendous problems that had beset Lugano and Herstatt, the Banque de Brussels, the Westdeutsche Landesbank, the Union Bank of Switzerland.

The E.E.C., however, is worried about the Treaty of Rome provisions on dominant market power. The British Bankers Association quotes guidelines. "Any discrimination that may exist, results directly from, and is inherent in the duty to exercise such strict controls, which is the duty of the Bank of England and in the interests of the European Economic Community."

As these guidelines were reached in consultation with the Bank of England, they may strengthen the E.E.C.'s qualms about the abuse of monopoly power, rather than weaken them.

What is certainly not in dispute is that Bank of England requests may have lacked the form, but had all the force, of law. How and in what form such requests will be made after the Banking Act is in operation, remains to be seen.

10.7 TARGETS

During the late 1970s, a new emphasis was laid on money supply. From 1976, a target figure was set for the maximum growth of money supply. A target that had to be altered became a *'rolling target.'* To achieve the objects of monetary policy (e.g. economic growth or the restraint of inflation) *intermediate targets* were used. These became the new 'in' words for money supply control or interest rate control. Operating targets were used to affect intermediate targets.

Thus, if the Government aimed to reduce interest rates or restrain the growth of monetary aggregates (*intermediate target*), it employed some monetary weapon or technique (e.g. open market operations). These techniques/weapons would work on the *operating targets* (short-term interest rates) to achieve the intermediate ones, and ultimately the policy goal (restraint of inflation/domestic expansion, etc.)

Different countries use different 'targets' and time spans. The Swiss concentrate on the narrow definition of money stock; the Germans on the broader definition. In France, the target is defined in terms of M2. The IMF imposed targets on Italy and the U.K. in 1976 and 1977 couched in terms of domestic credit expanison. In 1977—1978, the U.K. had a target range of between 13% (upper) and 9% (lower). A margin like this creates a big upswing or downswing as the target is approached. Financial markets know the authorities must react, and how. Institutions alter their portfolios accordingly. This is why the Germans use only a point, or single, target. The U.S. uses a 3 monthly target so that it can be revised in the light of economic events. The U.K. has adopted a six-month *rolling target*.

10.7.1 A ROLLING TARGET

If a fixed target for money supply growth of 10% for 12 months is announced (April to April) and by October the target growth has reached 8%, this allows only a 2% growth over the next six months before the overall 10% is reached. A six months' 'squeeze' of this stringency could have severe effects on the economy. This is why the U.K. has substituted a 'rolling target' for a fixed one. A target figure is set up in April and reviewed in mid-October when a new target is announced for the 12 months to the following October. Thus, if a 10% target were aimed at from April, and 7% already reached by mid-October, a target of 8% for the next 12 months would give an overall total of 15% for the 18 months — in line with the original 12 months target of 10% but without the need for such excessive restraint as would be necessary for the last six months of a *fixed target*.

10.8 HISTORY OF MONETARY POLICY IN THE U.K.

10.8.1 CHEAP MONEY, 1945—1951

During the 1940s, Keynes showed that unemployment could be long-lasting. It was not just a short-term phase caused by imperfections in the market. Demand management had to be used to cure it. This meant using the budget to raise or lower the level of investment and cause multiplied changes in the national income. Interest rates alone could not bring about these changes. Their influence on investment was not decisive enough. Nevertheless, post-war interest rates were kept low to lessen the cost of government borrowing during a period of social reforms and nationalization programmes. Short-term rates responded. Efforts to prevent long-term rates from rising were not so successful.

10.8.2. BANK RATE AND THE BALANCE OF PAYMENTS, 1951—1958

The 1949 devaluation naturally led to concern about the Balance of Payments and domestic inflation. A new government decided that monetary policy might have a restraining influence on the economy. Bank Rate was therefore used to control the growth of the money supply. Between 1952 and 1960, gross deposits of the clearing banks (the major part of the money stock) rose from £6083m to £7611m, an increase of 25.1% in 8 years, or just over 3% per year.

In spite of such success in controlling the growth of the money stock, some disquiet had been felt about the volatility of interest rates. What effect might this have on the maintenance of an orderly market in government stock?

Some other device or tool had to be found. Control of the money supply now gave way to control of *liquidity*.

10.8.3 RADCLIFFE AND LIQUIDITY

The Radcliffe Report of 1959 suggested influencing 'the general level of liquidity'. The Committee felt that in countries such as the U.K. with developed financial institutions, there were financial assets almost as good as money which people could hold instead of it. The existence of this quasi-money meant that (a) control on the money supply could be evaded by switching from money to quasi-money, and (b) interest rates would not work so well as a form of credit control. If high rates restricted bank loans, money would be raised elsewhere.

For these reasons, *direct controls* were introduced over (a) the amount of initial downpayment and length of repayment for instalment credit and (b) the volume of bank credit. This left interest rate as a method for influencing capital inflows and outflows.

During the 1950s, quantitative restraints on bank lending had been mild. Now they grew more severe. From 1965 until Competition and Credit Control in 1971, banks kept within a strict lending limit. Any contravention had to be explained to the authorities.

Banks, naturally, did not like these controls. Neither did industries supplying goods for the instalment credit market. Continual changes in the terms and amount of credit available, made long-term planning difficult for such industries.

Special Deposits were introduced in 1961 as an alternative to ceilings on loans. Banks, at that time, kept a minimum 30% (later 28%) liquidity to their deposit liabilities. 'Liquidity' meant cash (8%) plus assets easily turned into cash. Special deposits siphoned off a proportion of banks' assets, and 'froze' them into a special account at the Bank of England. These 'frozen' assets could not be counted as part of the banks' 28% liquidity ratio. But a shortage of one type of 'liquidity', such as Treasury Bills, was often made up by acquiring another, commercial bills. A new system was therefore adopted. After October 1973, interest was paid only on Special Deposits relating to *deposit account* liabilities (previously all Special Deposits earned interest at Treasury Bill rate). Thus, if a commercial bank had current account eligible liabilities of £1500m and deposit account liabilities of £1000m, with a 2% call for Special Deposits, it would give up 2% of £1500m and £1000m = £50m. But Treasury Bill rate would be paid only on 2% of £1000m (the deposit account liabilities) = £20m, and not, as formerly, on 2% of the combined totals. The penalty was withdrawn in November, 1974.

The Bank of England's main concern at this time was not to drive down gilt-edged prices and create a lack of confidence in the market. But restrictions on credit must lead to either rationing or higher interest rates. Hence special deposits were used as a control only when the authorities wished to indicate a tight credit attitude.

10.8.4 THE MONEY SUPPLY AND MONETARY TARGETS, 1968—1971

From 1945—1967, fiscal policy was the preferred method for influencing aggregate demand. Monetary policy seemed, by contrast, a clumsy macro-economic tool. After the 1967 devaluation of sterling, however, fiscal policy and a tight budget did not curb domestic demand. Neither did it improve the balance of payments. In America, too, the tax surcharge imposed by President Johnson proved similarly ineffective.

Economists (and others) were beginning to lose faith in fiscal weapons as a defence against inflation. Milton Friedman's writings emphasized the importance of the money stock. This helped to change the climate of opinion in favour of monetary policy. So too, did the I.M.F. policy advisers. They suggested a *monetary target* in terms of *Domestic Credit Expansion*. In a closed economy, increases in Domestic Credit Expansion are the same as increases in the money supply. In an open one, an increase in the money supply can be offset by a leak out in payments deficit. Hence, the money supply target was set in terms of DCE.

10.9 DOMESTIC CREDIT EXPANSION

This concept first appeared in 1969. It turned up again in 1977 when, in a Letter of Intent to the I.M.F., the government agreed to limit DCE to £9.6bn for 1976/77, £7.7bn for 1977/78 and £6bn for 1978/79. Domestic credit expansion can be seen as bank and overseas lending to the public sector plus bank lending in sterling to the private and overseas sectors plus changes in the public's holding of notes and coin.

A short way of summing up DCE is the increase in the money supply plus a balance of payments deficit, or minus a balance of payments surplus. Its usefulness is to show whether changes in the money supply have been generated internally, or are the result of changes in the balance of payments.

By 1971, the U.K. balance of payments had improved to such an extent that the concept of DCE languished. So too, did monetary policy. Efforts to control the money stock, to prevent fluctuations in gilt-edged prices and a balance of payments deficits, simultaneously, proved impossible. Monetary targets were abandoned. In came the new armoury of Competition and Credit Control. Domestic Credit Expansion was interred and heard of no more until 1977 when the I.M.F. resurrected and gave it a new lease of life.

Efforts to control the money stock by ceilings, (limits on lending), by quantitative and qualitative controls (limits on amounts and type of lending) by requests and directives; by hire purchase orders and by Special Deposits, had all proved *specifically* useful. Together, they had led to the misallocation of resources. They had also caused the growth of parallel markets unrestricted by the controls imposed on clearing banks.

A whole new philosophy of competition and credit control was therefore introduced into the banking system in 1971.

10.10 COMPETITION AND CREDIT CONTROL

10.10.1 BACKGROUND TO THE PROPOSALS

The Balance of payments took a turn for the better after the 1967 devaluation. Efforts to control the money stock therefore waned. Furthermore, it had been seen that monetary policy needed finer tools, if the targets aimed for were to be achieved.

Banks not subject to controls could increase their lending and so avoid the restrictions on the clearing banks. The clearing banks could offset a fall in their holding of Treasury bills, by an increase in commercial bills.

For efficient credit control, restrictions would have to apply to *all* institutions supplying credit. The *type* of assets held by banks against their liabilities would also have to be in the control of the Authorities: the Treasury and the Bank of England. But if credit 'rationing' went, what would take its place? Interest rates was the answer. They would act as the market mechanism bringing supply and demand into equilibrium.

For years, Bank Rate had been the signal to domestic and overseas viewers of the authorities' view of the economy. Now, it would have to go. But if Bank rate were abandoned, then the Bank of England's intervention in the gilt-edged market would also have to be jettisoned. And so it ultimately proved.

10.10.2 AIMS OF COMPETITION AND CREDIT CONTROL

The policy document, *Competition and Credit Control* (CCC), was published in May 1971 and the system introduced in September and October, 1971. Its general aims were to stimulate competition among all banks and to regulate the overall amount of credit granted by financial institutions.

Its specific aims were to:

(a) Make monetary policy more effective. *All* banks now had to keep a $12\frac{1}{2}$ % Reserve Asset Ratio against their Eligible Liabilities. The ratio for Finance Houses was 10%. Calls for Special Deposits would apply to them all.

(b) Prevent discrimination against the clearing banks in the total banking sector, by making *all* banks subject to the same lending restrictions.

(c) Control credit, not by ceilings on lending, but by market forces (i.e. interest rates). Other measures, e.g. Special Deposits, would be used when needed. Bank of England support for the gilt-edged market was withdrawn, so that prices and rates would find their own level. Minimum Lending Rate later replaced Bank Rate. The Bank reserved the right to raise MLR at any time, and first did so in November, 1973.

(d) Abolish the banks' interest rate agreement to encourage banks to compete more effectively with each other. This has, on the whole, been achieved, whereas the Credit Control measures have had to be strengthened by directives in 1972, 1973, 1974 and 1975. Calls for supplementary Special Deposits levied on the growth of interest-bearing balances were first imposed in 1973, and lifted in 1975.

10.10.3 THE TECHNIQUES OF CCC

Two new concepts came in with CCC. They were *Eligible Liabilities* and *Eligible Reserve Assets*.

Eligible liabilities can be briefly described as the short-term sterling deposits of the whole banking system. Together with eligible reserve assets, they are described more fully in Chapter 4. All banks had to keep a reserve asset ratio of a minimum of $12\frac{1}{2}$ % of their eligible liabilities.

Notes and coin held in bank tills did not count as reserve assets. The clearing banks agreed to maintain balances at the Bank of England at an average level of $1\frac{1}{2}$ % of eligible liabilities. The balances qualified as a reserve asset, but like the supplementary Special Deposits on interest-bearing liabilities, they earned no interest.

10.10.4 OTHER PROVISIONS

Although CCC dispensed with *quantitative* controls (limits on the amount of lending), qualitative controls could be used if required, and several followed in the next few years. So, too, did the corset. The scheme penalized banks for trying to win 'excessive' time deposits. It led to some hectic competition for *current* accounts with banks offering all kinds of inducements to potential customers. The scheme was suspended in 1975, but re-activated again later.

10.10.5 THE DISCOUNT MARKET

The authorities wished to secure some control over the use to which discount houses' funds were put. Discount houses were therefore asked to maintain at least 50% of their borrowed funds in specified public sector assets, principally Treasury Bills and short-term Government bonds. The object of this arrangement was to restrict the amount of funds which the discount houses could invest in the private sector, and so reinforce the Authorities' control over the supply of reserve assets. It proved too restrictive. Upward movements in interest rates can cause capital losses on portfolio holdings. Competitive bidding for a small issue of Treasury Bills drives prices upwards.

In July 1973, this restraint on the Houses' assets was altered. They were free to invest in any way they pleased, providing that the total of their 'non-specified assets' did not exceed more than 20 times the total of capital and reserves. The Bank agreed to continue its facility as lender of last resort to the discount houses.

10.10.6 FINANCE HOUSES

CCC brought finance houses into the orbit of ratio control for the first time. Previously, their lending had been subject to quantitative and legal restraints. Finance houses with liabilities of over £5m had to observe a 10% reserve asset ratio. Additionally, they could be asked for Special Deposits. These restrictions did not prove severe enough and extra controls had to be used sporadically thereafter.

10.10.7 COMPETITION

10.10.7.1 *The Clearing Banks*
As part of the new arrangements, the clearing banks discontinued their collective agreements on interest rates. When minimum lending rate changed, each bank could adjust its own deposit rates and the base rates on which it based its bending.

Base rates have kept more or less in line since CCC, a sign of perfect competition, declare some; of oligopoly, argue others. Only in December 1977, when MLR went up by 2% did the banks show an unusual disparity of rates. But the disparity did not last long. This seems to have been the pattern ever since.

10.10.7.2 *The gilt-edged market*
Under Competition and Credit Control the authorities withdrew their automatic official support from the gilt market. This move was to allow (a) interest rates to fluctuate more freely (even at the expense of a more volatile market in gilt-edged stocks) and (b) prevent money flowing into the banking system by Government purchases of stock at times when a tight money policy might be required.

10.10.7.3 *The discount houses*
The discount houses continued to underwrite the whole of the Treasury Bill issue, but not with a syndicated bid or at an agreed price.

10.10.8 ASSESSMENT OF COMPETITION AND CREDIT CONTROL
CCC was only a partial success. Increased competition among the banks helps the customer, but banks are at a disadvantage with other deposit media.

Banks must make their profits on their investments, and on the disparity between the cost of deposits and the price of lending. This is easy enough perhaps, in times of high interest rates and low costs; difficult when rates fall and costs rise. Whether all banks should have the same reserve ratio is a moot point.

Credit control has been less successful. Low interest rates and greater freedom of credit followed CCC. This was partly responsible for the property boom of 1972 and the subsequent collapse in 1974 of many fringe banks, when interest rates zoomed and cash flow fell. New credit controls had to be introduced after CCC and a limit placed on the amount of interest to be paid on bank deposits under £10,000, so that banks should not compete with building society investments within this limit.

10.11 LEGISLATIVE CONTROLS
The Authorities can use *administrative* controls such as CCC to influence the

availability and cost of credit. They can also use *legislative* controls. In the U.K. until 1979, these were minimal and mostly contained in the Bank of England Act 1946 and the Currency and Bank Notes Act 1954.

After the fringe bank crisis of 1973, concern was voiced about the traditional ratio of depositors' to shareholders' funds. Was share capital adequate in relation to this increased volume of deposits?

The U.K.'s entry into the E.E.C. with its more formalized banking arrangements further increased the need for greater U.K. banking supervision. In 1974, therefore, non-clearing banks were asked to provide the Bank of England every quarter with information on such items as: the maturity pattern of sterling deposits and claims; transactions with associated companies; provision for bad debts; depreciation of investment portfolios; and standby facilities with banks and other financial institutions.

In 1975, the Bank of England published a paper, *The capital and liquidity adequacy of banks*, agreed with the London and Scottish clearing banks. The paper proposed that the clearers would also have *balance sheet supervision*. The Bank would have annual discussions with each bank about its profitability, capital adequacy and liquidity.

The paper emphasized the need for adequate capital and reserves, and the prudence of keeping *free capital ratios* (equity and loan capital less infrastructure items such as premises, trade investments and investments in subsidiaries; and goodwill) as a percentage of deposits.

The liquidity position of a bank might also have to be evaluated by the separation of its sterling and foreign currencies. Similarly, a bank's retail book might have to be separated from its wholesale book. Satisfactory matching of liabilities and assets in the latter, should still be supplemented by standby facilities, to allow for default or late repayment.

The position of subsidiaries would be discussed by the Bank with the management of those companies; and of the clearing banks, with their representatives and those of the Banking Supervision Division of the Bank of England.

On 3rd August 1976, the Government's White Paper, *The Licensing and Supervision of Deposit Taking Institutions* proposed a distinction between licensed and unlicensed deposit-taking institutions. The guide lines of the White Paper, were followed in the Banking Act 1979.

10.12 MONETARY POLICY—SUMMARY AND CONCLUSION

Monetary policy has gone through many phases in the past decades. The Radcliffe Committee in 1959 saw the market for credit as a single market. Monetary policy had to be used to affect *liquidity*. By affecting liquidity and thus credit, total demand was affected. The mechanism which triggered off these changes was *interest rates*. "The authorities thus have to regard the structure of interest rates rather than the supply of money as the centre-piece of the monetary mechanism. This does not mean that the supply of money is unimportant, but that its control is incidental to interest rate policy." But interest rates, the Committee felt, were somewhat slow. The "quick substantial effects", they wrote, come from "*hire purchase controls*".

What, then, caused such a change from control of the *price* (interest rate) to control of the *quantity* (supply) of money? The answer was summed up in a speech by the Governor of the Bank of England on 9 February 1978: ". . .the acceleration of inflation." Expectation of future price rises influences not only inflation itself but wage claims and interest rates too. Monetary policy cannot, however, rest on *expectations*; on what the interest or inflation rate may be. It must rest on observation. Monetary aggregates can be observed. A specific level can be aimed at for some particular time and, if necessary, adjusted at an intermediate stage. This has been the thinking on monetary policy in the 1970's. As a result, publicly declared quantitative targets were introduced after 1976.

The achievement of such targets are only subsidiary or *proximate aims*. The idea of a target is to reach it in order to achieve the *main aims*. The Governor of the Bank of England gave as aims: economic growth, sufficient future investment, adequate employment opportunities; price stability; a prudent balance of payments—and a somewhat vague ambition—"maintaining an appropriate relation to the rest of the world."

But there are several monetary aggregates that can be chosen as an appropriate target for money supply control: M1, M3, PSBR, DCE. These aggregates vary. So does the accuracy with which they are forecast. Since 1974, bank lending has fluctuated from a normal monthly trend by as much as £100m. The mean error for PSBR given at the beginning of each financial year has been around £3bn. Forecasting techniques may be improved. Meanwhile by 1980, control of the money supply rested on three main techniques: open market operations (sale of government stock); high interest rates to stave off borrowing; and the corset to penalize 'excessive' deposits.

Other measures may have to take their place. The Green Paper (Cmd 7858) discussed whether stronger methods, such as monetary base control, were needed to regulate the money supply. The monetary base is usually classified as notes and coin held by the public and by the banks, and bankers' balances at the Bank of England. The public's holding of notes and coin is the largest component of such a base.

The advantage of monetary base control from the viewpoint of monetary policy, is that it gives the authorities a tighter control over the banks' reserve assets. Under CCC rules, the banks' $12\frac{1}{2}$ % reserve ratio (but 10% from 5 January 1981) is made up of assets largely held outside the banking system. Over these assets the authorities have only limited control. Further, when liquidity is tight, the Bank of England can enter the market to give temporary assistance to the discount houses, occasionally, to the banks, by buying their gilts, or releasing special deposits. In this way, high interest rates can be prevented from rising still higher.

If monetary base control were introduced which included notes and coin held by the public, movements of cash between the public and the banks could create different withdrawal patterns at different banks. The banking system would present a far less uniform picture, with unco-ordinated patterns of interest rates. During periods of inflation, the public is also likely to demand more cash. This too, would lead to a less orderly banking system.

If the monetary base were constructed with only bank cash and Bank of England balances, this might mean that different banks with different kinds of business and customers would need different cash ratios, but there would still be the same impetus to raise interest rates when banks were short of base money, and it would be more difficult for the authorities to engage in smoothing operations than at present.

Any monetary base control system must give the authorities greater power to regulate the volume of bank deposits and thus money supply. But such control is most likely to create an unacceptable volatility in interest rates. That, at least in 1980, was the current thinking of the Bank. Meanwhile the authorities are relying on market intervention to influence the rate of return on assets and thus the willingness of the public to hold them; and portfolio constraints which restrict the freedom of financial institutions, mainly banks, to acquire particular assets and liabilities.

TYPICAL QUESTION

Fiscal policy has been likened to heavy artillery in that it is 'slow to move and indiscriminate in its effect.' Discuss this view, and consider the extent to which fiscal policy has achieved its aims in any one country in recent years.

SUGGESTED ANSWER

Fiscal policy means using changes in Government spending and borrowing and taxation to achieve certain economic ends. The aims may change from year to year, e.g. the aim may be to expand exports, decrease prices, make a more equal distribution of income, but if the method of achieving these objectives is by taxation or Government borrowing and spending, then this is fiscal policy (as distinct from monetary policy which acts through the banking system on the money supply to achieve similar ends).

In Britain it has not been possible in post-war years to achieve simultaneously the general aims of most Governments, namely a high and stable level of employment; stable prices; stability of exchange rates with an increase in the reserves sufficient to allow for some overseas aid to be given. In recent years, employment prospects have worsened; the exchange rate has fluctuated; prices have increased. There is even some doubt whether there has been fairer distribution of wealth in spite of increases in various types of social benefit.

Fiscal policy is generally thought to be a slow and indiscriminate way of achieving Government objectives. But direct taxation changes can have a quantifiable effect; they can be levied on specific levels of income, and show up very quickly in disposable income and its multiplier effect. Similarly, taxation on goods will have an immediate effect on price levels and spending patterns. The effects are usually far more immediate than a similar change in interest rates, which have a pervasive effect on all industries, eventually.

Changes in investment grants, reliefs and subsidies can be used to affect not only particular goods, but also particular regions, e.g. selective employment tax penalized service industries and encouraged manufacturing ones, and, incidentally, tourist areas and industrial locations.

Because budgets have taken place usually only once a year, fiscal policy is slow to change in this respect. It cannot be altered quickly, as can changes in interest rates. In this regard it is slow, but the *impact* is usually quick as can be seen by comparing prices before and after a budget.

Summing up it can be said that fiscal policy takes time to initiate because it needs Parliamentary approval, though the 'regulator' allows some leeway. Furthermore, budgets cannot be introduced more than two or three times a year at most. But once the measures have been implemented they can take effect quite quickly, depending on the type of tax, investment incentives, reliefs and subsidies (which are a form of negative taxation). Changes in Government expenditure, however, unlike specific taxes, are indiscriminate in their effects, and take time to implement, particularly when capital expenditure decisions are being considered.

ADDITIONAL QUESTIONS

1. Explain the differences between fiscal and monetary policy, and discuss their relative advantages and disadvantages.

2. Describe the basic techniques by which central banks operate domestic monetary policy, and the relationship in which they must stand to the commercial banks if they are to do so effectively.

3. Distinguish between fiscal and monetary policy and discuss their relative advantages as means of controlling demand inflation.

4. To what extent in recent years have the objectives of monetary policy been achieved in Britain?

11 Public Finance

Public Finance deals with the income and expenditure of the public authorities. In the U.K., the public authorities comprise the central government,
local authorities and nationalized industries. The financial operations of this
group are of great importance, firstly because of their *size*. Public sector
spending accounts for so large a proportion of GNP (around 45% in the
U.K.) that its contraction or expansion affects output and employment levels
in the whole economy and thus the *value* of the wealth produced.

Secondly, public finance operations *transfer* purchasing power, changing
the *distribution* of wealth. Such alterations in the value and distribution of
the wealth produced are made for the maximum social advantage.

11.1 THE BUDGET

Government income comes from two main sources, taxation and borrowing.
Taxation is introduced or altered in the Budget, presented annually by the
Chancellor of the Exchequer. The Budget's main purpose used to be to
explain how the government would meet its expenditure for the next financial
year. Before Keynesian concepts of deficit financing, an 'unbalanced' budget
would have been considered very unsound accounting, and a Chancellor who
dared to present one, a shady character unfitted for public office.

The economic climate has changed since those days, but the Budget's
original purpose still remains: of explaining how the Government will cover
its spending by revenue. Additionally, the Government's borrowing requirement is given and economic policy reviewed. Tax and other changes may be
announced to alter the level of aggregate demand or the ratio of direct to
indirect taxation; to encourage or restrict the growth of particular industries;
obtain a fairer distribution of wealth; or to concern itself with energy saving,
the environment, transport policy and health.

Preparatory work for the March/April budget goes on throughout the
year. Various government departments, including the Inland Revenue and
Customs and Excise, estimate their tax receipts in the current financial year
and make forecasts for the next.

Any tax changes in the Budget statement get immediate statutory effect by
the Provisional Collection of Taxes Act. These changes, with other proposals
which need legislation, are embodied in the Finance Bill published some 6

weeks after Budget Day. If approved by Parliament, the Bill emerges as a new Finance Act.

V.A.T. rates can be varied by 20% and specific duties on oil, beer, etc., by 10% at any time by the use of the 'Regulator' (Finance Acts 1961, 1964, 1972). Further measures or another Budget to alter the economy in the direction required, can be brought in during the course of the year, although this would need a second Finance Act.

11.2 TAXATION

The purposes of taxation can be summed up as allocation, distribution and stabilization.

Allocation means that money must be raised for certain necessities of the state (national security: defence; internal security: law and order; social security: health, education and welfare.) 'Extras' of this kind are referred to as a 'social wage'.

Distribution means taking purchasing power from one group and transferring it to another, usually in the interests of social justice; sometimes to aid 'ailing' industries or regions by subsidies and grants; sometimes in the often illusory pursuit of economic efficiency.

Stabilization means using taxation (and its counterpart, subsidies) to regulate the economy for full employment, stable prices, economic growth or other objectives.

Income and spending match in both the allocation and distribution functions of taxation. They are unequal in the stabilization function. Thus, if the government wishes to spend £6m on defence (allocation), it raises £6m to match this spending. IF £6m is to be given to the poor by way of family allowances (distribution), £6m is similarly raised from taxes. But if the government wishes to expand the economy (raise the level of aggregate demand), it will spend more than its income; and contract the economy by spending less.

When Government revenue exceeds its spending, this is known as a *Budget surplus*. A surplus lessens total purchasing power. When Government spending exceeds its revenue, this is known as a *Budget deficit*. A deficit increases total purchasing power.

Using public spending as a countercyclical weapon for managing the economy is now often criticized. It is argued that there are large time lags between initiating projects and executing them. Bridges, roads, factories cannot be left half-finished. Hence, public spending restrictions are not always possible. Even when they are, tax changes might be more beneficial. Current thinking seems to be to divert purchasing power from the public sector into the private sector.

11.3 THE TAX AND PRICE INDEX

Consumer price movements are measured by the Retail Price Index. Changes in indirect taxes and in specific duties affect this index. Changes in National Insurance contributions and income tax (other than through the tax relief on mortgage interest) do not affect the R.P.I. The Tax and Price Index was first published in August 1979 and takes these changes into account. It incorporates changes in retail prices as well as changes in income tax and national insurance contributions. Thus, the Tax and Price Index measures changes in the purchasing power of gross (before tax) income whereas the Retail Price Index provides the basis for measuring changes in the purchasing power of net (after tax) income.

11.4 PRINCIPLES OF TAXATION

The principles (or 'canons') of taxation laid down by Adam Smith in 1776 are still used today. They are

(a) *Equity*. The tax should be fair ('contributions in proportion to their abilities').

(b) *Certainty*. The taxpayer should know what he has to pay. The sums should not be arbitrary.

(c) *Convenience*. The tax should be paid at a time and in a manner which gives the taxpayer least inconvenience. PAYE is such a tax.

(d) *Economy*. The tax should be cheap to collect.

Direct taxation is paid to the government directly by the person who bears, or should bear, the tax. A direct tax falls on the capital or income of persons and firms. Examples are income and corporation tax; capital transfer and gains taxes.

Indirect taxation goes to the government indirectly. The tax is demanded from one person who takes the *impact* of the tax, but who can shift it to another who bears the *burden* or *incidence* of paying it. Where there is an inelastic demand for a good, the incidence falls largely on the buyer; with an elastic demand, on the seller.

Indirect taxes are levied on goods or services. V.A.T. is such a tax. So are Customs and Excise duties.

Progressive taxation takes a higher proportion of income from those more able to pay. Tax rates increase steeply at higher income levels. There are also taxes on investment income, (though some might deem this a penalty for saving), on capital gains or profits.

Regressive taxation bears more heavily on people less able to pay. Road tax is an example. Not levied by engine size, or on the income of the driver, it is the same for a Rolls Royce, Mercedes or company car as for a second-hand Mini. A similarly regressive tax is a TV licence; or taxes which make no allowances for dependants and other necessary expenditure.

11.5 THE PATTERN OF TAXATION

Although (contrary to popular British belief) Britain's taxation is in line with other countries, inflation has caused a far heavier, impact on *direct* taxation. The main argument, apart from that of incentive, for switching from direct to indirect taxation, is that inflation drags lower income earners into the tax net (*fiscal drag*), but reduces the value of the fixed sums paid as tax or duty on goods ('*fiscal boost*').

National Insurance contributions are not regarded as taxes, but can act regressively on lower wages. A poll tax levied on the whole population is completely regressive. History provides so many examples of protests against unjust or regressive taxation that consideration is now given to the *taxable capacity* of a community which depends only partly on the amount of its wealth. Other considerations are: will the tax lead to internal unrest, evasion, inflation? Will it discourage enterprise?

11.6 RELATIONSHIP OF THE BUDGET TO THE BALANCE OF PAYMENTS

A reduction in taxes may have an adverse effect on the Balance of Payments. If the marginal propensity to import is high, and there are few spare domestic resources, then an increase in purchasing power (as will happen with reduced taxation) will result in higher imports and an adverse Balance of Payments. If the country has large reserves and a strong currency (the two usually go together), an adverse balance may be good for world trade. One country's debit balance is another country's credit. It is impossible for all countries to be in surplus together.

11.7 INCOME AND EXPENDITURE OF THE CENTRAL GOVERNMENT

As well as getting revenue by way of taxation, the government gets it by borrowing.

All Government revenue and expenditure used to go through one common fund, *The Consolidated Fund*, set up by the Customs and Excise Act 1787 as a 'Fund into which shall flow every stream of public revenue and from which shall come the supply for every service'.

The idea of a single Fund was breached, however, in 1932, 1947 and 1968. In 1968, *The National Loans Fund* was established to handle some of the receipts and payments that previously went through the Consolidated Fund. *The Exchange Equalization Account* was set up in 1932, for official dealings in the foreign exchange market. It draws sterling from the National Loans Fund to finance its purchases of gold or foreign currency and passes sale proceeds back. The EEA also lends working balances in sterling to the National Loans Fund as interest-free 'Ways and Means' advances. One other official account infringes the principle of consolidation: the *National Insurance Fund* established separately in 1947 so as to more easily relate insurance contributions to benefit income. (There are, of course, other

Government departments with their own subordinate accounts at the Bank of England.) *The Consolidated Fund* holds its balance in the Exchequer Account at the Bank of England. The two expressions, Consolidated Fund and Exchequer, are therefore often used interchangeably. Its revenue comes from taxation, Customs and Excise duties and other receipts. This revenue is used for *supply services*, authorized annually by Appropriation Acts; and *standing services* which have been authorized under Consolidated Fund Acts.

The *National Loans Fund* is one of several official accounts, and the Bank of England switches balances between the Consolidated and National Loans Funds so that a surplus on one finances a deficit on the other. The Bank also makes use of any temporary surpluses in accounts of subsidiary Government departments, or statutory funds (e.g. the National Insurance Fund) by exchanging the balances for tap Treasury Bills; or it credits the National Loans Fund and debits the lending account by interest-free Ways and Means advances (costs of servicing the debt is thereby reduced). Such lending is in the form of overnight assistance. It is used only occasionally if the anticipated daily needs of the Exchequer account have been miscalculated. Normal short-term forecasts of receipts and payments to show a deficit will be covered by Treasury Bill sales. The proceeds of such sales go to the N.L.F. Treasury Bills finance the Government's short-term debt throughout the year in this way. Fewer are required when tax or other receipts are heavy.

It is clear that when money flows into the government and a commensurate sum is not spent (Budget surplus), bank deposits will fall. There is an internal cash drain to the Government. An external drain of money overseas (sale of sterling for dollars) similarly lowers the level of U.K. bank deposits. The process is as follows: U.K. banks sell their sterling; it is bought by the Bank of England which credits the E.E.A. with the amount and debits the U.K. bank, which similarly debits its customer (commercial bank deposits and assets fall). The E.E.A. transfers the sterling acquired to the National Loans Fund and takes tap bills in lieu. The N.L.F. now has a surplus balance. Fewer Treasury bills need to be sold by the Exchequer. The external drain of the payments deficit has been mitigated by the internal drain into the N.L.F. (and the Exchequer), but domestic liquidity falls (fewer Treasury Bills in the market).

A summary of the relationships between the Funds is given below:

CONSOLIDATED FUND

REVENUE	*EXPENDITURE*
Inland Revenue	Supply Services (3)
Customs and Excise	Standing Services (4)
Vehicle Excise duties	Debt Interest
Broadcasting Receiving Licenses	Payments to Northern Ireland (5)
Interest and dividends (1)	Payments to E.E.C. etc.
Other receipts (2)	Contingencies Fund
	Other expenditure (6)

NATIONAL LOANS FUND

Any surplus income from Consolidated Fund (7)
Interest on past loans to nationalized industries, etc.
Interest on securities held by the Bank of England
Profit on note issue
Interest from Consolidated Fund (8)
Repayment of outstanding loans

National Debt: servicing
Loans to nationalized industries; public corporations and local authorities

(Exchange Equalization Account: changes in sterling capital)
Add surplus/deficit of National Insurance Fund; departmental balances; N. Ireland central government debt. = Central Government Borrowing Requirement

The revenue and expenditure of the Consolidated Fund are balanced; if there is a surplus it is passed to the National Loans Fund. This, together with other revenue, is balanced against expenditure; if there is a deficit, any surpluses from departmental balances and the National Insurance Fund will be added. The final total gives the Government's Borrowing Requirement. A negative figure means the Government will have the opportunity to repay some of the outstanding N.L.F. debt over the year or the N.L.F. surplus could increase the sterling capital of the Exchange Equalization Account. A positive total shows how much the Government must borrow in the forthcoming year: the shortfall between taxation/other revenue and expenditure.

Notes on the Accounts
1. Interest on economic aid voted out of the Consolidated Fund Supply Services and dividends on shares owned by the Government
2. Fees to public officials, e.g. Registrar of Births and Deaths; fines paid in courts, etc.
3. Defence and Civil Services of all kinds, voted annually.
4. Authorized under Consolidated Fund acts: includes incomes paid to members of the Royal Family (6) salaries and pensions of judges, certain M.P.'s etc.
5. Payments to Northern Ireland come from taxes collected there under an arrangement of 1921.
6. See Note 4 above
7. Any balance from the Consolidated Fund is used to offset the debt on the N.L.F.
8. From Standing services: note 4: debt interest

11.7.1 SOURCES OF BORROWING

Summarizing, the sources of borrowing available to the U.K. Government are:

(a) Balances of statutory funds such as those of the National Insurance Fund.

(b) Sterling Balances of the Exchange Equalization Account.

(c) Official accounts at the Bank of England other than the Exchequer Account.

(d) Statutory Funds (e.g. National Savings) which are invested by the National Debt Commissioners in Government Securities.

(e) The banking system, financial institutions and the public through holdings of Treasury Bills and other marketable debt. Roughly 20% of this debt is 'funded' which means the nominal value *may* be repaid at some future date. The other 80% is 'unfunded' which means the nominal value of the stock will be repaid on its maturity date.

(f) 'Unmarketable' debt such as National Savings Certificates, Premium and similar Bonds and tax certificates.

(g) Any increase in the holdings of bank notes.

Another source of borrowing is from overseas Governments and international monetary institutions. This source of borrowing does not, however, increase the net balances of the N.L.F. The Treasury technically *buys* (not borrows) foreign currency from e.g. the IMF, in exchange for sterling. It gives the foreign currency to the E.E.A. in exchange for tap Treasury bills. The I.M.F. lends back the sterling to the U.K. government in return for securities in the form of interest free notes. No cash outflow therefore comes from the N.L.F. The E.E.A. holds less Treasury bills and more foreign currency; the I.M.F. holds more U.K. government securities and the N.L.F. owes more (on the interest-free notes) to the I.M.F. and less on bills to the E.E.A.

11.8 THE PUBLIC SECTOR BORROWING REQUIREMENT (PSBR)

The PSBR arises mainly from budgetary decisions, i.e. the tax and spending policies of the Government. It can be defined as the excess of public sector spending over public sector revenue in one financial year. It includes the amount which the government borrows to lend; in other words it is the 'gross' borrowing requirement. The 'net' figure is called the public sector financial deficit. The biggest borrower in the public sector is, of course, the central government. Since the White Paper, 1978 (Cmd. 7049) the definition of public expenditure has been: the current and capital expenditure of central government and local authorities, excluding expenditure charged to the operating accounts of trading bodies; government finance in the form of grants, loans or public dividend capital provided towards the cost of capital investment by the nationalized industries and some other public corporations; the capital expenditure of the remaining public corporations; the contingency reserve and debt interest. In other words, the definition no longer includes, as formerly, all the capital expenditure of the nationalized industries, but only that part financed by grants, etc. from the public purse, i.e. by taxation or borrowing.

11.9 THE PUBLIC SECTOR BORROWING REQUIREMENT AND THE MONEY SUPPLY

As we have earlier seen, the money supply can be thought of as the purchasing power in the economy. When money supply increases, so does spending power. If the supply of home-produced goods does not increase to match the extra purchasing power, the price of domestic goods will rise. The volume of imports is likely to rise too. The balance of payments will worsen.

The Government therefore seeks to regulate money supply growth. In practice, the Bank of England supplies notes and coin to meet demand, so that money supply control means regulating the rate at which bank deposits grow. (Some economists might argue here for control on building society deposits, for they can be as liquid, if not as expansive, as banks deposits and when withdrawn add to purchasing power. They may even lead to an increase in house investment at the expense of industrial investment — or growth. But we are up against the definition of money supply which, as yet, does not include building society deposits.)

The public sector borrowing requirement is financed by three main methods. They are (a) borrowing from the non-bank private sector, which means borrowing from households and firms, (b) borrowing from the banking sector including the Bank of England, and (c) borrowing from external sources. Whether the money supply increases as a result of this borrowing depends on which of the three ways the Government finances its debt.

When the Government borrows from the non-bank public, the latter buy new securities from the Government, or take up other Government debt such as National savings of any kind. Public, i.e. government, deposits in the Bank of England go up: households and firms have drawn on their banking accounts to pay the Bank of England (acting for the government) the price of the securities bought, or switched their money into other Government debt. Bankers' deposits at the Bank of England go down, and so, therefore, does the money supply. What does the government do with the money it receives from the public? If the money is spent on transfer incomes and other non-investment, all that happens is that a redistribution of resources takes place: from one section of the public to another. If the government does not spend the money, there will be a reduction in the money supply from Bankers' deposits to Public, i.e. government, deposits.

If the Government cannot sell securities to the non-bank public or encourage them to take up other Government debt (National savings; Premium bonds, etc.), it may sell securities to the Bank of England. This means an exchange of securities for deposits. Thus, Public (government) deposits rise and — on the assets side — so do securities by the same amount. If the government spends the extra funds it has itself created, in the private sector, there will be an increase in bank deposits (liabilities) and the same rise in assets. But the ratio of the latter to deposits will have increased and the banks will therefore be in a position to expand advances or purchase investments. It can be seen then that public sector borrowing financed by the banking system increases the money supply. The banks may use the surplus cash for lending at call to the discount houses. The discount houses will use the money to buy Treasury bills. From the sales of the Treasury bills, the government will repay the Bank of England and so reduce its direct borrowing from the Bank. Thus, borrowing from the banking system can be by direct borrowing from the Bank of England (increase in money supply); from banks when they have surplus cash (change in bank asset structure and ultimately increase in money supply) or from banks' lending to discount houses to take up Treasury bills (increase in money supply).

The third way in which the public sector borrowing requirement can be financed is through external finance. If the Government sells securities abroad, there is no increase in the money supply. Similarly, when national-ized industries borrow abroad, but much depends on what is done with the money thereby gained. If it is used for industrial investment there may be a 'multiplier' effect and an ultimate increase in money supply. But this increase will be offset by the increase in fixed assets and cannot therefore be regarded as inflationary.

The PSBR invariably increases bank deposits. When the Government account is in deficit, more is being added to the bank accounts of those who supply goods and services to the government. Less goes to the government itself through tax revenue. Reductions in money supply come through any situation which lowers the volume of bank deposits. To finance the PSBR without inflating the money supply means persuading the non-bank public to buy enough Government securities to cover it so causing Bankers' deposits to fall and Public deposits to rise. If sales are insufficient, new policy measures will have to be found such as higher taxes or new ones; direct controls on bank lending or a new marketing approach for the sales of Government stock. Cuts in public spending itself are not always possible in the short-term and may be politically difficult to achieve.

11.10 LOCAL GOVERNMENT FINANCE

11.10.1 CURRENT EXPENDITURE

Local authorities have *current expenditure* for goods and services. These comprise wages for staff; grants and subsidies to individuals and local authority undertakings, (mainly housing and transport), and interest payments on past borrowings.

This current expenditure is financed by (a) rates, (b) central government grants and (c) other income.

11.10.2 CURRENT REVENUE

(a) *Rates* are local government taxes based on (i) the rateable value of property assessed by the Inland Revenue in England and Wales and special assessors in Scotland; and on (ii) rate poundage declared locally, which is the amount per £ the occupier has to pay on the rateable value of the property. There are various reliefs.

(b) *Central government grants* are (i) specific and supplementary for expenditure on specified services, (ii) a rate support grant paid to support local authority revenue. The Government assesses the national total of rate support and other revenue grants and then shares this among the local authorities on the basis of three 'elements', (1) the *needs* element to compensate for different spending needs, e.g. education, (2) the *resources* element to compensate for the different tax raising capacity of local authorities and (3) the *domestic* element to compensate for local authority reliefs given on certain domestic rates.

(c) *Other income* arises from trading surplus on local authority enterprises and from payments of rents and interest on loans.

11.10.3 CAPITAL EXPENDITURE

Capital expenditure is that spent on housing, buildings and equipment for education; roads, lighting; and mortgages for house purchase. *Revenue for capital expenditure* comes from (a) central government and other borrowing, such as local authority stocks, (b) internal financing such as any surplus from the current account.

11.11 THE NATIONAL DEBT

The National Debt represents the liabilities of the National Loans Fund. This Fund services the National Debt and lends money to the nationalized industries and local authorities. Much of this lending is for investment in assets such as roads, housing, schools, hospitals, defence installations and the like.

11.11.1 OWNERSHIP OF THE NATIONAL DEBT

Most people have holdings, at least indirectly, in the National Debt, through pension or trade union investment in Government stocks. Direct ownership of the Debt arises through personal ownership of government securities, Premium, Retirement and other Bonds or National Savings.

Official holdings of the Debt include the National Insurance and other funds held for investment by the National Debt Commissioners; those held by the Bank of England (Issue Department) as 'backing' for notes (the fiduciary issue) and by the Banking Department as assets. Other holders of the Debt include private funds and trusts, banks, insurance companies, building societies, pension funds, overseas central banks and international organizations.

11.11.2 MARKETABLE DEBT

The National Debt is said to be marketable when it can be bought and sold in the money markets and the Stock Exchange. Examples are Treasury Bills and Government stock. The latter is often referred to as 'gilt-edged' or 'gilts'.

When the whole of a gilt-edged issue is not taken up by the market, the Bank of England sells them over a period of time as demand develops. The issue is then known as a 'tap' issue.

11.11.3 NON-MARKETABLE DEBT

Non-marketable debt consists of those government-sponsored assets that cannot be sold on the money markets or Stock Exchange, and which have to be redeemed by the owner and cannot be sold or transferred. The various types of Bonds (Premium, Retirement, Savings), Savings Certificates, National Savings Bank deposits and the Save-As-You-Earn schemes.

11.11.4 IS THE NATIONAL DEBT A BURDEN?

Any increase in the National Debt means that more has to be borrowed from the citizens of the country or from abroad. In the former case, this will affect income distribution and the level of taxation. What is taken from one group by taxation, however, will be passed on to other groups or individuals as dividends, interest or social welfare payments (transfer incomes). No addition thereby arises on national resources, though enterprise may be discouraged if the tax burden for transfer incomes grows excessively.

Where any part of the National Debt is raised abroad, e.g. by selling stock to overseas buyers, this does represent a drain on resources. Interest payments have to be met, and capital eventually repaid. Meanwhile, however, the Government, as with any borrower, can invest or squander the borrowed money as it chooses. So the 'drain' on resources is only as bad or good as the use made of the money that has been lent.

11.12 DEBT MANAGEMENT POLICY

Debt management policy has two main aims. They are to absorb the total of all the debt instruments: long-term, marketable and non-marketable debt, short-term bills and notes and coin — without causing undesirable effects on monetary policy in general and the liquidity of the banks in particular.

When any part of the debt is financed by the Bank of England, the government is paid by an increase in Public Deposits at the Bank. Money supply and bank liquidity become harder to control. An absorption of Treasury Bills by sales to the banking system has the same effect of increasing the money supply.

Conversion of short-term debt into long-term debt is called funding. The Government seeks to sell long-dated gilts for several reasons. One is to smooth out the level of liquidity in the market. If a tight monetary policy was being called for by the government at a time when a very large issue of government stock was reaching maturity, holders of the stock would receive cash.

This injection of money into the economy would conflict with the deflationary policy desired. The holders of such stock may not take their money at the maturity date if some more attractive investment became available. The operation of funding helps the authorities in raising finance for the government within the framework of an orderly capital market.

Short- and long-term debt can be sold to the non-bank public. This reduces the money supply, but may mean very high interest rates in order to sell sufficient stock. The government has used the following techniques to sell stock to the public: (a) sales by tender, (b) sales of variable rate stock, (c) sales of low coupon stock for high tax payers, and (d) sales of partly paid stock with calls for the remainder in ensuing months. Other marketing variants may follow.

11.13 FISCAL POLICY (A BRIEF ANALYSIS)

The economy is in neutral equilibrium when Income = Expenditure and Injections (Exports, Investment, Government Spending) = Withdrawals (Savings, Imports Taxation). National Income at this level may be fully using the country's resources or there may be a *deflationary gap* (unemployed resources) or an *inflationary gap* (the equilibrium level of output cannot be reached).

Fiscal policy means using the budget to remove the deflationary or inflationary gap to get full utilization of resources. Equilibrium takes place when $S + M + T = I + X + C$. The Government can control Taxation (T) and Government Spending (G). By altering either of these variables, the government can alter the level of national income. If taxation (T) exceeds Government spending (G), a budget surplus will arise. If G exceeds T, there will be a budget deficit.

Keynesian remedies for an inflationary or deflationary gap worked very well in the post-war decades. Management of aggregate demand seemed the answer to all economic problems. The problem during the decade 1970—80 has been inflation with unemployed resources and so far the only solution put forward has been the monetarist one.

11.14 FISCAL POLICY—MONETARY POLICY (ADVANTAGES/ DISADVANTAGES)

Whereas monetary policy acts on the supply and cost of credit, fiscal policy acts through taxation *and* government borrowing and spending. The aims of fiscal policy are much the same as those of monetary policy: full employment, stable prices and a balance of payments surplus. Because fiscal policy can be *specific* in its effect, it is often used additionally for directional objectives such as regional growth, or the stimulation of special sectors of the economy. As with monetary policy, however, the aims of fiscal policy can be mutually exclusive. Stimulation of the economy to boost employment, tends to lead to inflation and/or a balance of payments surplus, and so on.

A combination of policies is often used together because each has certain advantages. Thus, tax changes (fiscal policy) show up quickly in consumer's expenditure (or lack of it). Because they must have Parliamentary approval, (with a few exceptions) they take time to implement, possibly only twice a year. By contrast, changes in the money supply take time before their effects are felt, though interest changes which can effect the money supply, can be changed overnight. So can changes in qualitative controls which can have similar effects as taxes and subsidies (fiscal policy). Changes in government expenditure may be difficult to bring in because of political implications, or because projects cannot be stopped halfway. Monetary policy has not usually been used to alter the overall level of demand in an economy; whereas this was for many years the main thrust of all fiscal policy.

TYPICAL QUESTION

Outline the main methods by which the British Government may borrow from the public, showing how any securities concerned are issued. Which types are marketable and which are held as assets by the commercial banks?

SUGGESTED ANSWER

The Government borrows from the public through marketable and non-marketable debt. In the first category come Treasury Bills which are issued by the Government to the highest bidders at a weekly tender, or at a rate of discount fixed by the Treasury. The latter type, known as 'tap bills', are generally issued only to Government departments and the Issue department of the Bank of England.

The public obtain their bills by purchase in the market. Some of these bills may have originally been issued as tap bills, but there is nothing to distinguish them as such.

Also in the marketable category are gilt-edged securities. These are fixed interest government bonds issued to the public mainly through the Stock Exchange. The National Savings Department, formerly the Post Office Savings Department, will also buy or sell gilt-edged securities on their Register which, in practice, means most gilt-edged stock.

As well as borrowing from the public by marketable debt, the Government issues non-marketable debt. This covers many varieties of small savings. The funds of the Trustee Savings Bank and departments of the National Savings Bank ordinary accounts are placed at the Government's disposal by the National Debt Office who invest them in marketable bonds and non-negotiable securities.

Current balances of the National Insurance funds to which, the public contribute by way of their weekly stamp may be lent to the National Loans Fund as a Ways and Means Advance or to acquire tap bills.

Other groups of non-negotiable debt are savings certificates and bonds and, until recently, tax reserve certificates. These certificates and various types of non-negotiable bonds are issued by the Department of National Savings. Tax reserve certificates on which tax-free interest was paid could be bought from the Bank of England, acting for the Treasury, by companies and individuals for the payment of tax. The purchase price was paid by the Bank of England into the National Loans Fund and in this way provided the Government with a short-term loan.

Commercial banks hold only that part of government debt which they find liquid and profitable. In practice, this means (a) funds which can be included in their reserve asset ratio: Treasury Bills and short-dated government bonds, both of which are marketable, and (b) longer-term government bonds which are marketable and, if prices hold up, profitable, but which do not form part of their reserve asset ratio, being one group of assets in their investment portfolio.

ADDITIONAL QUESTIONS

1. Who are the main holders of the U.K.'s national debt?
In what circumstances is a country's national debt a burden?

2. How are the commercial banks in a country affected by the fiscal policy of the government of that country?

3. Outline the various considerations which influence the concept of a government's budget.

4. Write brief notes on regressive taxation.

5. Give a brief analysis — as distinct from a list of particular taxes — of the various ways in which a government may obtain revenue by taxation.

6. In what ways is fiscal policy used to influence the British economy?

12 International Trade and the Balance of Payments

12.1 COMPARISON OF DOMESTIC AND INTERNATIONAL TRADE

(a) International trade differs from the domestic variety firstly in that there are no restrictions on movement within national (democractic) boundaries. Internationally, there *are* restrictions on the movement of people and of capital.

(b) The second main difference is that sovereign states control their own territory. Within that area, they operate rules for the benefit of their citizens. They protect home-produced goods. The government introduces fiscal measures to change taxes or the level of government spending. These changes alter incomes and thus the demand for goods and services. Monetary policy is adjusted. It operates on the supply of money and its costs. The amounts that people spend or borrow are affected.

Such domestic measures may be good for the short-term benefit of the country. But, if they restrict the flow of international trade, they will ultimately damage the country itself and the rest of the world. Countries nevertheless use controls over money, goods and factor prices to (i) raise revenue, (ii) protect infant industries, (iii) maintain full employment, (iv) avoid dependence on other countries, (v) strengthen relations with other countries, (vi) prevent outflows of money.

(c) The third and most important difference however, between domestic and international trade is that each state controls the issue and type of money to be used in its own country. National money is not usually acceptable as a medium of exchange outside its own borders. Countries therefore concern themselves with the value of their own currency in regard to others. This leads to various systems for making international payments and to different prices of exchange rates for national currencies.

12.2 THE LAW OF COMPARATIVE COSTS

This demonstrates how countries gain by trade with each other. Even when one country is rich enough to produce everything more cheaply than a poorer neighbour, the law of comparative costs still holds good. This law is based on the principle of *specialization*. It states that a country gains by specializing in the production of those goods in which it has the greatest comparative advantage or the least comparative disadvantage.

Comparative advantage operates when one country (Country A) has a lower opportunity cost in the production of a commodity than does Country B. *Opportunity cost* (the alternative foregone) is the amount of a commodity which must be given up in order to produce an extra amount of another commodity.

Absolute advantage is another term used in·the theory of international trade. Any country that can produce more of a commodity than another country with the same resources is said to have an absolute advantage over the second country.

Examples
(i) *Absolute advantage in one commodity*
Countries A and B produce two commodities, clothes units and food units. In country A, 1 day's labour produces 100 clothes units, or 200 food units. In country B the same labour produces 200 clothes units or 100 food units:

	Country A	Country B
Clothes units	100	200
Food units	200	100

Absolute advantage
Country A has an absolute advantage in the production of food; Country B has an absolute advantage in the production of clothes.

Opportunity cost
For country A, the opportunity cost of 1 clothes unit is 2 food units.
For country B, the opportunity cost of 1 clothes unit is $\frac{1}{2}$ food unit.
For country A, the opportunity cost of 1 food unit is $\frac{1}{2}$ clothes unit.
For country B, the opportunity cost of 1 food unit is 2 clothes units.

Comparative advantage
Country A has a comparative advantage in the production of food units (opportunity cost is least).
Country B has a comparative advantage in the production of clothes (opportunity cost is least).

Specialization
If A specializes in food, and B in clothes, total production of both commodities will increase. The switch of one worker in A from clothes to food production means the loss of 100 clothes units but a gain of 200 food units. In B, a worker moving from food production to that of clothes means a loss of 100 food units and a gain of 200 clothes units. The rate of exchange between the two countries will lie between 1 unit of clothing to $\frac{1}{2}$ /2 units of food. Country A gains more the nearer the rate is to 1 unit of clothes for $\frac{1}{2}$ unit of food. B gains more the nearer the rate is to 1 unit of clothes to 2 units of food. Where the rate actually settles will be determined by the relative strengths of demand by the two countries for each commodity.

(ii) *Absolute advantage in both commodities*

	Country A	Country B
Clothes units	100	50
Food units	200	150

Although country A has an absolute advantage in both commodities, the opportunity costs are different:

Opportunity cost

For country A, the opportunity cost of producing 1 clothes unit is 2 food units.

For country B, the opportunity cost of producing 1 clothes unit is 3 food units.

For country A, the opportunity cost of producing 1 food unit is $\frac{1}{2}$ clothes unit.

For country B, the opportunity cost of producing 1 food unit $\frac{1}{2}$ clothes unit.

Comparative advantage

Country A has a comparative advantage in the production of clothes (opportunity cost is least). Country B has a comparative advantage in the production of food (opportunity cost is least).

Specialization

If A specializes in clothes and B in food, both countries gain. The rate of exchange will lie between 1 clothes unit for $\frac{2}{3}$ food units. The nearer the rate is to 1 clothes to 3 food, the greater the benefit to Country A. The closer the rate is to 1 clothes to 2 food, the greater the benefit to Country B. Where the rate settles, depends on the relative strength of demand for the commodities in each country.

(iii) *Opportunity costs equal*

When opportunity costs are equal, no gains result from specialization, no matter where the absolute advantage lies.

	Country A	Country B
Clothes	100	200
Food	200	400

Absolute advantage

Country B has an absolute advantage in the production of both commodities.

Opportunity costs

For country A, the opportunity costs of producing 1 clothes unit is 2 food units.

For country B, the opportunity costs of producing 1 clothes unit is 2 food units.

Specialization will *not* increase the total production because opportunity costs are equal in both countries. If A specializes in clothes, 1 extra clothes unit loses 2 food units. If B specializes in food production, a gain of 2 extra food units means a loss of 1 clothes unit. If A specializes in food, 2 extra food units will lose 1 unit of clothes. If B specializes in clothes, 1 extra clothes unit loses 2 units of food. There is thus no gain in specialization, and no inducement to international trade unless each country needs the other's goods. Then trade will operate on a kind of barter system 1:1 converted into the appropriate currency.

In all the examples above, certain additional costs have been ignored.

12.3 TRANSPORT COSTS

These may offset the comparative advantage enjoyed by one country over another, and make it more profitable to produce goods at home, or to trade with another country where transport costs are less. The development of railways in the U.S. combined with speedier/cheaper sea travel made the shipment of wheat to Liverpool in the 19th century a practicable and profitable proposition. Fast refrigerated ships brought dairy produce from Australia and New Zealand into competition with European markets. Such falls in transport costs can stimulate new types of trade often to the disadvantage of a previously existing industry.

12.4 PRODUCTION COSTS

If production costs change with increasing or decreasing returns, benefits will still accrue from international trade, providing the opportunity costs differ in each country.

12.5 TERMS OF TRADE

By terms of trade is meant the ratio of export to import prices. In order to calculate this ratio, a base year is used with the formula as below:

$$\frac{\text{Price index of exports}}{\text{Price index of imports}} \times 100.$$

Changes in the terms of trade can then be measured from year to year. If we start with 100 as both the import and export price index, then we get the result 100 from the above formula:

$$\frac{100}{100} \times 100 = 100.$$

If the index of imports or exports changes, so will the result. If it falls below 100, the terms of trade have become less favourable. If the figure goes above 100, the terms of trade have become more favourable. Thus,

$$\frac{120 \text{ (Price index of exports)}}{100 \text{ (Price index of imports)}} \times 100 = 120.$$

The higher figure of 120 shows that the terms of trade have become more favourable: more imports can be bought for the same volume of exports. Or,

$$\frac{100 \text{ (Price index of exports)}}{125 \text{ (Price index of imports)}} \times 100 = 80.$$

The lower figure of 80 shows that the terms of trade have become less favourable: less imports can be bought for the same volume of exports.

12.6 TERMS OF TRADE AND BALANCE OF TRADE

An improvement in the terms of trade may or may not lead to an improvement in the balance of trade (trade export payments less trade import payments). If export prices rise relative to import prices (improved terms of trade) and volumes are unchanged, the balance of trade also improves. But price changes usually affect the volume of goods bought and sold, and will certainly do so in the long term.

A long-term improvement in the balance of trade depends not only on the terms of trade but on the relative elasticities for imports and exports. If export prices rise (improved terms of trade) and there is an elastic demand for exports, the volume of goods sold at the higher price will soon fall. So too, will receipts.

Simply put: 10 goods sold abroad for £1 got £10 (or the foreign exchange equivalent) in payment. If the price rises to £2 and customers still buy the goods, (inelastic demand) receipts go up to £20. But if only 4 goods are now sold (elastic demand) receipts fall to £8. On the other hand, with a price fall to 50p at least 40 goods must be sold (very elastic demand) to get the former £20 in receipts.

These examples show that price changes do not automatically worsen or improve the balance of trade. Increased revenue depends not merely on price, but on the elasticities of demand and supply.

12.7 THE BALANCE OF PAYMENTS

The balance of payments is an account of one country's financial dealings with others over a particular period of time. In Britain, the figures are produced quarterly and are grouped into four basic sections plus a Balancing Item:

(a) the Current Balance
(b) Investment and other Capital Flows
BALANCING ITEM
(c) Balance for Official Financing
(d) Official Financing

12.7.1 THE CURRENT BALANCE

This is made up of two parts (a) the trade (or visible) balance and (b) the balance of invisibles.

12.7.1.1 *The visible balance or balance of trade*

The visible balance arises from the export earnings of, and import payments for, (visible) goods. For over 200 years, with a few exceptions (1956, 1958, 1971 and the last quarter of 1977), Britain's spending on visibles has exceeded its revenue from visibles. Usually this net deficit on trade has been more than balanced by the very large invisible surplus. The position altered in 1973. The overall current account balance (visibles and invisibles) dived deeply into deficit. The heavy trade deficit was not balanced by earnings on invisibles. In 1977, the position again changed. North Sea oil helped the current balance into surplus.

A balance of trade *trend* can be distorted by sales or purchases of large single items. Ships, aircraft, North Sea installations, precious stones are costly goods. The inclusion of one aircraft, ship or North Sea platform can make a large difference to the balance of trade figures. They are now being listed separately. To get a true picture of the balance of trade figures for one particular year, the import and export of goods must be analysed into their component parts. Projections of future trends must also allow for variations made by large costly items and changing demand/supply patterns for different types of goods.

Strikes in industries with a large external trade can affect the current balance in strange ways, e.g. a dock strike in a country with a consistently large import bill will be as good (or as bad) temporarily as an increase in quotas or tariffs or an import surcharge.

C.i.F. and F.o.B.

These odd hieroglyphics also have strange effects on the current account balance. Imports are usually valued C.i.F. (cost, insurance, freight). This is their value on arrival plus the cost of insurance and freight between ports of arrival/departure. Exports are valued free on board: (F.o.B) their value on shipment including any expenses up to that point. Due allowance must be made for these variations to get a true picture of the trade balance. In West Germany, the difference between C.i.F. and F.o.B. valuations of imports in 1976, amounted to over $5 bn: roughly 6% of the total C.i.F. import bill.

Insurance and freight costs are therefore deducted from import costs. If paid by the importer they figure as an outgoing payment on the balance of invisibles, and as an additional receipt on the invisible balance of the exporting country.

12.7.1.2 *The balance of invisibles*

The U.K. share accounts for about 9% of the world's invisible earnings, more than any other country except the United States.

Within the general section of invisibles are included payments for and earnings from services such as shipping, aviation, insurance, banking and tourism; interest, profits and dividends earned by British investments abroad, and by foreign investments in Britain; Government current spending abroad for the operating costs of embassies, trade missions, consulates, etc., for grants to developing countries; transfer payments to and from the E.E.C. and transfer payments such as gifts or pensions to people living overseas or to people in Britain from relatives living abroad.

The items mainly responsible for the invisibles surpluses of recent years include earnings by way of commissions, royalties, patents and fees for financial and technical services as well as overseas construction work. The largest earnings within this sector of 'other private services', and those which provide the greatest benefit to the balance of payments come from the financial and allied services connected with the City of London.

Shipping, once a big earner, and still comprising 25% of the invisibles sector has, in recent years, shown a small deficit. The deficits on government services and transfers and on public sector interest, have also grown, but to a much larger extent in recent years. However, these perennial lossmakers have been more than compensated by the large increase in earnings from aviation and tourism.

12.7.2 INVESTMENT AND OTHER CAPITAL FLOWS

The current balance shows a country's trading position: the deficit or surplus sustained on goods (visibles) and services (invisibles) bought or sold. The capital account (investment and other capital flows) shows the inflow and outflow of capital: how much is being lent and borrowed and by whom. Lending causes an outflow of capital and is marked with a minus in the capital account. Borrowing causes an inflow of capital and is marked with a plus. The Government is a large borrower; so are nationalized industries and local authorities. Government stock bought by overseas citizens creates an inflow into the investment account, while interest paid on these stocks appears as a debit on the invisibles account.

Money for private investment in stocks and shares (portfolio investment) and direct investment by companies in factories and plant (direct investment) go into the account. Euro-dollar borrowing is marked with a plus; when used for investment abroad, the Euro-dollar sum is prefixed with a minus. Credit given and received on import and exports cannot be ignored.

Until 1976, all borrowing by the public sector under the exchange cover scheme used to be presented in the *capital* account (investment and other capital flows). After 1976, such borrowing went into the official financing section. The reason for the change in presentation was this: all transactions which are outside the direct supervision of the authorities (visibles, invisibles, investment and capital flows) go into their respective sector of the balance of payments. All transactions which are of a financing nature and under the control of the monetary authorities go into another sector, official financing. Difficulties naturally arise over where a particular transaction goes. (Special Drawing Rights, subscriptions to the I.M.F. are examples — both go in the Capital Flows account.) Foreign currency for the exchange cover scheme is supervised and added to the reserves; hence it was felt that this item should more properly be included in the balance for official financing.

All these capital flows from individuals, firms and institutions adding to or taking from their U.K. bank balances are added together. The result gives the total for investment and other capital flows. This sum is added to the current account. The grand total is called the balance for official financing. It should match the figure of official financing which shows how a deficit is financed or a surplus spent. Any discrepancy appears in the balancing item.

12.7.3 BALANCING ITEM

When the total of capital flows is added to the current balance, the figure should equal the exact amount of foreign currency which the country has gained or lost. This happy result is never achieved, but the discrepancy is not forgotten. It appears in the balancing item. Why should the figures not exactly match? The reason is that transactions are not all recorded at the exact time they took place. A credit card transaction abroad may not get into the U.K. figures for three months. If the foreign currency appreciates meanwhile, the U.K. debtor will have to pay the difference. Government spending is easier to record exactly than the spending of foreign visitors in the U.K. or U.K. visitors abroad. There are other timing variations: exports which go out in December may not be paid for until January or February of the following year.

Allowance is made for these various time lags, but exact recording is not possible. The balancing item gives the yearly error. Over a period of time these errors tend to balance themselves out.

12.7.4 OFFICIAL FINANCING

This section shows how a deficit is financed or a surplus used. As an example, the figures for 1979 follow.

		£m
(a)	Current Balance	− 2,437
(b)	Investment and Other Capital Flows	+ 3,525
	Balancing Item	+ 623
(c)	Balance for official financing	+ 1,711
	Allocation of Special Drawing Rights	+ 195

In this year the U.K. had a surplus balance of £1,711m. The Official Financing sector shows how the £1,711 was used. (It should be noted that in this year the U.K. received £195m in S.D.Rs which accommodated some of the surplus and allowed greater additions to the official reserves.)

Everything paid out from the £1,711 balance goes into the Official Financing Account. If the balance for official financing is in surplus, as in the above example, the Official Financing sector will show the same figure with a minus, and vice versa thus:

(d) *Total Official financing*   − £1,711m

The breakdown of the total (excluding the £195m S.D.Rs) is as follows

		£m
1.	Net transactions with I.M.F.	− 596
2.	Other monetary authorities	0
3.	Foreign currency borrowing by: H.M. Government	0
4.	Public sector under the exchange cover scheme	− 251
5.	Official reserves (drawings on, +; additions to, −)	− 1,059
(d)	Total Official Financing	− 1,711
	Special Drawing Rights	− 195

Notes on the accounts
1 and 2 shows money being paid back to the I.M.F. and/or other monetary authorities after previous borrowing arrangements
3. Shows (unusually) no foreign currency borrowing by the Government
4. Shows foreign currency lending to the public sector being paid back.
5. Shows that a total amount of £1,711 (excluding the S.D.Rs) was added to the reserves.
a + b + c show a deficit, which has been the more usual pattern over the past decades, the balance for official financing (c) will show a minus figure, and official financing (d), a plus. This can be seen in the figures for 1978 (below). A large deficit current account was financed by drawings from the I.M.F., public sector borrowing, and use of the official reserves:

1978 balance of payments summary

(a)	Current balance	+ 932	Net visible balance + net invisible balance
(b)	Investment and other capital flows	− 3,199	
	Balancing item	+ 1,141	
(c)	Balance for official financing	− 1,126	

(d)Official financing

	1. Transactions with I.M.F.	− 1,016
	2. Foreign currency borrowing.	− 378
+ = drawings on	3. Borrowing H.M. Government.	+ 191
− = additions to	4. Official Reserves.	+ 2,329
Total official financing		+ 1,126

12.8 BALANCE OF PAYMENTS AND DOMESTIC FINANCIAL ACCOUNTS

The initial domestic effects of balance of payments flows depend on their distribution between the private, public and banking sectors. Table 12.1 allows most of these flows to be followed.

Table 12.1 *Currency flows in the balance of payments.*

1. Current account
2. Overseas investment in U.K. public sector
3. Overseas investment in U.K. private sector

4. U.K. private investment overseas
5. Overseas currency borrowing or lending net by U.K. banks
    (a) to finance U.K. investment overseas
    (b) other
6. Exchange reserves held in sterling (including international organizations)
    (a) British Government securities
    (b) banking and money market liabilities
7. Other banking and money market liabilities in sterling
8. Import credit
9. Export Credit
10. Other short-term flows
11. Balancing item

Sub Total   Balance for official financing

12. Public sector borrowing under the exchange cover scheme

Total   Total currency flow (as defined in financial sector accounts

---

Notes
3, 4, 8 and 11 are almost all flows between the overseas and the U.K. non-bank private sector. Though the balancing item 11 represents unidentified flows, these are allocated to the private sector as the public sector can be more easily monitored, and timing errors, etc. are more likely to arise in the private sector.
2. Flows between overseas and public sectors.
1. Mainly private and overseas sectors; but also includes public sector and U.K. bank sector.
5. Flows between non-residents and the U.K. private, banking or public sectors.
6. Changes in Government securities, Treasury bills held as exchange reserves reflect flows between the overseas and public sectors; between Treasury bills and external £ deposits, flows between the overseas sectors and U.K. banks.
7. Largely flows between overseas and U.K. banks, and a small proportion between overseas and public sectors.
9. Flows between overseas and U.K. private, banking and public sectors.
10. Flows between overseas and U.K. private, banking and public sectors.
11. Flows between overseas and public sectors; if through U.K. banks then a flow between overseas and U.K. banks.

Table 12.2 *Balance of Payment Flows by Sector*
Source: Treasury Working Paper No. 5 (Rachel Lomax and Colin Mowl).
The balance of payments flows can be broken down by sector. For internal monetary forecasting and policy analysis, the Treasury and the Bank of England rearrange Table 12.1 as in Table 12.2.

Balance of Payments Flows by Sector
(a) *Current balance*
(b) Flows to public sector

THEORY AND PRACTICE OF MONEY

(i) Contributing to PSBR
    (1) Government lending and investment
    (2) Public corporations' lending and investment
(ii) Financing the PSBR
    (1) Central Government:
        a. Treasury bills
        b. British government securities
        c. Direct borrowing (net)
    (2) Local authorities
    (3) Public corporations
(c) *Flows to banks*
    (i) Non-resident £ deposits
    (ii) £ lending to non-residents
    (iii) Non-resident foreign citizens (f.c.) claims net of deposits:
        (1) On-lent to H.M. Government
        (2) On-lent to rest of public sector
        (3) Other
(d) *Flows to non-bank private sector*
    (i) U.K. private investment overseas
    (ii) Overseas investment in U.K. private sector
    (iii) Portfolio (net) and direct share transactions
    (iv) Deposits with non-bank financial institutions
    (v) Balancing item
(e) *External liabilities and Claims/Banking Adjustment**
(f) Total currency flow (= a + b + c + d + e)

12.9 ECONOMIC POLICY AND THE BALANCE OF PAYMENTS

Most countries try to achieve some kind of equilibrium in their balance of payments over a period of time. But between deficits and surpluses, they prefer the latter. Surpluses spell strength. Money will flow into strong currency countries as inevitably as a river to the sea.

For more common is the situation where a country is in *deficit*. If a country buys more abroad than it sells, the deficit has to be made up somehow. The country will have to use some of its reserves or borrow externally. If it continues to borrow, its credit is going to run out, or the terms of borrowing become more stringent. Its exchange rate will fall. Imports will rise in price and, in time, be prohibitive to buy. Unless the country can get more foreign currency or become more self-sufficient, its standard of living will fall.

A Letter of Intent to the I.M.F. by an established borrower often improves

---

*This is an adjustment to reconcile differences of coverage, etc. between figures of U.K. banks' net external liabilities as used in the balance of payments accounts and those used in the financial accounts.

a country's balance of payments because its economic policy becomes less expansive and is seen to be so. Developing countries, however, can rarely have a more restrictive policy, and their chances of borrowing are negligible. The only solution for this kind of situation is for the I.M.F. to impose an international 'corset' similar to the one used in the U.K. for domestic banks. The country that makes the biggest average increase in its reserves in any 2 to 3 year period must give up an agreed proportion to the country with the smallest per capita income over the same time scale. But how should such a scheme be enforced? It could be incorporated in the I.M.F.'s articles, and those who do not keep the rules must leave the Club.

Many kinds of policies are tried to achieve a current account equilibrium. But a 'favourable' balance of payments is not always beneficial. It may mean that the country is piling up reserves far in excess of its actual needs, to safeguard its exchange rate. The reserves can be used for 'undesirable' investments abroad; or the 'favourable' balance may have been earned only by a lower standard of living at home.

Similarly, an 'unfavourable' balance may be due to a temporary situation such as a bad harvest, droughts or strikes. The country can run down its reserves to increase its imports of certain vital goods, or stock up for a better tomorrow. A developing country may borrow for domestic capital formation. But, as we have shown above, a deficit cannot be continued indefinitely. When reserves and borrowing facilities end, the country must pay its way or go without. More foreign currency must be earned or less spent. This can be done by what economists call expenditure-changing devices or expenditure-switching devices. The former change the demand for imports/exports; the latter, their relative prices.

12.9.1 EXPENDITURE-CHANGING DEVICES

These change the pattern and volume of spending and are usually introduced by variations in fiscal or monetary policy. Extra taxation reduces the level of spending. Higher interest rates restrict borrowing and ultimately, spending. If such policies do not reduce imports, arguments for controls will be voiced. These are often against international agreement and can cause retaliation. For a country in continuous deficit they may seem the only way to a surplus. Incomes policy to combat inflation may also be used to bring down the demand for imports. If import prices are cheaper than at home, however, people are likely to buy more of them if their incomes fall.

12.9.2 EXPENDITURE-SWITCHING DEVICES

These alter prices. Devaluation (or depreciation of a floating currency) alters the price (exchange rate) for domestic currency. It thus alters the prices of imports and exports. The former get dearer; the latter, cheaper. Devaluation will prove unsuccessful, however, in a country with excess demand. The increased demand for exports resulting from devaluation would raise internal prices still more. Inflation then offsets the effect of devaluation. Devaluation is also of little help to a country with an inflexible economy that cannot switch its production or manpower to export-orientated industries.

Devaluation results in more foreign currency earnings when there is an elastic demand for exports and supply conditions at home are flexible enough to meet the increased demand. Less foreign currency will be spent after devaluation if demand for imports is elastic and the foreign producer can switch to other types of production or markets.

12.9.3 THE J CURVE

The *immediate* effect of a devaluation is to increase import prices. The balance on current account deteriorates, going downwards like the initial downward slope of the letter J. If the elasticities are right (import and export demand both elastic), however, a gradual improvement takes place, leading to the upturned stroke of the J.

12.9.4 CORRECTING AND FINANCING A DEFICIT

There are three main ways of financing a deficit balance of payments: by gifts, by sales of assets or by borrowing. At some time these must stop. If the creditor does not wish to continue lending, and no other source of finance can be found, the debtor country will have to try to correct the deficit. For poorer countries, the 'remedies' of currency depreciation and expenditure switching or changing, may be economically or politically impossible. The task of correcting a deficit by restricting imports or increasing exports could lead to chaos and/or still greater reductions in already impoverished living standards.

12.9.5 TRADE BARRIERS

The fewer trade barriers there are, the freer does international trade become. The General Agreement on Tariffs and Trade, concluded in 1947, was accepted by more than ninety countries. Later agreements were made to reduce tariffs by the Kennedy Round and the Tokyo Round. In 1980, the latter led to an agreement by the United States, Japan and the E.E.C. to reduce tariffs by one-third in the next eight years. Barriers to trade are normally directed at specific countries' exports of specific goods. Less obvious, but equally 'pernicious', are state organizations allowed only to buy home-produced goods. These non-tariff barriers are harder to remove than the more obvious import restrictions.

Arguments advanced to explain the need for quotas or tariffs are to (a) prevent exploitation, (b) raise living standards, (c) achieve non-economic aims, or (d) a surplus balance of payments. High-wage countries want tariffs against low-wage countries. Developing countries want protection against developed ones. International trade should benefit all. How the gains are shared depends on exchange rates and mutual agreements.

TYPICAL QUESTION

Countries often try to correct a deficit in their current balance of payments by allowing the value of their currency to depreciate on the foreign exchange market. What conditions are necessary in a country's internal and external situations for such a measure to be successful?

SUGGESTED ANSWER

When a country's currency depreciates, more has to be given up in exchange for other currencies. The immediate impact of depreciation is to make exports of the depreciating country cheaper, and imports dearer. Such a policy will only be successful if the elasticities of supply and demand are appropriate: the elasticity of demand for exports and imports must be greater than 1.

To take an easy example: £1 = $1; after depreciation £1 = 50 cents. Britain sells £500 goods to the U.S.A.

(a) *Exports*
    Before depreciation of the £   this brings in £500 = $500
    After depreciation of the £   "   "   " £500 = $250
therefore Britain's exports will have to double in volume to make up for the halving in revenue caused by depreciation of the £.

(b) *Imports*
    Before depreciation of the £
    Britain imports 500 goods at 500 dollars = £500 (cost to the importer).
    After depreciation of the £
Britain's imports will cost 500 dollars = £1,000 (cost to the importer).
Unless the imports are halved, depreciation will prove a costly policy.

Depreciation (of a floating rate currency) or devaluation of a fixed exchange rate will only be an effective policy measure if the depreciating country is (a) not liable to suffer excess demand or (b) has a flexible economy, (c) is not subject to official restrictions (quotas, tariffs, etc.) which have already reduced imports to bare necessities and finally, (d) if the depreciating country is not subject to a wage—price spiral.

ADDITIONAL QUESTIONS

1. Distinguish between (a) 'terms of trade' and (b) 'balance of trade'. How is a country's balance of trade affected by changes in its terms of trade.

2. 'The external receipts and payments of a country, in total, must balance.' Explain this statement illustrating your answer by reference to the United Kingdom.

3. The figures below are taken from the annual balance of payments of Ruritania. Prepare:

(a) Ruritania's balance of visible trade:

(b) Ruritania's balance of payments on current account.

Do these figures support the contention that Ruritania is a developing country, and not highly industrialized? Give reasons for your answer.

	Million Rurits
Banking earnings (net)	− 30
Capital movements (net inflow)	+ 1,280
Insurance earnings (net)	− 20
Interest paid abroad	− 1,400
Interest received from abroad	+ 30
Manufactured goods:	
exports (f.o.b.)	+ 120
imports (f.o.b.)	− 2,000
Raw materials and fuel:	
exports (f.o.b.)	+ 3,000
imports (f.o.b.)	− 1,000
Shipping earnings (net)	− 80
Tourist earnings (net)	+ 100

Note: there were no changes in Ruritania's official reserves during the year.

13 Exchange Rates

An exchange rate is the price of one currency in terms of another. If a currency is in demand for (a) trade, (b) investment, (c) speculation, its price will go up. More of other currencies will be exchanged for it.

From the early 19th century, the U.K. was on the gold standard. This is a fixed exchange-rate system in which a country's currency is related to a given weight of gold. In the U.K. £1 equalled 0.257 standard ounces of gold. Any other currency with a gold-related currency therefore had a fixed exchange rate with the £ sterling. In 1914, on the outbreak of war, the gold standard ended. In 1925, a gold 'bullion' standard came in: the Bank of England bought gold at £4.2409 per fine ounce and sold it at £4.2477. (The U.S. Treasury bought and sold at $20.67 per fine ounce.) In the U.K. only large amounts were exchangeable, hence Gold Bullion standard.

In 1931, Britain went off this gold bullion standard. Flexible rates were introduced. The Government used the newly set-up Exchange Equalization Account to stabilize the exchange rate of the £ within the limits thought desirable.

From 1945 to 1971, under the Bretton Woods system, the U.K. was again on what amounted to a fixed-rate system. The £ was related to the dollar at a fixed rate (par value) with a 1% fluctuation allowed up or down from the 'par' value. The value of the dollar was fixed at 35 dollars to 1 ounce of gold. Dollars were convertible into gold for international settlements. This arose out of the I.M.F. system by which each member established a par value for its currency and undertook to maintain market exchange rates within 1% of this declared par value. Countries that freely bought and sold gold in settlement of international transactions were 'deemed' to be adhering to the requirement of maintaining exchange rates within the 1% margins. The U.S.A., the only country that met this condition, was not expected to intervene in the foreign exchange markets. Other countries were. By buying or selling dollars against their own currencies they would keep their rates within 1% of their parities with the dollar.

In 1945, the £'s value was $4.03 dollars; in 1949 $2.80; after devaluation in 1967 it was $2.40. The Bank of England's intervention points were slightly narrower than the I.M.F.'s ceiling of $2.40 plus 1% of $2.40, i.e. $2.424, and the I.M.F.'s floor, $2.40 minus 1% of 2.40 = $2.38.

To sell a wanted currency is easy. For a country to buy its own unwanted currency is a different matter altogether. This was the U.K. position for much of the 1960's and 1970's. When a country buys its own currency, reserves of other currencies or gold, are needed. If these are not available, then a country on a fixed exchange rate must borrow.

No economy has unlimited access to convertible reserves. No country can continue to borrow indefinitely. The U.K. tried numerous policies: even for a short time a surcharge on imports (outlawed by the General Agreement on Tariffs and Trade). Though these helped temporarily, deflation was used to re-inforce devaluation. Protectionist measures were not permissible so full employment and economic growth were sacrificed for a stable exchange rate.

13.1 TYPES OF EXCHANGE RATE

13.1.1 FIXED

The most inflexible type of fixed exchange rate is the gold standard, since any currencies fixed to a common standard are fixed to each other.

The next type of fixed exchange rate (used in the Bretton Woods I.M.F. system) is sometimes called flexible (which it is not), or managed (which it is). The rate is fixed or managed within a narrow band. The European snake was another variant of this narrow-band fixed exchange rate with a 1.125% variation either side of a fixed rate. The wider band suggested by the Smithsonian meeting was so wide (in total 4.5%) that it really deserved the epithet 'flexible'.

13.1.2 FLOATING

Floating rates are those in which currencies are allowed to float up or down in accordance with market forces. Governments who do not like the effect of market forces on their currency, can intervene, buying or selling in the market as they see fit. This is known as a *'dirty'* float. A *'clean'* float has had no official intervention.

13.1.3 OTHER

Other types of exchange rate are the *crawling* or *adjustable* peg, which has been introduced in Brazil, Chile and Israel. Such a system allows small devaluations or revaluations, usually in line with the changing internal value of a currency. In Brazil, the crawling peg was introduced after 1964 with a number of other devices such as indexation, legal wage formulae, tax reforms and the stimulation of savings. Devaluation took place at uncertain intervals in small steps to prevent currency speculation. The rate was based on the rise of the internal wholesale price level, after deducting the estimated average rate of inflation in Brazil's main trading partners. The steps were always kept below the current market interest rate so as to discourage borrowing for foreign currency speculation. The time intervals varied, depending on the behaviour of exports and the position of the reserves. The measures seem to have been successful, for the rate of inflation abated from 100% in 1964 to 40% in 1965/6 and in the range of 15/20 in 1972/3. Some inflation recurred in 1974 but the economic growth rate had been extremely high.

13.2 PURCHASING POWER PARITY

Another way of comparing the relative value of different currencies is to analyse how many units of each currency would be needed to buy the same basket of goods. If it cost £1 in the U.K. to buy a basket of goods that cost 5DM in Germany, the consumer purchasing power parity of £1 = 5DM. If the exchange rates do not reflect these values they are not correctly aligned, at least from the consumer's point of view. Thus, if the exchange rate of £1 is less than the purchasing power parity (5DM in our example) purchases in the foreign country will appear expensive. Gustav Cassel (1866—1945) originated this theory but it needs careful interpretation.

13.3 THE EFFECTIVE EXCHANGE RATE FOR STERLING

This is a phrase sometimes used by financial journalists. It is the rate which links sterling's worth with the currencies of 21 of Britain's major trading partners. Between 1945 and 1971, the exchange rates of major currencies were fairly stable. Since 1971, exchange rates against the dollar have varied from country to country, often with wide margins. Thus, the dollar depreciated against the European 'snake' at the beginning of 1975; yet sterling which also depreciated against the snake, appreciated against the dollar. These variations obscure the overall picture of one currency's changing worth against others.

To get a clearer comparison, a group of currencies are taken, suitably weighted in terms of their relative importance, from a given base year.

The kind of weighting used must be related to the purpose for which the comparison is required. If the effect of a change in exchange rates on the balance of trade is wanted, then trade weighting is best. If it is the effect of a change in exchange rates on the domestic price level that is wanted, a purchasing power index would be more suitable.

The I.M.F. has a multilateral exchange rate: MERM* based on 21 countries and currencies. The U.K. uses this model to get its own effective exchange rate index which can be defined as a geometrically weighted average of sterling exchange rates with 20 other currencies expressed as a ratio to 18 December 1971 base values, with the weights of the averaging process derived from the I.M.F.'s MERM, and using 1972 trade flows.

---

*Multilateral exchange rate model.

13.4 EXCHANGE CONTROLS

Countries control the movement of capital or the import of goods to equalize their payment balances, stabilize their currencies or protect their reserves. Emigrants may take out only a proportion of their funds; tourists and business men are limited in their foreign currency purchases. Companies may buy foreign currency only under certain rules and with the permission of the authorities. Sometimes countries with strong currencies even charge interest on foreign capital deposits because inflows can have as destabilizing an effect on the exchange rate as money moving out.

In the U.K., the Exchange Control Act 1947, imposed restrictions on financial transactions with residents outside the Scheduled Territories. These Scheduled Territories comprised the U.K., the Isle of Man, the Channel Islands, Ireland and Gibraltar.

For the E.E.C. and the overseas sterling area (which roughly embraces the former Commonwealth countries) there were different rules. They related to inward direct investment, emigration and cash gifts.

Free movement of capital was one of the aims of the E.E.C. Before becoming a member, Britain introduced some freedom in this direction in 1972. Companies could spend £1m a year on direct investment on any project in the E.E.C. They were exempted from the 'super-criterion' restriction whereby a direct investment abroad was limited to a sum of £250,000 and had to pay for itself in balance of payment terms in 18 months.

In 1974, the Government ended the £1m exemption. In December 1977, with the balance of payments improving, some minor easing of controls took place. Direct investment under the 'super-criterion' rule, went up to £500,000 or in the case of E.E.C. schemes to 50% of the total cost. The time in which the investment had to justify itself was raised to 3 years. Indirect investment (i.e. the purchase of securities) still had to be financed out of the 'investment currency pool', or market.

The investment currency market was a fund of foreign money accumulated by the sale of properties and investments abroad owned by U.K. residents. The market originated as a result of exchange control regulations. After the Second World War official exchange was not available for portfolio investment in foreign currency securities. U.K. residents who wished to make certain foreign capital transactions had to pay a premium for the investment currency used. This premium: ('the dollar premium') was an amount that had to be paid over the normal exchange rate for the purchase of currency from the investment currency pool. The premium went up when the pool was nearly dry; down when the pool was full and was also affected by the worth of the floating £. Exchange controls were lifted in 1979.

13.5 REMOVAL OF EXCHANGE CONTROLS

On 24 October 1979 exchange controls in the U.K., were removed. There was complete freedom to retain and use foreign currency for any purpose. Bank accounts could be kept in the U.K. or abroad, and applications for travel funds no longer had to be made to the Bank of England. As a result of the abolition of exchange controls, outward direct investment no longer needed permission; 'investment' currency, and the requirement to deposit foreign currency securities with an authorized depositary were abolished. For the first time in 40 years there was complete freedom on investment decisions.

13.6 SOME EXCHANGE CONTROL LANDMARKS

(a) Defence (Finance) Regulations under the Emergency Powers (Defence) Act 1939: first imposed controls.

(b) Exchange Control Act 1947 gave the Treasury extensive powers (largely delegated to the Bank of England) to control most transactions between the U.K. and countries overseas, except the Scheduled Territories. These originally comprised most of the Commonwealth and a few other countries, all of which were previously known as the Sterling Area.

(c) The U.K. accepted Article VIII of the I.M.F. Agreement in February 1961 and allowed freedom on current payments. From 1966—1970 an I.M.F. waiver covered a £50 annual travel allowance but since that date there have been no absolute limits on travel expenditure abroad.

(d) Controls on capital movements could not be lessened because of various economic crises. In July 1961, restrictions were imposed on the financing of outward direct investment; these were strengthened in 1965, and extended on a voluntary basis to investments in the main developed countries of the Scheduled Territories in May 1966.

(e) As a result of the sterling crisis in June 1972, exchange control was extended to virtually all the members of the Sterling Area. The Scheduled Territories now consisted of the United Kingdom (with the Channel Islands and the Isle of Man) and the Irish Republic. Malta returned shortly afterwards.

(f) The U.K. joined the Common Market, 1 January 1973, and agreed to liberalize capital movements (with certain transitional arrangements). Concessions were introduced for direct investment in Community countries by U.K. residents.

(g) Because of balance of payments difficulties, the above concessions were withdrawn in 1974 as were certain concessions for capital transactions with the Overseas Sterling Area. Controls were further tightened in November 1976; sterling was no longer available for the refinancing by U.K. residents of 'merchanting' trade (trade between third countries).

(h) Liberalization of controls resumed in the latter part of 1977. On 1 January 1978, the 25% 'surrender' rule, introduced in April 1965, was withdrawn. In June 1979, the first steps came to dismantle the exchange controls; these mainly concerned the financing of outward investment and levels of personal allowances, including those for emigration purposes. Further measures came in July, with official exchange made available for payment of most securities denominated in E.E.C. currencies and for foreign currency securities issued by international organizations of which the U.K. was a member.

(i) All remaining exchange controls removed in 1979.

The reasoning behind the abolition of exchange controls is as follows. Too much money has been flowing into U.K. banks. The banks have therefore lent more to the public (loans, overdrafts, credit cards). Increased demand, not matched by an increase in supply of British goods has caused an increase in imports. With exchange controls abolished, investment funds can flow freely outwards, so reducing U.K. bank deposits. The outward flow of sterling should also, in theory, reduce the external value of the currency making imports dearer, and so curbing the demand for them. At the same time, a fall in the exchange value of the £ should make British goods more competitive. The free market philosophy may also have a bearing.

13.7 OTHER TYPES OF EXCHANGE CONTROL

In non-capitalist countries, exchange controls take different forms: usually over imports and exports as well as capital transfers. Administrative controls on the trade balance try to match foreign currency expenditure with foreign currency income. If this is not successful there will be a cutback in imports. As foreign capital investment in industry is prohibited, the problem of capital movements is largely avoided. Blocked accounts ensure that foreign earnings in such countries, e.g. sale of copyright on books, films, songs, (when royalties are paid) must be spent within the country. But if desired goods are not available there, individuals or countries with inconvertible currency are left with an unusable surplus. Barter deals may then be arranged between surplus and deficit countries. Centred on Zurich, they are known as switch dealing: a long and tortuous 'solution' to the problem of inconvertible currencies and trade imbalances.

13.8 LEADS AND LAGS

13.8.1 LEADS

Payments in currencies which appear likely to appreciate are often made *earlier* than they need to be. If the currency does go up, the purchaser pays less than if he had delayed payment. These early purchases, *'leads'* as they are called, of an appreciating currency exaggerate still further its upward movement.

13.8.2 LAGS

If a currency looks likely to depreciate, people *delay* payment for as long as possible. A time *lag* even of a few weeks depresses the currency still more.

Multinational companies must take a view of the future course of exchange rates when moving funds between their various global subsidiaries. They speed up payments in appreciating currencies, delay them in depreciating ones.

In the home market, it is, unfortunately, a common custom for some large firms and local authorities to delay payment of their bills for services, projects, materials. These delays have serious consequences for the smaller concern, particularly builders, some of whom are unable to survive the time lag, and may well go into liquidation. Delays in the foreign exchange market where bills have to be paid in foreign exchange, can have equally damaging, though different, effects, for they exaggerate an observed tendency in an exchange rate.

13.9 THE FORWARD MARKET

The repercussions of leads and lags are felt most strongly in the 'spot' exchange rate quoted for current transactions. But foreign exchange for future transactions will be affected by the spot rate as well as by market expectations. If a British importer has to pay $5000 in one month's time for the delivery of U.S. machines, he can buy the currency today (spot) or at today's price for forward delivery in, e.g. one month's time. A premium will be quoted which might be 2 or 3 cents dearer than the spot rate. But no matter what happens to the dollar meanwhile, he knows how much the transaction will cost him. The penalty of not getting sums right in the foreign exchange market, is high, particularly when very large sums are involved.

Example
A company executive wants deutschmarks. The rate is $1 = 3.93DM. He takes a forward contract and pays $100,000 for 393,000DM. The deutschmark appreciates (or is revalued) by 10%. The rate is now 3.60DM. The company has gained 393,000 − 360,000 = 33,000 deutschmarks which at the rate of $1 = 3.60DM = $9,166.66, for the cost of the forward premium.

13.10 THE FOREIGN EXCHANGE MARKET AND THE MONEY SUPPLY

Changes in sentiment towards a currency on the foreign exchange affect the money supply in two ways. If, e.g. sterling appreciates, this tends to increase the demand of domestic non-bank investors for gilt-edged stock, and so depress the money supply. Secondly, the inflow of currency across the exchanges affects the level of *domestic liquidity*. These flows are examined in more detail below.

13.10.1 THE FLOW OF FUNDS

Sterling M3 is defined as notes and coin in circulation with the public plus net sterling bank deposits of all *U.K. residents*. An inflow of funds into sterling which takes the form of an increase in an *overseas residents'* sterling deposits does not therefore add directly to the U.K.'s money supply. Overseas buying of private sector securities does increase it; so does any other inflow which increases residents, bank deposits in the U.K. The impact of external flows on the domestic money supply is shown in the table below. It is assumed that there is an *inflow* of funds. (An outflow would have a different effect.)

Table 13.1   *External Flows and Money Supply*

Inflow of Funds	Money Supply (sterling M3)
1. Overseas investment in new U.K. public sector securities	No increase in money supply
2. Overseas investment in U.K. bank deposits	No increase in money supply But see Note 2 below.
3. Overseas investment in non-bank private sector securities or purchases of securities from non-bank investors	Equal increase in money supply
4. Public sector borrowing overseas	No increase in money supply
5. U.K. non-bank residents switch deposits from foreign currencies to sterling	Equal increase in money supply

In all the examples listed above there will usually be a rise in the official reserves.

Notes

1. Overseas investment in new U.K. public sector securities (e.g. gilt 'taps' or Treasury bills) increases the level of U.K. official reserves. The authorities finance this increase through the sales of their new securities. They do not borrow domestically to finance the inflow. There is no impact on sterling M3.

2. Foreign-held deposits with U.K. banks are not included in sterling M3. Overseas investment in U.K. bank deposits therefore have no *direct impact* on the money supply. There is however, a secondary effect. The banks use the surplus sterling resources, arising from the inflow of overseas funds into the official reserves, to invest in Treasury bills. The consequent increase in the banks' reserve asset ratio can generate a secondary expansion of the money supply, for the banks, with a higher asset base, can increase their lending (unless constrained by any Supplementary Deposits scheme in operation).

3. If foreigners buy U.K. equities or property, or extend credit to U.K. customers, the sterling bank deposits of U.K. residents will rise. A similar result ensues from gilt sales by private non-bank investors to overseas purchasers.

The U.K. residents credit the resultant proceeds to their bank accounts. The U.K. authorities then have to finance an increase in the reserves. Unless they eliminate the excess sterling bank deposits generated by the inflow (through sales of gilts/public sector debt to non-bank investors) there will be an increase in the money supply.

4. Public sector borrowing overseas (e.g. in Euro-currencies) has a similar impact to 1. above. The rise in official reserves is financed by public sector borrowing and there is no increase in the money supply.

5. If U.K. non-bank residents switch their foreign currency deposits or securities into sterling

deposits or securities, there will be an increase in the *sterling* bank deposits of U.K. residents. Unless the authorities sell public sector debt to non-bank private residents to eliminate the excess sterling bank deposits (thereby reducing Bankers' Deposits and increasing Public Deposits at the Bank of England), there will be an increase in the money supply.

Even when there is a very large inflow of funds, the expansionary impact on the money supply can be small or even neutral if there is (a) a low public sector borrowing requirement and (b) a large sale of gilts to U.K. private sector non-bank investors.

The net impact of currency flows on sterling M3 is shown in 3. and 5. in Table 13.1. In spite of a large currency inflow into the U.K., the effect on the money supply was broadly neutral. The increase in banks' deposits did not lead to a secondary expansion of the money supply because their reserve asset holdings fell in line with the decrease in domestic deposits.

It can be seen therefore that changes in the exchange rates and/or official reserves affect the money supply if they alter the level of U.K. residents' bank deposits or, as a secondary effect, if the level of the banks' reserve base is changed, so that banks expand (or contract) their lending.

13.11 EFFECTS OF BALANCE OF PAYMENTS FLOWS UPON THE MONETARY AGGREGATES (M1, M3, M3 STERLING AND DCE)—A SUMMARY

Balance of payments flows usually have a greater effect on the money supply under a fixed exchange rate. A floating exchange rate normally insulates the domestic money supply from external influences. However, the overall effect depends on (a) what flows are involved (b) how money supply is defined and (c) indirect effects of external flows upon (b) (Table 13.2).

Under *fixed exchange rates*, an inflow represents a movement of funds from the overseas to the domestic sector of the economy. Such a flow increases money supply only if it expands private sector bank deposits. If it increases non-resident holdings of public sector debt or non-resident bank deposits, the money supply remains unaffected.

Under *floating exchange rates*, the exchange rate adjusts to match outflows with inflows. If, however, the flows affect the allocation of total funds between money and other financial assets, the money supply may alter.

Domestic Credit Expansion should theoretically be unaffected by whatever type of exchange rate operates. In practice, capital inflows appear to affect DCE *indirectly,* by, e.g. generating greater confidence — leading to higher sales of public sector debt to the non-bank private sector and thus a fall in DCE.

In summary, the effect of external flows on the monetary aggregates depends ultimately on the reaction of banks, private sector and overseas residents and the monetary authorities. Inflows usually increase banks' reserve ratios. Whether this leads to a multiple credit expansion depends on the banks' original reserve asset ratio, the scope for deposit expansion, and any change in demand for bank credit.* If the authorities are aiming for a sterling M3 target, they will want to offset the increase in DCE caused by the

---

*(See P.D. Spencer: *Precautionary and Speculative Aspects of Bank Behaviour in the UK under Competition and Credit Control 1972 – 1977.* Internal Treasury Paper January 1978.)

Table 13.2. Summary of effects of balance of payments flows on the monetary aggregates
SOURCE: *Balance of Payments Flows and the Monetary Aggregates in the United Kingdom* (Rachel Lomax and Colin Mowl) (Treasury Working Paper No. 5)

	Exchange rate regime	DCE	£M3	Reserve assets	Net f.c. ('switched position)	Eligible liabilities			Reserve ratio
						Resident £ deposits	Non-resident £ deposits	IBELS	
(a) *100 inflow to private sector**									
Counterpart outflow:									
(i) None	Fixed	—	+100	+100	—	+100	—	+100	↑
(ii) 100 private sector	Floating	—	—	—	—	—	—	—	—
(iii) 100 £ bank deposits	Floating	—	+100	—	—	+100	-100	—	—
(iv) 100 public sector	Floating	—	+100	+100	—	+100	—	+100	↑
(b) *100 inflow to £ bank deposits*									
Counterpart outflow									
(i) None	Fixed	—	—	+100	—	—	+100	+100	↑
(ii) 100 private sector	Floating	—	-100	—	—	-100	+100	—	—
(iii) 100 £ bank deposits	Floating	—	—	—	—	—	—	—	—
(iv) 100 public sector	Floating	—	—	+100	—	—	+100	+100	↑
(c) *100 inflow to public sector:*									
Counterpart outflow:									
(i) None	Fixed	—	—	—	—	—	—	—	—
(ii) 100 private sector	Floating	-100	-100	-100	—	-100	—	-100	→
(iii) 100 £ bank deposits	Floating	—	—	-100	—	—	-100	-100	→
(iv) 100 public sector	Floating	—	—	—	—	—	—	—	—
(d) *100 increase in banks' net external f.c. liabilities:*									
Associated f.c. transactions:									
(i) Banks sell f.c. to E.E.A.	Fixed	—	—	+100	100 into £	—	—	+100	↑
(ii) f.c. loan to resident for overseas investment	Fixed	—	—	—	—	—	—	—	—
(iii) f.c. loan to resident for domestic use	Fixed	—	+100	+100	—	+100	—	+100	↑

* either private sector component of current account or capital inflow to private sector
all assumed to be interest-bearing

inflow. They will therefore try to sell public sector debt to the non-bank private sector and/or increase interest rates. The latter will reduce the demand for bank credit, but such higher rates may, unfortunately for the authorities' attempt at 'sterilization', induce further capital inflows. Their effort to keep DCE down will then be in vain.

When *supplementary special deposits* are in operation, the above effects are modified. The private sector will be encouraged to hold short-term public sector debt and less bank deposits by changes in interest rate differentials, a process known as disintermediation. A cutback in sterling lending will have the same effect as disintermediation in reducing DCE and the money supply.

13.12 THE MECHANICS OF THE EXCHANGE EQUALIZATION ACCOUNT

If there is an *increase* in the demand for British goods, exporters will pay into their banks, the foreign currency earned. The banks sell the currency for sterling to the Exchange Equalization Account. Sterling bank deposits rise. The small working balance of the E.E.A. falls. The E.E.A. recalls some of its Ways and Means advances to the National Loans Fund, or sells some of its tap Treasury bills to finance the purchase of sterling and replenish its working balance. Because the National Loans Fund has paid cash to the E.E.A., it needs additional finance. The N.L.F. gets this by sales of new Treasury Bills in the market. This helps to absorb the surplus cash of the clearing banks and make good the outflow from the National Loans Fund. The increase in Treasury bills can have an expansionary effect on bank credit, however, unless the authorities sell gilts to the non-bank public, thus partly covering the borrowing requirement without an expansion in the money supply.

If there is a *decrease* in the demand for British goods (or any other reason why sterling holders want to exchange it for another currency) banks will acquire pounds and exchange them for (say) dollars. The Exchange Equalization Account takes in sterling (from the banks) for dollars. The pounds which the E.E.A. has acquired are lent to the Exchequer in return for tap bills. Alternatively, Treasury bills will be bought in the market. As a result the Exchequer's need for Treasury bills is lessened. There will be fewer issued. The banks get fewer Treasury bills. They have less potential for lending. Overall liquidity falls.

13.13 SUMMARY OF THE ADVANTAGES AND DISADVANTAGES OF DIFFERENT TYPES OF EXCHANGE RATES

ADVANTAGES	DISADVANTAGES
Floating Rates	
1. A Payments equilibrium is automatically established, for the market mechanism adjusts the currency price.	1. Uncertainty of future prices may cause traders to (a) lessen their international trade, (b) buy forward cover, (c) speculate.

ADVANTAGES	DISADVANTAGES
2. The exchange reserves change very little so that there is no need to keep large reserves.	2. Domestic policies may be pursued irresponsibly regardless of falls in the exchange rate and of future prospects.
3. The need for a large volume of international liquidity is reduced.	3. Some intervention by authorities still needed to smooth out excessive short-term changes in the exchange rate.
4. Domestic policies can be pursued without regard to the exchange rate or the level of currency reserves.	
5. Freedom from control encourages world trade.	4. Though freedom from control could encourage world trade, controls on capital movement are still enforced even with floating currencies in operation.
	5. Where forward cover is expensive, international trading is inhibited.

Fixed
Gold Standard

1. Stability in international trade/investment/domestic finance.	1. Restricts freedom on domestic policies.
2. Encourages international economic integration.	2. Supply of gold is too limited for international trade, or may be limited for political reasons.
3. Prevents inflation because loss of reserves will cause corrective action.	3. Gold as a reserve currency is too costly to produce, too heavy/risky to move, too wasteful to store.
4. Monetary base not so easily expanded as is a paper/bookkeeping one.	

Fixed (Bretton Woods Adjustable Peg)

1. Easy to understand.	1. Causes delays in adjustment of the exchange rate.
2. A measure of discipline with opportunities for alteration if necessary.	2. Possibility of devaluation encourages speculation.
3. Price certainty in international trade.	3. Large reserves needed, or ability to borrow.
4. = 2 under Gold standard (above)	4. Loses gold standard certainty without gaining flexibility.
	5. Restricts freedom in domestic policies.
	6. Deficit countries must adjust; surplus countries need not.
	7. Encourages inflation (over-consumption) when deficits are financed by international borrowing.

ADVANTAGES   DISADVANTAGES

Flexible

Crawling Peg

1. Adjustment plus certainty: high   1. Limitations on interest rate free-
   interest rates for depreciating cur-   dom could deter long-term invest-
   rency; low rates for appreciating   ment.
   ones.
2. Restricts speculation.

TYPICAL QUESTION

Describe and criticize the international system of exchange rates and parities
which has operated since the Second World War. Outline briefly the main
alternative arrangements which have been suggested.

SUGGESTED ANSWER

The international system of exchange rates and parities which operated after
the end of the Second World War was one of fixed exchange rates with a small
margin of flexibility.

The official or par value of each currency, though usually expressed in
U.S. dollars, was based, until 1971, on a specific amount of gold. On either
side of the par value were narrow margins within which central banks
stabilized the value of their currencies. In the United Kingdom before the
1967 devaluation, the rate was £1 = $2.40 with a movement of 1% on either
side before the central bank intervened either to buy pounds with their reserve
of gold and dollars and so support the rate, or to sell pounds and depress it.

Exchange stability was encouraged by the International Monetary Fund
which provided borrowing facilities for countries with temporary balance of
payments difficulties.

The fixed rate system with an adjustable peg operated fairly well in the
early years after 1947, but revealed major disadvantages subsequently. It
needed large amounts of official liquidity, eased but not remedied by the
introduction of Special Drawing Rights in 1970. Adjustments of the
exchange rates tended to be delayed, especially by reserve currency countries.
During financial crises when parities were under pressure, fixed exchange
rates encouraged speculation and so led to devaluation and competitive over-
devaluation.

However, fixed exchange rates did impose restraints on domestic policy,
and so prevented prices and economics of different countries from getting
too far out of line with one another.

Alternative systems to the fixed rates of the 1947—1971 era are:

(a) *Wider bands*, among whose advocates have been Torrens in 1819, Keynes
in 1930, the Joint Economic Committee of U.S. Congress, the British Treasury and the Bank of England, 1952 – 5. The main advantage claimed for the

system is that it stabilizes speculation and gives protection from imported inflation.

(b) *Step-by-Step or Sliding Parity*, sometimes known as *the crawling peg*, by which exchange rates are adjusted at periodic intervals by a certain percentage according to their moving average in some past period such as the previous year. Although this system allows for automatic adjustment, it is somewhat complex to operate. Professor James Meade suggested changes of a maximum 1/6% per month which could be required of any country that was a net borrower from the I.M.F. Speculation would be minimized; the system would be consistent with I.M.F. rules, but internal interest rates would have to be controlled at a rate to offset any depreciation of currency by this method.

(c) Finally, there is the system of floating rates (to which Britain switched after the currency outflow in June 1972). The advantages claimed for floating rates are (i) optimum resource allocation, (ii) freedom for domestic policies, (iii) no official reserves needed, and (iv) speculation against currency is avoided. The disadvantages are that the complexities of assessment may cause isolationist policies; and domestic monetary policies have to be far more active to induce inflows or outflows of capital.

ADDITIONAL QUESTIONS

1. Write brief notes on 'leads and lags'.

2. Why has the international system of fixed exchange rates which has operated since the Second World War been widely replaced by floating rates?

3. Discuss the relative merits of fixed and floating exchange rate systems.

14 International Liquidity

Liquid resources give their owner immediate and unconditional purchasing power. International liquidity similarly gives the owner immediate purchasing power internationallly. It can therefore be defined as the *total means of payments accceptable for international settlements over which the world's monetary authorities have immediate and unconditional command*.

This sum comprises (a) gold and convertible foreign exchange reserves held by the countries of the world, (b) SDRs, (c) official borrowing facilities held with the I.M.F.

This definition of international liquidity used by the I.M.F. has two advantages (a) it is statistically calculable, (b) it excludes borrowing potential dependent on bilateral and multilateral agreements which cannot, in their nature, be available to all, and may never be taken up. Such agreements help trade, but, as with gifts from relatives or friends, they come only at specific times, and only to a chosen few.

14.1 PURPOSE OF OFFICIAL RESERVES

Official reserves help overcome balance of payments difficulties. A country with insufficient reserves to offset a deficit, may have to introduce a restrictive domestic credit policy and/or import or exchange controls. Such restrictions harm world trade.

What alternatives are there for a country importing more than it can pay for in exports, if its monetary reserves are too small to cover the balance? It can buy less, restrict imports, adjust its internal economy, allow its exchange rate to fall (and this will not be a remedy if demand for imports/exports is inelastic), sell overseas investments, or borrow external finance to continue trading? If the latter method is chosen, how long will the creditors oblige?

Every flow of goods has a parallel flow of money. Thus, in 1972, Russia imported grain in which it was deficient, from the U.S.A. which had a surplus. Payment was in gold. If the Russians had no gold for payment (or other acceptable exchange media such as minerals or oil), should no grain have been bought?

This was the kind of problem the I.M.F. faced during the 1960s when the ratio of world liquidity to world imports fell from 68% in 1954 to 43% in 1964, and it was thought that there was not enough money of the right kind (acceptable to all) to finance the growth of world trade.

Dollars and gold were taking over sterling's role as an international currency. But gold production was not keeping up with the increase in world trade, and the dollar, in such short supply after World War Two, became a much less wanted currency in the 1960s with the U.S.A. going into deficit each year. Yet, if the U.S.A. adopted protectionist measures and achieved a surplus for itself, a world recession could easily result.

As a temporary solution to this dilemna, the I.M.F. created additional borrowing facilities and SDRs. Floating exchange rates, adopted by many countries after the Smithsonian meeting of December 1971, also took the strain off reserves, though such measures may well have added fuel to the domestic inflationary fires that began for the U.K. in 1973 and did not abate for several years thereafter.

The Committee of Twenty that had been set up in 1972 to reform the world monetary system was wound up in June 1974. The issues it faced (a) international liquidity and the replacement of the dollar as the world's main reserve asset, and (b) the persistent balance of payments deficit of the U.K. and the U.S.A. were no longer relevant to the new problems of world energy and huge imbalances caused by a four-fold increase in oil prices.

14.2 CONCLUSIONS

International experience of the 1950s and 1960s has shown that the 'problem' of international liquidity revolves round three points: the *level* of world reserves, their *distribution* and their *quality*. A decline in international reserves appears to be not a cause of diminishing world trade, but an effect. Greater flexibility in exchange rates helps to avoid payments difficulties and trade restrictions. So too, do international borrowing facilities such as those provided by the I.M.F. Both, however, delay corrective domestic measures being taken.

The distribution of reserve currencies is never going to be easy, for who is going to penalize a country persistently in surplus, and how? The scarce currency provision clause in the Bretton Woods-system for such a situation has made no impact whatsoever. Progress has been made with the introduction of SDRs. International co-operation might now be tried on the levels of interest rates. These have important effects on domestic prices and investment, and what may be even more important in the future, on international flows of money.

14.3 FORMS OF INTERNATIONAL LIQUIDITY

14.3.1 STERLING

Some national currencies serve, like gold, as international money: they act as a store of wealth, a medium of exchange, a standard for deferred payments and a unit of account. Countries settle payments between each other in these currencies and also hold them as part of their monetary reserves. A country which issues these currencies loses *and* gains from the role of international banker. It may postpone a necessary devaluation. It may institute a policy of deflation contrary to the national interest. On the other hand, the country can use money which flows in to whatever advantage it sees fit. If money flows out, however, sufficient reserves must be found to offset the drain. This is no easy balance to maintain and proved too difficult for Britain in the 1960s and 1970s.

14.3.1.1 *History*

During the 19th century, sterling was used as an international and trading currency. When countries bought and sold goods, they paid and were paid in sterling. Their central banks held their official reserves in this form, or in gold, and kept the balances in the Bank of England to be withdrawn when needed.

In 1931, when Britain came off the gold standard, which had lasted for nearly a century, three kinds of trading areas developed:

(a) The sterling bloc, which fixed their currencies in relation to sterling.

(b) The gold bloc, which fixed their currencies in gold terms.

(c) The dollar bloc, which fixed their currencies in terms of the dollar.

On the outbreak of war in 1939, Britain introduced exchange controls. The sterling area countries kept their reserves in Britain. They pooled their resources and bought and sold foreign currency within the pool. In this way, Britain obtained credit to fight the war when the rest of Europe was under Hitler's yoke, and the U.S.A. had not yet become embroiled in the struggle.

The U.K. Exchange Act 1947 continued restrictions on capital transactions for countries outside the sterling area. These had kept their own controls. In 1958, the controls were lifted. The major European currencies, including the £, became convertible. This meant that any country, (not just those in the sterling area) which held pounds, could change them into dollars, marks, francs and so on.

Holders of funds could switch from one financial centre (and currency) to another, as it suited them. France devalued by 14.7% (December 1959) only a few months after devaluing by 16.7% (August). The mark and the gilder were later (1961) to revalue, and Canada to float.

Britain had paid dearly for its struggle in World War Two. Official reserves and foreign investments were depleted. Liabilities of over £3000 million had been incurred. In spite of this, many countries still kept their balances in London. Even in the 1960s, when many former colonies had gained their independence, 30% of world trade was financed in sterling, and 60 countries had their official reserves in Britain.

These balances helped to disguise the fact of Britain's declining exports. Britain's reserves were affected not only by the *capital movements* of sterling, but by the *current balances* of sterling area countries. When these were in surplus, Britain's reserves (and liabilities) increased; when in deficit, Britains reserves (and liabilities) fell. Britain's surplus balance of £600m in 1962 plunged to a £650m deficit in 1964, and the £ visibly weakened. Injections of aid from the I.M.F. with a standby credit of $1bn in August, and $500m 'swap' credits through the BIS, nursed sterling through the crisis.

Fixed exchange rates, introduced at Bretton Woods, had many advantages so economists then averred. But such a system made it difficult for countries to change their parities smoothly. Countries in deficit, or whose exchange rate looked overpriced, found the supply of their currency increasing, and its demand falling relative to other currencies. More people wanted to sell than hold or buy it. So it now was with sterling. But if the pound became under pressure, so too, did Bretton Woods.

Just as Russia proved the unlikely, but temporary, saviour of gold, so central banks, through the BIS, proved the unlikely saviours of the I.M.F. fixed exchange rate system. They devised international credit arrangements. Devaluation of sterling, too long delayed, finally took place in 1967. It reduced the parity of the £ from £1 = $2.80 to £1 = $2.40. Holders of sterling had gained by the higher interest rate paid on sterling compared with other countries, but this did not mitigate for most of them, the capital loss entailed by sterling's devaluation. What was the future to hold? How were those countries holding large sterling balances (like Hong Kong with £800m) to get out of sterling without changing its parity again? Heavy sales of a security depress its price. This truth holds good for currencies too.

To help sterling's reserve position, the central banks of the Group of Ten countries, plus Austria, Denmark and Switzerland, negotiated a further standby credit of $2000m in 1968.

The arrangement had two parts:

(a) Whenever U.K. reserves were depleted, the central banks would top them up to an agreed limit.

(b) Sterling area countries got a guarantee which covered 10% of their total reserves against any fall in value, providing they kept that (10%) *minimum proportion in sterling*. Sterling area countries achieved large surpluses in 1970. The total of their sterling balances held in Britain naturally also went up. This was not the object of the Basle agreement and when it was renewed in 1971, the guaranteed proportion was reduced. In 1972, the £ floated, and new exchange controls effectively reduced the sterling area to Britain, the Channel Islands, Eire and the Isle of Man. In January 1977, a medium-term financing facility backed by the U.S.A., Japan, West Germany, Belgium, Canada, Sweden, the Netherlands and Switzerland was introduced to help Britain cover withdrawals of sterling balances held by foreigners in London. The facility provided a $3bn standby credit at 5% for up to 7 years to cover the *official holdings*. Unlike private holdings of sterling, official holdings have proved to be very volatile. This was emphasized after the oil crisis when inflows of OPEC money helped Britain buy with credit what could not have been bought otherwise.

Holders of sterling could convert their money into British Government bonds denominated in dollars on market-related terms. The 1977 Basle agreement gave Britain time to match her external liabilities and assets until North Sea oil revenues enabled debts be repaid. The Basle Agreement also helped Britain to slough off honourably, and almost painlessly, the international role that no country now wants: that of reserve currency banker for the rest of the world.

14.3.2 GOLD

Whatever form of money a country uses, some control must be exercised over the quantity issued: too much and prices soar, too little and they sink. For centuries, the advantage of gold as a currency was its stability: caused by the high scarcity value of the metal in relation to its volume and weight.

Throughout the nineteenth and early twentieth centuries, gold was seen as a generally stabilizing force on the value of money and international exchange rates. From Bretton Woods onwards, those in favour of demonetising gold (no longer using it as money), gathered strength. By the end of the 1970s, it looked as if they might banish it from the monetary scene altogether.

But gold is a great survivor, perhaps because of its remarkable qualities. Easy to count, pleasant to touch, an imperishable conductor, gold will not rust or spoil. Whenever currency crises threaten, people and nations revert to gold as a medium of exchange and a store of wealth.

The full gold standard used by many nations, including the U.K. until 1914, was a fixed exchange rate system. It provided an automatic mechanism for adjusting price levels to cure balance of payments disequilibria. If the U.K. had an adverse balance, gold would go out to pay overseas debts. This outflow of gold caused a reduction in the quantity of money, a restriction of credit and a fall in domestic prices below that of other countries. The lower price level then stimulated exports and decreased imports, correcting the adverse balance. Countries with surpluses, experienced the opposite effects: the inflow of gold increased the money supply; credit expanded, domestic prices rose and were followed by a fall in exports and a rise in imports. For this full standard to operate three conditions were necessary:

(a) The unit of account had to be a fixed weight of gold of declared fineness.

(b) Paper money had to be freely convertible into gold though gold coins need not actually circulate.

(c) No restrictions were allowed on the import and export of gold.

When war broke out in 1914, the U.K. abandoned the full gold standard, and returned in 1925 to a *Gold Bullion Standard*. The Gold Standard Act of 1925 compelled the Bank to sell gold at £3.17.10$\frac{1}{2}$ d per troy ounce, but only in the form of bars of 400 troy ounces of gold (the standard size bar used by central banks in their transactions). The Currency and Bank Notes Act of 1928 resumed the full gold standard until the Gold Standard Act of 1931.

Both the gold and gold bullion standards fixed exchange values of national currencies by their weight in terms of gold. One pound sterling weighed 0.257 standard ounces. One dollar weighed 0.053 standard ounces. Therefore £1 equalled 0.257/0.053 = 4.86 dollars. This rate was known as the *mint par of exchange*. The market rate could not move far from this rate, for debts could be settled either in gold or currency. If the rate of exchange fell below £1 to 4.84 dollars (known as the export gold point), it paid the British importer to buy and transmit gold. An American, importing goods from Britain could pay in gold or pounds. When the exchange rate equalled £1 to 4.88 dollars (known in Britain as the gold import point), it paid the American to buy and transmit gold. Thus, the rate of exchange with the U.S.A. was fixed between £1 equalled 4.84 dollars (gold export point) and 4.88 dollars (gold import point.)

In 1931, Britain came off the gold standard. The pound had been overvalued when sterling returned to gold in 1925. Internal costs could not be brought down. Protectionism flourished. It reduced international trade and the level of U.K. reserves. The £ was therefore floated. The bulk of Britain's reserves were transferred to the Exchange Equalization account. From 1932 to 1939, the E.E.A. operated a system of *managed flexibility*. Though the sterling/dollar rate was allowed to fluctuate (often significantly) from day to day, the E.E.A. intervened to offset speculative or temporary changes in the exchange rate.

In 1934, the U.S.A. raised the price of gold from 20.67 to 35 dollars an ounce. This rate became the basis for the *Gold Exchange Standard* set up at Bretton Woods, which operated for most of the western nations from 1944 until 1971. *A Gold Exchange Standard* economizes the use of gold. Countries fix their exchange rates to another country that is on the gold standard. America was prepared to exchange dollars into gold at the rate of $35 for one ounce. Countries, not themselves on the gold standard, could thus keep their reserves in dollars and change them into gold when they wanted.

The danger of such a system is that, if confidence in exchange paper wanes, the race to get out of the weakening currency into gold, becomes a stampede. So it was to prove with the dollar in 1971, when 65 bn paper dollars were held against $10bn worth of gold in Fort Knox. But there had been earlier hazards. The market for gold is both an industrial and monetary one. This has always been a problem for the supporters of monetary gold. How can the two markets be insulated, one from the other? Should they both have the same price? If so, gold-based money could have its values altered purely by industrial buying.

Demand for gold comes from speculators or hoarders, industry and central banks; *supply* from South Africa and Russia, the largest producers, followed by Canada, Australia, and West Africa.

The London gold market, closed on the outbreak of war in 1939, reopened in 1954, and soon overtook Zurich, which had become the main centre for the purchase and sale of gold. When, in 1958, the £ became convertible, the European currencies strengthened and the dollar weakened. Everybody holding dollars tried to change them into gold.

The gold price rose from \$35 – \$40. Official selling drove the price down. Central banks now began the first of several operations to stabilize the gold price. The Gold Pool was set up in 1961 by the central banks of Belgium, France, the Netherlands, West Germany, Britain, Switzerland and Italy. They formed a sales consortium with the U.S. Federal Reserve Bank of New York. The Bank of England organized the sales, drawing on supplies of gold from other members to steady the market. Ouotas were agreed among the group, with the U.S.A. providing half of the total supply. The Gold Pool kept the price down – and later up – to 35 dollars. But after maintaining the gold price within the agreed limit for a few years, the Pool collapsed in 1968.

Though it had survived several squalls, the devaluation of sterling in 1967 acted like the breaking of a dam. In the first 10 weeks of 1968, the Pool had supplied the market with 45 million ounces of gold, the equivalent of the western world's entire output for one year. Nevertheless central banks had learnt a very important lesson, which they were to put into practice more frequently in the next decades, namely that unity is strength.

The gold market opened again in 1968 with a two-tier price structure: (a) For *official gold* at 35 dollars an ounce to settle payment balances. (b) *industrial gold* at a price which would fluctuate with the forces of demand and supply. Such a system could only last if the free market price did not gyrate too much above the official price.

Seven central banks, including France, undertook to refrain from sales or purchases of gold on the free market so as to keep the gold price stable. But the huge payments deficit of the U.S.A. in 1970, and widening interest rate differentials between that country and Europe, led to disenchantment with the dollar. By 1971, the U.S.A. faced the risk of a major run on its gold stock or a massive buildup of U.S. debt in foreign currencies. In August, President Nixon suspended the convertibility of the dollar into gold.

In December, the 10 countries ('Group of Ten') participating in the *General Arrangements to Borrow* (GAB) met in Washington at the Smithsonian Institute to discuss new exchange rates and other measures. Part of the package was the devaluation of the dollar to 38 dollars an ounce of gold. New 'central' rates were agreed between members. The success of the meeting can be judged by the fact that only a year later Britain had to 'float' its currency, and the market price of gold had risen to 90 dollars an ounce. In February 1973, the dollar was devalued to \$42.22 an ounce of gold against a market price of \$130 an ounce. The difficulty was a new crisis of liquidity which the I.M.F. tackled by the Witteveen proposals. The valuation of paper gold (Special Drawing Rights) was also changed. Based on a 'basket' of currencies, SDRs were to be weighted so that revaluation would have a much greater impact than devaluation. This, plus an interest rate of 5% was intended to make them a more valuable asset to hold than gold.

A further agreement allowed gold reserves to be revalued at current market prices as security for international borrowing. This particularly helped Italy, but France also decided, in January 1975, to quote her gold reserves at the market price of $170.40 instead of $42.22. In that month, it was additionally agreed to end the obligation of I.M.F. members to pay 25% of their quotas in gold. The role of monetary gold in the world economy was to be further reduced by the gradual sale of the I.M.F.'s holdings of gold. Central banks agreed to buy and sell gold among themselves and on the open market at free market prices instead of the old official price for a two-year period provided there was no net accrual of gold to the countries concerned. They also agreed to report to the I.M.F. and the B.I.S. the total amount of gold bought and sold.

In January 1976, at a meeting of the I.M.F. in Kingston Jamaica, the plan to finish gold was finalized. One sixth of the I.M.F.'s gold would be sold (25m ounces) the profits put into a trust fund and the profits used for the benefit of developing countries. Another one sixth was to be sold to members of the Fund, in proportion to their quotas, at $35 an ounce, (more than $100 below the then market price.) This 'restitution' as it was somewhat oddly named, began in 1978 with 5bn ounces to 112 countries.

Following the Kingston agreement, the I.M.F. held its first auction of gold in June 1976. The price fell to $104, gold's lowest value for 3 years. Five further auctions took place in that year each of 780,000 ounces of gold, realizing $320m. By 1978, there had been two disbursements from the trust fund to 24 members mainly in Africa, India and the Far East.

The real aim of the sales, however, was to phase gold out of the monetary system forever. This policy may well succeed during a period of international recession. But what happens when/if world trade increases? Will there be cries again about insufficient liquidity? Will the SDR fit the bill as an international trading currency or will people and countries go on hoarding the 'barbaric relic' of gold? The Report of the Group of Ten in 1964 stated that "gold will continue to be the ultimate international reserve asset." Other upholders of the metal claim that it will never be dislodged from the monetary scene because gold:

(a)   Keeps exchange rates stable, and such stability fosters international trade.

(b)   Prevents exchange speculation

(c)   Is in short enough supply to maintain its value.

(d)   Flows between countries, and ensures an equilibrium without government interference. Furthermore, deficits cannot be continued indefinitely without some efforts being made to adjust the national economy.

The arguments against gold are formidable:

(i)   There is insufficient gold to maintain the system. Gold backing for a currency needs enormous quantities of gold.

(ii)   Gold cannot be 'managed' in the same way as can a paper currency. It costs a great deal to import and export, whereas paper is almost costless.

(iii)   Distribution of gold could be restricted because of political or other non-economic considerations by the major suppliers. This indeed is the strongest argument against the use of gold as an international currency. It would put the supply and control of world money into areas which have been geologically favoured by deposits of gold. The change of fortune which the OPEC countries have made for themselves by the oil price increase, has been grudgingly accepted by the countries needing energy. Would a rise in the prices of a commodity money such as gold be accepted by the world who lacked it, with such equanimity?

14.3.3 THE DOLLAR

During the nineteenth century when America was developing as a homogeneous nation, Britain was becoming the workshop of the world. London, pre-eminent in trade, also grew pre-eminent in finance. Because the capital city attracted specialist financial institutions, international trade became invoiced and paid for in sterling. In this way, sterling developed as an international trading and reserve currency.

After the two world wars, London's role in international trade and finance diminished. Even by the later 1950s, however, sterling was still financing 25% of world trade.

How did America, and the dollar, eventually take over sterling's role as a trading and reserve currency? For a currency to become commonly used in trade, there must be institutions which offer services in that currency. The currency must be sought after, but not too desirable, otherwise it will be *held* for its appreciating merit rather than *used*. When it is *held* either by institutions or individuals, it becomes a *reserve* currency, a store of value. A store which depreciates is discarded; which appreciates, is kept. A currency therefore has two conflicting pulls when it is being used both for trade and as a reserve. The *past* is important for a *trading* currency; the *future* for a *reserve* one. How the currency performed in the *past*, affects its present trading role; what its value is likely to be in the *future*, affects its reserve role. At times, the two roles must conflict.

The conditions necessary for a currency to be used in trade, namely a stable exchange value and institutions accepting it, operated for the dollar at the end of World War Two. The Marshall Aid programme, U.S. military aid and investment caused millions of dollars to circulate throughout the world. Countries were happy to use them. Only America could produce the equipment needed to rebuild Europe and Japan. Only America could produce the goods needed by developing countries. The dollar thus became a source of additional liquidity for the world. It was better than gold. Gold had one fixed price; the dollar did not. The dollar earned interest, gold did not and, of course, in emergency, the dollar could always be changed into gold, or so it was thought by those who held the American currency. As the economies of Europe and America recovered from the ravages of war, the dollar position changed. In 1964, for the first time, dollar liabilities of the U.S.A. to foreign official institutions, exceeded U.S.A. gold holdings. The

U.S.A. balance of payments deficit caused by the Vietnam War, grew worse until in 1971, a 10% surcharge on imports was made. The convertibility of the dollar into gold was ended, and the dollar devalued to $38 an ounce of gold. Two years later it went down to $42.22.

Within the space of twenty years, the dollar had proved as vulnerable as sterling for use as a trading and reserve currency.

14.3.3.1 *Conclusion*
National currencies will continue to be held as reserve and trading currencies. Their use aids international liquidity. Problems come when confidence fails. This lack of confidence can arise as a result of economic or political weakness of the user, who may then remove his holdings at short notice.

Under a *fixed exchange* rate system, a country can run up deficits, as did the U.S.A. in the Vietnam war, instead of using domestic financing (e.g. higher taxes). This can be good or bad, depending on the recovery potential of the country concerned. Too many deficits must ultimately lead to devaluation.

Under a *floating exchange rate system,* the reserve currency role confers no real advantages on a country like the U.S.A. "The U.S. need not be dependent on foreign borrowing in the form of increased dollar reserves held by foreign monetary authorities, to carry out its international responsibilities." On other reserve currencies, as we have seen, international money flows can have a severe impact on exchange rates, and consequently international trade. The larger the flow, the greater the pressure.

One solution to the problem is for national holdings of official reserves over a given figure to be hived off to the safekeeping of the I.M.F. The I.M.F. could convert these national assets into its own 'currency' so that it would then truly function as an international bank. A different solution was provided by Special Drawing Rights, a new international reserve asset introduced on 1 January 1970. The sale of gold by the I.M.F. could, therefore, be premature. It would be better for the I.M.F. to hold gold as 'backing' for its SDR issues. When confidence goes and paper assets becomes unwanted, gold is the asset to which people and nations return. Gold gives stability to a currency. Why it should do so is a question of psychology rather than economics, but attitudes, converted into demand and supply stances, have a way of changing prices more quickly than a new technology.

TYPICAL QUESTION
Write a brief history of sterling as a trading and reserve currency over the past 15 years showing the underlying factors which have been operating.

SUGGESTED ANSWER
Sterling developed as an international currency during the 19th century. Overseas governments and merchants kept their reserves in sterling in

London and used it for international transactions. Sterling therefore became both a reserve and a trading currency.

Countries using sterling in this way grew into a recognizable group pooling their reserves in London, with freedom of current and some capital movements between each other, but with exchange control between non-members. Control was lifted in 1958. From then on, the United Kingdom's balance of payments gradually worsened until the 1967 devaluation, when holders of sterling suffered a capital loss.

To help sterling readjust its reserve currency role, the Basle Agreements of 1968 arranged for a standby credit of $2,000m from the central banks of the U.S.A. Germany, Holland, Belgium, Switzerland, Italy, France, Austria, Sweden, Canada and Japan. This credit facility could be drawn over a three-year period, and was meant to be the final part of a series of plans to relieve sterling of the burden of being the currency of a temporarily deficit country and a long-term reserve currency.

In return for a dollar exchange guarantee from the United Kingdom, the sterling area countries agreed to keep a certain proportion of their reserves in sterling. This increased the balances. The floating of sterling, June 72, and Britain's entry into the common market meant the virtual winding up of the sterling area. A standby facility of $3000m was arranged by the Bank for International Settlements in January 1977 to finance official sterling balances under certain safeguards. Private sterling balances are not covered by the scheme.

ADDITIONAL QUESTIONS

1. How is Britain's balance of payments affected by the use of sterling as a reserve currency?

2. Write brief notes on: (a) The price of gold. (b) Sterling balances.

3. The following data, representing the total reserves of member countries of the I.M.F., are for the end of each of the years shown and are expressed in thousand millions of SDRs (used as international units of account).

	1955	1960	1965	1970	1976
Gold	35.0	37.7	41.5	37.0	35.4
Special drawing rights (SDRs)	–	–	–	3.1	8.7
Foreign exchange	16.8	18.5	24.0	45.4	160.3
Reserve position in the Fund	1.9	3.6	5.4	7.7	17.7
Total international liquidity	53.7	59.8	70.9	93.2	222.1

Using these statistics as a guide, explain what has been described as, 'the problem of international 'liquidity'. What further information would you need to write a full appraisal of the problem?

15 International Monetary Institutions

15.1 THE INTERNATIONAL MONETARY FUND (I.M.F.)

While the Second World War was being waged, statesmen were already considering problems of the peace to come. Discussions began in 1941 to set up an international body which would help countries with their balance of payment problems. The main protagonists were Harry Dexter White of the U.S. Treasury and John Maynard Keynes of the U.K. Treasury. They were (according to J. Keith Horsefield) "animated by a belief that the economic distresses of the interwar years could be avoided after the end of World War Two only by international co-operation on a previously untried scale."

Agreement was reached at a conference in Bretton Woods, New Hampshire, U.S.A. in 1944, to set up the International Monetary Fund, which began operations in December, 1945. There were initially 30 members. By 1977, a further 100 countries had joined.

15.1.1 STRUCTURE OF THE FUND

Each member can appoint a Governor and an Alternate to the Board of Governors, the Fund's highest authority, which meets usually every autumn. It makes a report on the year's events and suggestions for the coming year.

Decisions reserved to the governors include (a) a general revision of quotas which has to be approved by $\frac{4}{5}$ of the total voting power; (b) a rise in the world price of gold, and (c) a change in the Articles of Agreement.

The Articles of the Fund, it has been said, contain "the most elaborate provisions on voting of all international charters". (Joseph Gold, The International Monetary Fund and International Law. IMF., 1965, page 10). Only two amendments to the Articles were made in over 30 years. The first in 1968 introduced SDRs. The second in 1975 was a fundamental change: (a) to legitimize the floating exchange rates adopted by many countries after 1971, and (b) to improve the Fund's operations, voting rules and procedures.

The Board of Governors appoint the Executive Board of 20 directors at the I.M.F. headquarters in Washington. This is the main body responsible for supervising the Fund's activities. Five member countries with the largest membership fee (the U.S.A., the U.K., West Germany, France and Japan) each appoint one executive director. The other 15 are elected from groups of other countries. Executive directors serve for two year terms.

15.1.2 AIMS OF THE FUND

The aims of the Fund, set out in the second of the Fund's Articles of Agreement, were:

(a) *To promote international monetary co-operation* through a permanent institution which provides the machinery for consultation and collaboration on international monetary problems.

(b) *To faclilitate the expansion and balanced growth of world trade international trade,* and to contribute thereby to the promotion and maintenance of high levels of employment and real income and to the development of the productive resources of all members as primary objectives of economic policy.

(c) *To promote exchange stability,* to maintain orderly exchange arrangements among members and to avoid competitive exchange depreciation.

(d) *To assist in the establishment of a multilateral system of payments* in respect of current transactions between members and in the elimination of foreign exchange restrictions which hamper the growth of world trade.

(e) *To give confidence to members by making the general resources of the Fund temporarily available to them under adequate safeguards,* thus providing them with opportunity to correct maladjustments in their balance of payments without resorting to measures destructive of national or international prosperity.

(f) *To shorten the duration and lessen the degree of disequilibrium in the international balances of payments of members.*

15.1.3 METHODS FOR ACHIEVING THESE AIMS

15.1.3.1 *Fixed Exchange rates*
Each member had to fix the par (exchange) value of its currency in terms of gold or U.S.A. dollars, at the rate of 35 dollars to one ounce of gold. A fluctuation of 1% up or down was allowed. By 1949, however, it was realized that several currencies were out of line, and at the fourth annual general meeting, large devaluations were made. A few later alignments took place: Britain and France devalued; Germany revalued and Canada floated. But, excepting for these and a few later changes, fairly stable parities were maintained from 1945 to 1971. International currency movements became freeer and, by 1958, convertibility for all major currencies for current transactions had been established.

15.1.3.2 *Finance from the fund – the quota system*
Funds for maladjustments in payment balances were to be obtained from the Fund firstly by its quota system. When members joined, they paid a

membership fee or *quota*. This quota reflected the economic size and trading importance of the country. Voting power was also determined by the size of the quota, a system that has met with increasing opposition over the years both from the less developed nations and from the oil-rich countries.

Three-quarters of the quota was to be paid in the member's own currency. The remaining 25% had to be paid in gold and was known as the *gold* (or reserve) *tranche*. The Fund is now committed to phasing gold from the international monetary system and accepts the 25% in currency or S.D.R.s. Fund financing by the quota system works in the following manner. A country in balance of payments difficulties buys from the Fund, the foreign currency it needs, by offering more of its own currency. Technically, therefore, the debit country is not *borrowing* but *buying* the wanted currency in return for its own, which has to be repurchased within 3 – 5 years. Interest at rather less than market rates, is paid by the borrowing country on the Fund's surplus holdings of its currency.

In accordance with article (e) 'adequate safeguards' must be observed when making the resources of the Fund 'temporarily available' to members. The credit tranche system provides these safeguards. The 25% gold tranche can be drawn (against balance of payments needs) without question. The I.M.F. then holds 100% of the member's quota, all in currency. A further 25% can be fairly easily drawn but borrowing conditions for the next three permitted tranches of 25% become successively more stringent until the I.M.F. holds 200% of the country's quota.

The higher tranches are usually made under *standby arrangements*. The requests for credit are examined by the Fund. Discussions take place about the balance of payments and other adjustments that have to be made by the borrowing country, whose government agrees in a *Letter of Intent* to the conditions imposed. Such conditions usually ask for 'performance criteria': economic targets that must be met if the credit is to continue. Performance criteria were first set out in 1957 and were very lengthy. Today, the most important are limits on domestic credit and on public sector borrowing. Other conditions might be exchange rate adjustments, abolition of subsidies and price controls, fewer trade restrictions, and quite often a public sector wages policy. It is not therefore surprising that standby amounts are rarely drawn in full. Indeed in fiscal 1976 – 1977 only 25% of the total standby credit approved by the I.M.F., was actually taken. *The general review of 1976*, the sixth since the I.M.F. was founded, increased total quotas from SDR 29.2 bn to SDR 39.0 bn. Britain's quota increase of $4\frac{1}{2}$% acutally decreased her credit ceiling by about 1bn S.D.R.s and the U.S.A. had a very slight quota decrease of from just over 20% to just under 20%. German and Japanese quotas were, not surprisingly, above the general average increase of $33\frac{1}{2}$% while that of Saudi Arabia went up by more than four times. Under the rules of the I.M.F. no quota increase can take place until ratified by members holding at least 75% of the total I.M.F. quotas. This situation was reached in November 1980. If all the countries agree to the increase and pay the extra contributions, the total increase in I.M.F. quotas could go up from S.D.R. 39.7 billion to S.D.R. 60 billion.

15.1.3.3 *Other financing*

General arrangements to borrow
In the early days of the I.M.F., smaller countries were the main borrowers. In 1962, it was realized that, if the industrialized countries needed finance, more resources would be needed than those that came from subscriptions. Ten countries with the largest quotas (U.S.A., U.K., West Germany, France, Japan, Canada, Italy, Netherlands, Belgium, Sweden) and, later, Switzerland, agreed to lend $6bn to the Fund to help finance a drawing by any others in the group. In 1978, the G.A.B. amounted to around $7 $\frac{1}{2}$ bn.

The Compensatory Financing Facility
The facility was set up in 1963 to help members whose exports consisted mainly of primary products. When export earnings fall heavily, C.F.F. helps the balance of payments deficit which results. Increases in this facility were allowed in 1975: up to 50% of quota in any one year with a maximum of 75% and without any restriction on the entitlement to normal financing facilities. Drawings in 1976 amounted to $2.50bn of which $1.75bn was taken up by non-oil producing nations. In 1977, drawings were lower at 240m S.D.R.s (the average of 1 S.D.R. in 1977 was $1.17) because of commodity price rises.

The Extended Financing Facility
This provides finance for countries with payments problems that take a longer time to solve and for whom, therefore, longer loans are needed than those provided under the credit tranche system. Borrowing conditions are very tight so that although 140% of quota rather than the three normal tranches of 25% each is allowed, few countries wish to commit themselves to such stringent conditions for three years ahead.

The Buffer Stock Facility
This is another form of lending to help finance members' contributions to approved buffer stocks of commodities. Like the *Trust Loan Fund*, financed partly by the I.M.F. gold sales, it is only of marginal help.

The Oil Facility
Many industrialised countries experienced huge current account deficits as a result of the oil price increase in 1973 after the Middle East War. The estimated surplus of oil producers in 1974 rose by £25 billion to £27bn, while the industrial countries moved from a surplus of £4bn in 1973 to a deficit of £13bn in 1974, with different countries being affected in diffferent degrees, e.g. U.K. and Italy, along with many developing countries, had their payments difficulties exacerbated, while Germany's surplus actually rose.

A less emphasized, but equally important, problem resulting from the oil price increase was the massive accumulation of funds in certain O.P.E.C. countries. Where was the money to be invested? What country, or institution, desired such large inflows of capital on which interest would have to be paid, and which could be withdrawn at fairly short notice? How could the oil-rich producers absorb enough imports to balance the oil-related deficits of other countries?

International consortia of banking institutions got together to recycle the 'petro-dollars' as they came to be called. Meanwhile, the Oil Facility financed by contributions from surplus countries provided $8bn in 1974 and 1975 to finance oil deficits (including $1,160m drawn by the U.K.) Repayments of drawings under the oil facility had to be made within 4 – 7 years instead of the normal 3 – 5, and had already begun by 1978. Interest rates were less favourable being nearer general market rates. Access to the oil facility was closed in 1976.

The "Witteveen" or Supplementary Facility
The I.M.F.'s ability to help members depends on having enough funds. In August 1977, at a meeting in Paris, 14 countries, including seven oil-producing nations, added a further $10bn to its resources. This Supplementary Facility became known as the Witteveen facility because Johannes Witteveen was, at that time, Managing Director of the Fund. It counted as part of the reserves of the countries contributing it and also as part of the world's money supply against which additional credit could be generated. But 90% of the facility was subject to stringent lending conditions.

Saudi Arabia, having contributed the major part of the financing facility (nearly twice as much as the U.S.A.) naturally hoped for greater representation on the I.M.F. executive board. The Americans did not want any increase in the number of seats. Perhaps as a compromise, the 6th quota review boosted the oil producers' quota, while lessening that of the U.K., and (marginally) the U.S.

The Supplementary Facility added 12.5% of quota to the first credit tranche, bringing it up to 36.5% of quota; and 30% to each of the three successive tranches, so roughly doubling the permitted total. It can also be used to double the Extended Facility to 280% of quota, or, exceptionally, even more.

15.1.4 GOVERNMENT OF THE FUND (See also Section 15.11)
The main supervision of the I.M.F.'s activities is exercised by the Executive Board, appointed by the Board of Governors. The U.K.'s Governor and Alternate are the Chancellor of the Exchequer and a director of the Bank of England. Annual meetings of the members and governors take place in different countries each year.

15.1.5 THE UNITED KINGDOM AND THE FUND

Under a standby which was agreed in December 1975, the U.K. drew a credit tranche of $800 million in May 1976 with three further tranches agreed for future years. The drawings were intended to help finance the U.K.'s deficit balance until the North Sea oil revenues changed the current account deficit into a surplus. The policies agreed by the Chancellor of the Exchequer and the I.M.F. were set out in a Letter of Intent, 15 December 1976. As a result sterling strengthened and in the next 10 months the reserves increased from $4bn to $20bn so that, in 1977, sterling needed no external support.

15.1.6 SPECIAL DRAWING RIGHTS

In the 1960s, the reserves held by countries for settling international balances were thought to be insufficient for the expected growth of world trade. A scheme was sought for increasing world liquidity. Special Drawing Rights (S.D.R.s) seemed to be the answer. After the first amendment to the Fund's Articles of Agreement in 1968, they were introduced on 1 January 1970. Until then, all borrowings from the I.M.F. had had to be repaid, whereas of the new Drawing Rights, only part had to be repaid. The rest was, in effect, a newly created asset. The Fund was acting like a bank in *creating* money.

The first distribution of SDRs agreed by the I.M.F. at its 24th annual meeting in September, 1969, amounted to $9,500m. Of this amount $3,500m was distributed in 1970, the rest spread over 1971 and 1972. The U.K.'s allocation was $410m.

15.1.6.1 *Method of use*
The S.D.R.s could be used in three ways:
  (a) Added to a country's gold and foreign exchange reserves.
  (b) Used by central banks to settle debts directly with each other.
  (c) Used by central banks through the I.M.F. with the Fund designating a particular country to receive the S.D.R.s in exchange for its own currency.
In whichever way S.D.R.s were used, they were subject to a 70% rule: all countries were allowed to keep an average of 70% of the S.D.R.s they were credited with over the three-year period. Britain had $410m S.D.R.s. Of that amount, 70% ($287m) was a permanent addition to her reserves, while the remaining 30% ($123m) was a temporary loan that had to be repaid.

When S.D.R.s were first issued, they were given a value of one U.S. dollar = 0.8887 grams of gold. The dollar was devalued twice thereafter, and floating exchange rates adopted by many countries after 1972. In 1974, S.D.R.s were also 'floated'. They have now become a 'basket' of the 16 major currencies which each have a share of 1% or more in world trade. The weighting in the 'basket' is based on their average shares over the 5 years 1968 to 1972. The I.M.F. makes a daily calculation of the SDR in terms of the U.S. $. It takes the market exchange rates of the dollar against each of the other 15 currencies; these dollar equivalents (i.e. 16 amounts of U.S. cents) are added together to give the U.S. dollar value of the basket and therefore of the SDR. The other 15 currencies can then be converted into S.D.R.s at the appropriate rate. Daily values for the S.D.R. are published in I.M.F. publications as well as in *The Times* and the *Financial Times*.

Making the S.D.R. into a basket of currencies, has given it a more stable purchasing power than one national currency can hope to have. By using S.D.R.s as a medium of exchange, therefore, a country gets a fairer purchasing power payment for its goods than from a currency that may, for all sorts of reasons, tumble downwards before payment is made. As a result, the S.D.R. is becoming more widely used as a unit of account for international payments. The first Euro-bonds denominated in S.D.R.s were issued in June 1975, although payments and receipts were to be in U.S. dollars. When the Suez canal was reopened in the same month, tolls were denominated in S.D.R.s, although payment was again in U.S. dollars. The ultimate aim of the I.M.F. is to make the S.D.R. an important, preferably the principal, asset in the monetary system. Their development as an international unit of acccount is certainly increasing, particularly since the second amendment to the Fund's Articles (1976) agreed to "reduce the role of gold and increase the usability of the S.D.R.s". Discussions have since taken place on linking S.D.R.s with aid to the developing countries. (The 'Link' proposal) but the I.M.F. gold auctions have caused this idea to be temporarily abandoned.

In September 1978, the Interim Committee of the I.M.F. recommended a further allocation of S.D.R.s. Accordingly, it was agreed to make a second allocation amounting to 12bn S.D.R.s. These would be distributed in three equal annual instalments over the years 1979–81. The first allocation was given out in January 1979, and the U.K.'s share was S.D.R. 304m.

Changes of the Articles of Agreement of the I.M.F. agreed to in April 1978 had the effect of modifying the S.D.R. provisions. It was hoped to make them a principal reserve asset in the international monetary system. The main changes were as follows:

(a) Prior authority is no longer required from the I.M.F. for spot exchanges of S.D.R.s with participating members' currencies. The only condition is that the correct rate of exchange must be used. The ways in which S.D.R.s can be used has been expanded. They can be used for loans; as security in transfer-retransfer agreements; or in payment of debt. The use of S.D.R.s in swaps and forward transactions will be considered by the I.M.F. Board.

(b) From 1st January 1979, the minimum required level of average holdings over any five-year period was reduced to 15%. S.D.R.s may be held by 'official entities' such as international development institutions. So far, official institutions are using the S.D.R. more as a unit of account than a store of value.

15.1.6.2 *Valuation of the S.D.R.*

On 1 July 1978, a new valuation for the S.D.R. was introduced, based on statistics for the years 1972 – 1976. The weightings reflected the issuing countries' share of world trade except for the U.S.A., whose weighting was adjusted to reflect the importance of the dollar in world trade. Two currencies in the previous 'basket', the Danish krone and the South African rand were taken out. Two new currencies, the Saudi Arabian riyal and the Iranian rial joined the basket to bring the numbers up to the original 16. The relative weightings in the basket were also altered.

It was intended that the valuation should be adjusted at 5 year intervals beginning on 1 July 1983, and that the 16 member countries with the largest export of goods should be included. However, the I.M.F. decided that, as from 1 January 1981, the S.D.R. was to be valued against a basket of 5 currencies, not 16. They were, with their respective weightings, the U.S. dollar (42%), the German mark (19%), the French franc (13%), the Japanese yen (13%), and £ sterling (13%).

The change is expected to make the S.D.R. simpler to understand and more attractive to hold.

15.1.7 ASSESSMENTS OF THE I.M.F.

Criticisms of the I.M.F. naturally revolve round its lending policy. The I.M.F. has to ensure that there is sufficient liquidity for international trade, that adjustments in exchange rates can be smoothly made and that the confidence in the world's monetary system, and particularly in reserve currencies, is maintained. The I.M.F. treats but does not cure the cause of a country's deficit. Its 'medicine' may well depress another country which will need great reserve strength if it, too, is not to be brought low.

The second criticism of the I.M.F. is that action recommended for a debtor country may be so painful that it causes unfavourable side-effects. Living standards could fall precipitately. Suffering may ensue and lead to such a change in the body politic that the last state of the erstwhile patient is worse than the first.

The third criticism of the I.M.F. is that its medicine is always the same, which is hardly surprising as the sickness itself never changes, and neither (on the whole) do the physicians.

Other criticisms are more subjective, often with political overtones, e.g. the I.M.F. should/should not lend to those countries approved/disapproved by others. The main fault of the I.M.F., however, is that it has responsibility with power only over the weak, not the strong. Thus, there can be comment and report on exchange rate policies, nothing more though the second amendment allows for exchange-rate surveillance. The I.M.F. may cajole countries with surpluses, it cannot coerce them. These criticisms should not detract from some of the solid achievements.

For over 25 years, the I.M.F. supported fixed exchange rates, and so provided stability in international trade. If devaluations had been effected more quickly and less publicly, some of the worst speculative excesses could have been avoided. If further, creditor countries had revalued earlier, or imported more, large disequilibria in international payments could similarly have been avoided. But I.M.F. penalties for countries in persistent credit are, naturally, minimal. And countries in such a situation are unlikely to get domestic support for policy measures which will reverse the trend, unless the Government *and* the electorate are exceptionally liberal *and* rich.

The Fund has helped many countries out of balance of payments difficulties and, by 1968, it had lent over $14,000m to more than 40 countries.

It has provided a central meeting place where international monetary discussions can take place, and has been a constant source of advice for all members, whatever their state of economic development. Finally, the introduction of S.D.R.s has created a new monetary unit. This could take the place of a convertible currency as a unit of account or even a medium of exchange in the international monetary scene. But, as a store of value, gold is unlikely to be displaced by S.D.R.s, particularly during financial crises.

15.2 OTHER INTERNATIONAL MONETARY INSTITUTIONS

The I.M.F. is probably the best known of all the international monetary institutions. The *International Bank for Reconstruction and Development* comes a close second. The Fund acts like a bank, while the Bank acts like a fund. It provides resources for development projects throughout the world. *The International Finance Corporation* and the *International Development Association* operate in a similar way. Other international lending agencies have since been set up to arrange finance for development projects on a regional basis. Examples include the Asian, Caribbean, African and Inter-American Development Banks. The Kuwait Fund, established in 1961 was one of the earliest to offer loans for Arab, African and Asian projects. The oil revenues of the 1970s stimulated others in the same area.

The European Investment Bank makes funds available for various European schemes. It is described in Chapter 16. *The Bank for International Settlements* is more akin to the I.M.F. Its main purpose is not, as with the development banks, the provision of funds for regional growth, but of financial facilities mainly to industrialized central banks.

The work of the international lending agencies (or development banks) is summarized in Table 15.1 and is followed by descriptions, in more detail, of the World Bank, the I.D.A., I.F.C. and B.I.S.

15.3 THE WORLD BANK

The International Bank for Reconstruction and Development is commonly known as the World Bank. Set up as a result of the Bretton Woods Conference, it began operations in June 1946, with 58 member countries. Its

Table 15.1 Guide to International Agencies.

Name	First year of operation	Rate of loan approvals	Membership	Area of activity	General terms of loans*
World Bank International Bank for Reconstruction & Development (I.B.R.D.)	1946 (I.B.R.D.)	$8.4bn (1977 – 78)	132 countries including the U.K.	World-wide	Hard loans through I.B.R.D. Soft loans through I.D.A.
International Development Association (I.D.A.)	1960 (I.D.A.)				to poorest members.
African Development Bank/ Fund (A.f.D.B.)	1964 (Bank) 1972 (Fund)	$325.59m (1977) Priority given for projects involving several countries. Communications structure has received most loans.	47 countries including the U.K. Original membership: 29 African states	Independent African states	Hard loans through Bank. Soft loans through Fund to poorest members: interest-free for 50 years

Table 15.1 Guide to International Agencies. (cont'd)

Name	First year of operation	Rate of loan approvals	Membership	Area of activity	General terms of loans*
Asian Development Bank (A.D.B.)	1966	$775.90m (1976)	42 countries including the U.K. and 25 L.D.C.'s	South and South-East Asia Funds for development projects with technical aid for their formation and assistance	Hard loans to member countries Soft loans to poorer members.
Caribbean Development Bank (C.D.B.)	1970	$28.98m (1977)	20 countries including the U.K.	Caribbean	Hard loans to member countries Soft loans to poorest members
Inter-American Development Bank (I.D.B.)	1959	$1.86bn (1977)	41 countries including the U.K.	North and South America except Cuba	Hard loans to member countries Soft loans to poorest members
Abu Dhabi Fund for Arab Economic Development (A.D.F.A.E.D.)	1974	$169.5m (1976)	Abu Dhabi government	Arab Africa and Asia	Fairly hard loans.
Arab Bank for Economic Development in Africa (A.B.E.D.A/B.A.D.E.A.)	1974	$66.29m (1977)	Most members of the Arab League	Africa	Soft – medium loans

Name	First year of operation	Rate of loan approvals	Membership	Area of activity	General terms of loans*
Arab Fund for Economic and Social Development (A.F.E.S.D.)	1973	$350m (1977)	20 Arab states	Arab Africa and Asia	Soft – medium loans
Islamic Development Bank (Is.D.B.)	1975	$71m (1977)	27 Islamic states	Islamic world	Soft loans
Kuwait Fund for Arab Economic Development (K.F.A.E.D.)	1961	$265.6m (1977)	Kuwait Government	Arab Africa and Asia	Soft – medium loans
Saudi Fund for Development (S.F.D.)	1975	$382m (January – June 1977)	Saudi Government	Arab Africa and Asia	Soft-medium loans
European Development Fund IV (E.D.F.IV.)	1975	3.5bn Units of Account (about £2.4bn) to be disbursed between 1975 and 1980	E.E.C. countries including the U.K.	53 African, Caribbean and Pacific (ACP) countries worldwide	Mostly grants but some Soft loans

Table 15.1 Guide to International Agencies. (*cont'd*)

Name	First year of operation	Rate of loan approvals	Membership	Area of activity	General terms of loans*
Inter-American Development Bank	1959		Originally 22 American countries; Canada joined 1972; other countries including U.K. 1976		Loans to governments and public/private enterprises (repayable in currency lent for specific projects (10 – 25 year loans)

*Terms vary from bank to bank and from year to year. Hard loans resemble those available from commercial banks, but are used for funding high-risk or non-productive projects. Soft loans are usually long-term, low interest-bearing or interest-free (with a small annual service charge). They usually provide for generous 'grace periods' before repayments start.

Use of consultants by Bank/Fund	General terms of Consultants' tenders	General terms of suppliers' tenders	Further information
Employs own experts and outside consultants from time to time. Advises borrowers on employment of consultants and choice is subject to Bank's approval.	By international competitive tender. Consultants must register with: The Consultant Services Advisor, World Bank, 1818 H Street NW Washington DC 20433.	By international competitive tender. Details may be required from applicants regarding financial status and past experience.	*Monthly Operational Survey; Guidelines for Procurement; Use of Consultants by the World Bank.* Contact: World Bank, 66 avenue d'Iena, 75116 Paris.
Works closely with World Bank, employs own experts and outside consultants from time to time. Advises borrowers on employment of consultants.	By international competitive tender among member countries. Consultants must register in French with: Banque Africaine de Developpement, BP 1387, Abidjan, Ivory Coast.	By international competitive tender among member countries.	Contact: Banque Africaine de Developpement, BP 1387, Abidjan, Ivory Coast.
Works closely with the World Bank, employs own experts and outside consultants from time to time. Advises borrowers on employment of consultants and choice is subject to A.D.B. approval.	By international competitive tender among member countries. Consultants must register with: The Asian Development Bank, P.O.Box 789, Manila Philippines.	By international competitive tender among member countries.	*Guidelines for Procurement; Uses of Consultants;* Contact: The Information Office, Asian Development Bank, P.O.Box 789, Manila, Philippines.

Table 15.1 Guide to International Agencies. (*cont'd*)

Use of consultants by Bank/Fund	General terms of Consultants' tenders	General terms of suppliers' tenders	Further information
Works closely with the World Bank, employs own experts and outside consultants from time to time.	By international competitive tender among member countries. Consultants must register with: The Caribbean Development Bank, P.O.Box 408, Bridgetown, Barbados.	By international competitive tender among member countries. Suppliers must register with: The Caribbean Development Bank, P.O.Box 408, Bridgetown, Barbados.	*Guidelines for Procurement; Guidelines for choice of Consultants;* Contact: The Information Office, Caribbean Development Bank, P.O.Box 408, Bridgetown, Barbados.
Works closely with the World Bank employs own experts and outside consultants from time to time.	By international competitive tender among member countries. Consultants must register with: The Office of Professional Services, Inter-American Development Bank, 808 17th Street NW, Washington DC 20577.	By international competitive tender among member countries.	*Guidelines for Procurement; Use of Consulting Firms;* Contact: Office of Information Inter-American Development Bank, 808 17th Street NW. Washington DC 20577.

Use of consultants by Bank/Fund	General terms of Consultants' tenders	General terms of suppliers' tenders	Further information
The Arab funds work closely with each other and with I.L.A.s, notably the World Bank and the African Development Bank. For some time they channelled the vast majority of their funds through other established agencies, but they have been rapidly establishing their own appraisal and consultative apparatus. Now all the Arab funds have their own experts, employ outside consultants from time to time and advise borrowers on their choice of consultants.	Procedural rules and regulations are generally at the discretion of the borrowing government. Consultants and suppliers must be confident that they can fulfil the requirements demanded from all potential traders with the Middle East and Arab countries, especially that they are not included on any trading boycott list. Consultants are not always obliged to register but it is advised that they make their interests known.		Contact: Information Officer, A.D.F.A.E.D., P.O.Box 814, Abu Dhabi, Contact: B.A.D.E.A.,, P.O.Box 2640, Khartoum, Sudan. Contact: Information Office, A.F.E.S.D., P.O.Box 21923, Kuwait. Contact: Information Office, Islamic Development Bank, P.O.Box 5925, Jeddah, Saudi Arabia.

Table 15.1 Guide to International Agencies. (cont'd)

Use of consultants by Bank/Fund	General terms of Consultants' tenders	General terms of suppliers' tenders	Further information
			Contact: Director General, Kuwait Fund for Arab Economic Development, P.O.Box 2921, Kuwait.
			Contact: The Director, Saudi Fund for Development, P.O.Box 5711, Riyadh, Saudi Arabia
E.D.F.IV is administered through the European Commission mainly through its delegations throughout the world. Delegations and the Commission use own experts and outside consultants from time to time. Advises borrowers on choice of consultants and the choice is subject to Commission's approval.	By international competitive tender among E.E.C and A.C.P. states. Consultants must register with: Director General Directorate General VIII, (European Development Fund), 200 rue de la Loi, Brussels 1040, Belgium.	By international competitive tender among E.E.C. and A.C.P. states.	*Journal of European Community; Access to Contracts; Programme of Projects; The Courier;* Contact: Centre for Industrial Development, 451 Avenue George Henri, 1200 Brussels, Belgium.

first aim was to provide finance for the countries devastated by World War Two. John Maynard Keynes emphasized this in his opening address at the first meeting of the Bretton Woods Commission on the Bank: "It is likely, in my judgement, that the field of reconstruction from the consequences of war will mainly occupy the proposed Bank in its early days. But as soon as possible and with increasing emphasis as time goes on, there is a second primary duty laid upon it, namely to develop the resources and productive capacity of the world, with special reference to the less developed countries."

The Bank's current aims are the economic development and an increased standard of living for its members, and the long-term growth of international trade, primarily by providing loans for specific projects with related technical assistance.

15.3.1 STRUCTURE

The bank's membership consists of *governments*: 134 of them around the world. Subscriptions to the Bank's capital stock are based on each member's quota in the I.M.F. Every member has 250 votes plus an extra vote for each additional $100,000 of capital stock subscribed. Voting rights were altered in 1979 when the Bank's authorized capital stock was increased by $40,000m. Each member country was given an additional 250 shares without any increase in subscription. Though the shares did not count as part of the Bank's capital base for purposes of lending authority, they increased the voting power of the smaller and poorer countries. Only 7.5% of the increase in the authorized $40,000m was to be paid in, with 92.5% to be called in if required by the Bank to meet its obligations on borrowings.

15.3.2 SOURCES OF FUNDS

The Bank is corporate in form. Member governments own its capital stock. Part only of this capital is paid in. The remainder can be called up, if required, to meet liabilities arising out of borrowing or guaranteeing loans. This financial structure provides the Bank with loan resources from its paid-up capital as well as guarantees for securities which can be sold to private investors. Capital issues are the Bank's largest single source of funds. A substantial contribution to the Bank's resources also comes from its retained earnings and the repayment flows from loans.

15.3.3 LENDING POLICY

Because the Bank relies mainly upon private investors for its financial resources, there are restrictions on its lending. Without these safeguards, the Bank would find it difficult, if not impossible, to raise the funds needed to implement its policy. The safeguards emphasize that:

(a) The Bank's loans must be for high priority productive purposes and used to meet the foreign exchange requirements of specific (not general) projects.

(b) If the borrower is other than a government, the loan must be guaranteed by the member country in whose territory the project is to be located or by its central bank or comparable agency.

(c) The Bank must pay regard to whether the borrower or guarantor will be able to fulfil the obligations undertaken.

(d) The Bank must be satisfied that the borrower cannot raise the capital reasonably elsewhere.

(e) 'Tied' loans are prohibited so that no conditions must be imposed which require loans to be spent in any particular country or countries.

(f) Only economic considerations should govern the Bank's decisions; it must not be influenced by the political character of the member or members concerned.

15.3.4 EARLY ACHIEVEMENTS OF THE BANK

In spite of the restrictions imposed on its lending policy, and the charging of near-market rates for its loans, the World Bank achieved a great deal in its first 20 years of operation. By the end of 1967, it had helped the reconstruction of Europe, and made 527 loans totalling over $10,000m in 82 countries. Asia and the Middle East accounted for $4215m, and electric power development absorbed more borrowing than any other sector.

Criticisms of the Bank are that

(a) Its lending policy is too 'safe'.

(b) Loans should not only be for specific projects.

(c) Interest charges are too high.

(d) Voting strength is largely in the hands of the richest nations with 500 million people, while the 6 poorest nations (and the most populous) have only 8% of the votes.

(e) Emphasis has been placed mainly on industrial activities to get the largest return on capital employed. This gives little share in development benefits to the poorest groups.

15.3.5 ASSESSMENT OF THE WORLD BANK

The World Bank is an international institution whose main purpose is the economic development of its members by the provision of loans. It naturally suffers from the problem of having too many wanting to borrow, too few wishing to lend. Some of its earlier defects such as the necessity for government guarantee on loans and a higher rate of interest to poorer countries than charity. . .or even justice. . .demanded, are being remedied by affiliate organizations such as the I.D.A. and the I.F.C.

More has been spent on *agriculture*. During the 17 years from 1946 to 1963, a total of $456m was spent on agricultural projects. Since 1970, that sum has been spent on agricultural projects *every year*, and for 1979, the sum expended was $2,521m. *Education* took $5m between 1946 and 1963; $157m between 1964 and 1968; and a total of $496m in 1979.

The above allocations reflect a new direction in the Bank's *lending policy*. Until 1964, a third of its lending was to the developed countries. Between 1964 and 1968, two-thirds of the total lending went on infrastructure projects (transport, power, communication), whereas today the largest proportion goes into rural development, industry, education, water supply, nutrition and population projects as part of a direct attack on poverty.

The old 'trickle-down' spending (so called because it was hoped that benefits from capital intensive projects would trickle down to the poor), has been abandoned. The emphasis is now on direct participation, with the linking of health and farming and family welfare in the centre of planning. There has been a gradual phasing out too, of aid to 'richer' countries, (those with per capita income above $1000 a year) in favour of the poorest countries, particularly since the *'Third Window'* scheme proposed in January 1975. This provides terms for development aid halfway between those charged by the World Bank, and its soft-loan affiliate, the I.D.A.

A further change has been in *recruitment*. In 1968 the percentage of professional staff from developing countries was around 20%. In 1979, of the total specialist level staff in the Bank, 32.5% were nationals from the developing countries.

Too much cannot be expected of one institution. Even if the developing countries doubled their per capita growth rate, and that of the industrial countries remained static, it would still take a century to close the absolute income gap between them. The Third World nations have achieved together a very great growth rate in the past 25 years. Though their population increased by 1000 million, income per head rose at an average annual rate of 3.4% between 1950 and 1975. If China is excluded, the growth rate drops to 3%. The industrialized nations during the same rich period, had an estimated average growth rate of 3.2%.

Social progress has also improved in the Third World. Average life expectancy has moved up from 40 to 50 years, a rate of progress that took the industrialized nations 100 years to achieve. And though population has grown, there is rather more food available than previously; more children attend primary schools; literacy has increased and so has calorie consumption. When Robert Macnamara, President of the World Bank, pointed out this paradox at the joint annual meeting of the I.M.F. and the I.B.D.R. in 1977, he emphasized that 'closing the gap' between poor and rich nations was never a feasible objective. The uneven growth between different developing nations was similar to the huge disparity between the rich and poor countries, per capita incomes which at its extremes ranges in money terms to more than $8000 per capita.

The aims therefore of the World Bank should not be to close the gap between the high incomes enjoyed in the west, and the poor ones obtaining in the developing countries. It should be, so Mr. Macnamara averred, a 'basic needs' approach: providing essentials like food, health services, education and similar programmes by trying directly to raise employment, income and productivity levels of the poorest social groups.

Through its own resources and those of its affiliate bodies, the I.D.A. and the I.F.C., the Bank has shown ingenuity and administrative finesse in helping to solve some of the economic problems of its members. By 1979, loans and disbursements amounted to over $10,000m for 142 approved operations. They were for drainage, irrigation, for rural development and education, for water supply and sewerage, the construction of ports and electric power stations, for tourism and teacher training. This is no mean achievement.

15.3.6 INTERLINKED MEMBERSHIP

Legally and financially, the two affiliates of the World Bank, namely the I.D.A and I.F.C., are separate but linked institutions. Only members of the I.M.F. can be members of the World Bank, and only members of the World Bank can be members of the I.D.A. and I.F.C.

The President of the Bank is chairman of the Board of Directors of I.D.A. and I.F.C. The Governors and Executive Directors of the Bank also serve on the I.D.A. and I.F.C. (if their countries are members of both institutions.) The I.F.C. has its own operating and legal staff; but shares the Bank's administrative and other services. The I.D.A. and the Bank have the same staff.

15.4 THE INTERNATIONAL FINANCE CORPORATION

The World Bank's Articles require it to obtain a government guarantee for loans to private enterprise. Business men are not always willing to accept these loans, even on the rare occasions when governments are willing or able to provide them. Furthermore, the Bank makes loans on fixed interest terms and cannot subscribe to equity shares or similar risk capital.

For these reasons, the International Finance Corporation was established in 1956 to supplement the work of the Bank. Its aim is to stimulate investment in the less developed countries by investing, without government guarantee, in private enterprise with private investors.

The I.F.C.'s loans can cover up to a maximum of 50% of the cost of the enterprise, though 25% is the usual amount. Competent management must be assured and the I.F.C. exercises no voting rights. The I.F.C. recoups its funds by selling its holdings to private investors when the project reaches fruition.

As well as providing finance for investment, the I.F.C. also acts as an underwriter. Like the Bank, it has powers to raise funds on the world's capital markets. It began with an authorized capital of $100 million, and 85 members. By 1967, it had invested over $240m in 36 different countries. By 1979, membership had increased to 109 countries.

Its functions can be summed up as follows:

(a) It provides equity and loan capital for private enterprise in association with private capital.

(b) It stimulates the international flow of private risk captial.

(c) It encourages the development of local capital markets.

(d) By providing technical assistance and finance with local knowledge, the I.F.C. helps to develop entrepreneurial and managerial talent.

15.5 THE INTERNATIONAL DEVELOPMENT ASSOCIATION (I.D.A.)

Soon after the World Bank was set up, it became obvious that many countries were going to need external borrowings on cheaper terms than those available from the Bank. The emergence of newly independent countries in Africa in the early 1960s further emphasized this need. They lacked the credit rating of the Powers with which they were formerly associated, yet needed finance on concessionary terms. It was to fulfil this need of cheap long-term loans for priority projects in developing countries, that the International Development Association began operations in 1960.

Loans can be up to 50 years. There is often no interest charge; only a service charge of under 1% with an initial ten-year grace period. Thus, a loan made to India in 1962 for the expansion of electrical power required no repayment before 1972, then 1% of the principal per annum for ten years, then 3% for the final 30 years. The general idea behind these loans is to delay repayment until the completion of the project, and then to spread them over its productive life.

By mid 1979, I.D.A.'s lending resources which goes on concessionary terms to the world's poorest countries only, amounted to $3021.5m. Subscriptions of the 121 member countries provide some part of the I.D.A.'s finances. Developed (Part 1) and developing members (Part 2) pay differing subscriptions, and loans are made only to governments. Further resources come from grants made by the World Bank and the sale of I.D.A. credits. Because of the uncommercial terms charged for loans, it is thought impracticable to raise funds from private investors, and the I.D.A. relies primarily on its richer members for funds.

Joint financing by the World Bank, the I.D.A. and government lenders increases the flow of capital to developing countries and promotes its more effective use. Such co-financing of Bank-supported and I.D.A.-supported projects amounted to $3,248m in fiscal 1979, $469m up on the previous year.

15.6 THE BANK FOR INTERNATIONAL SETTLEMENTS

1929 was the year when the U.S. index of common stocks began its fall from 225 in September, 1929 (1926 = 100) to 32 in June, 1932. Meanwhile, Austria's largest bank had suspended payments; German banks soon followed, and in March 1933, all American banks closed, opening only gradually when they could show they could meet their liabilities.

Against that dismal background, the Bank for International Settlements was conceived. Dr H.Jalmar Schacht, interwar head of the German Reichsbank, but then an unappreciated monetary genius, helped to pioneer the establishment of the Bank. It was set up in 1930, conveniently in a hotel by the rail junction at Basle, Switzerland. By 1931, central banks from 21 European countries including Latvia, Lithuania and Estonia were shareholders.

Although around 25% of its shareholdings are held privately, the Bank is an institution owned by *central banks* and its directors are all governors of central banks. Members include central banks from every country in east and west Europe, except the Soviet Union, East Germany and Albania. The U.S.A., Canada, Japan, Australia, and South Africa are also members.

The first aim of B.I.S. was a purely practical one: to administer the refunding of Germany's reparation payments of the post-1914 war (the Dawes Loan, 1924 and the Young Loan, 1930). The annual reports of B.I.S. used to include a section on the management of these early debt-refunding operations. Theorists and practising bankers later developed other, usually conflicting aims: The Bank should provide loans and stabilization aid; it should be a super central bank. B.I.S. itself suggested that it should act as an agency for bookkeeping transfers anticipating similar ideas set forth some decades later by Professor Triffin.

World economic opinion was not yet ready for an international central bank. B.I.S. remained in the background providing short-term bridging loans. Recipients in the past decade include the central banks of the U.K., Portugal, Turkey, Belgium and Sweden. The Bank is forbidden by statute to lend money to governments. It supervised the various loans to the European Coal and Steel Community. It became the technical agent for the European Payments Union which began in 1950 as a financial clearing arrangement between the various European countries. During the series of currency crises in the 1960s, the Bank arranged financing facilities which helped countries suffering from speculative and other outflows.

The outflows were relent by the creditor country to the debtor for three months; alternatively the creditor bank agreed not to convert the received currency into its own. Both methods lessened the impact of a heavy withdrawal of funds on a countries' reserves. The first such financing arrangement followed the revaluation of the mark in 1961 and the consequent drain on sterling.

Such 'swap' arrangements were used several times thereafter — hurriedly in 1961 (more formally in 1968 and 1972) either in standby arrangements or as reciprocal credits. They continued up to the standby credit of 1977, the object of which was to phase the sterling balances smoothly away from Britain. B.I.S. agreed to provide a $3bn medium-term standby credit facility to the Bank of England if the sterling balances fell below $2165m.

B.I.S.'s functions as trustee for reparation payments was suspended in

1931 under the Hoover Moratorium. Its main functions are now (a) to encourage co-operation between central banks by monthly meetings of directors (b) to provide facilities for international co-operation. Examples are the help given to the central banks of Austria, Hungary and Yugoslavia in 1931; the 'safety net' for sterling (described above) in 1977. (c) To act as agent for various international agencies. It has acted so for the Universal Postal Union, the International Telecommunication Union, and the European Coal and Steel Community. It also acts as an agent for the short-term support mechanism of the European Economic Community, administering financial transactions of the European Monetary Compensation Fund.

B.I.S. publishes monthly statistics on the Euro-currency short-term market and takes an active role in the gold and Euro-currency markets. Its balance sheet is expressed in 1930 gold Swiss francs and in 1980 totalled $45bn. Its liabilities of $40bn are mostly from central banks. The advantages of B.I.S. to the countries using its facilities are: (a) Anonymity, for central banks do not always wish to advertise the movement of their funds, particularly during times of crisis. (b) Risk spreading, for the deposits of the B.I.S. are highly liquid: 77% of the B.I.S. assets have maturities of under three months, and deposits placed with the B.I.S. usually can be withdrawn at under two days' notice.

The constitution is somewhat odd. Voting rights are reserved forever to the central banks of the countries where the shares were orginally issued, in spite of what wars and other crises may have done to the countries since. None of the developing countries is a member, not even the oil-exporting countries, but this may be remedied in time. In spite of these defects, the B.I.S. has done much useful work since its inception. In its annual report, it provides an outspoken analysis of the year's successes in economic and financial policy.

The Bank has shown ingenuity in re-routing international monetary flows and so helped to avert or soften the impact of monetary crises.

TYPICAL QUESTION

Assess the role played by special drawing rights in the contemporary international financial system. Do you agree that they will eventually become the principal international reserve asset? Give reasons for your answer.

SUGGESTED ANSWER

In the 1960s the reserve held by countries for settling international balances was thought to be insufficient for the growing volume of world trade. A device was sought for increasing world liquidity. Special Drawing Rights seemed to be the answer. They were introduced on 1 January 1970. Until then, all borrowings from the I.M.F. had to be repaid. Only part of the new drawing rights had to be repaid. The rest was, in effect, a newly created asset. The Fund was acting like a bank in *creating* money. The first distribution of SDRs, agreed by the IMF at its 24th annual meeting in September 1969, amounted to $9,500 million. Of this, $3,500 million was distributed in 1970, the rest spread over 1971 and 1972. The U.K.'s allocation was $410 million.

The S.D.R.s could be used in three ways: (a) added to a country's gold and exchange reserves, (b) used by central banks to settle debts directly with each other, and (c) used by central banks through the I.M.F. with the Fund designating a particular country to receive the S.D.R.s in exchange for its own currency.

In whichever the way the S.D.R.s were used, they were all subject to a 70% rule, i.e. countries were allowed to keep an average of 70% of the S.D.R.s they were credited with over the three-year period. Britain had $410 million S.D.R.s but, of that amount, 70% was a permanent addition to her reserves; the rest was a temporary loan that had to be repaid.

When S.D.R.s were first issued they were given a value of one U.S. dollar defined in gold terms*. The dollar was devalued in December 1971 and floating currencies – with some exceptions such as the European snake – took the place of Bretton Woods fixed exchange system. In 1974, S.D.R.s were therefore also 'floated'. They became a unit made up of a 'basket' of 16 major currencies each of which had a share of 7% or more in world trade. In 1981 the 16 currencies were pared down to 5. The S.D.R. is now sometimes used as a unit of account for international payments so that buyers and sellers receive or give amounts equal to the value of S.D.R.s in whichever currency they agree to use.

Another issue of S.D.R.s was made in January 1979 and further instalments are planned to 1981. The development of the S.D.R. as an international unit of account is increasing.

ADDITIONAL QUESTIONS

1. Describe the methods by which the International Bank for Reconstruction and Development seeks to achieve its present-day purposes (ignoring its role in post-war reconstruction) and to overcome the problems it has encountered.

2. Write brief notes on the Bank for International Settlements.

3. Describe the operations and financing of the World Bank (International Bank for Reconstruction and Development) and its subsidiaries.

4. How does the IMF obtain the funds which it makes available to member countries in balance-of-payments difficulties? Are the resources which it can use sufficient to meet potential demands for assistance?

---

* 0.8887 grams ≡ U.S. $1.

5. Write an account of the role of S.D.R.s (special drawing rights) in the international monetary system over the past ten years.

6. Write short notes on. . .IMF quotas.

16 The Common Market: Economic and Monetary Union

Many people have dreamed of European unity. The 20th century effort towards the union of Western Europe took a big leap forward with the formation of a financial clearing arrangement, the European Payments Union, between six European countries in 1950. Today there are legally three European communities. They share the same institutions.

(a) *The European Coal and Steel Community* was set up by the Paris Treaty, April 18, 1951. It began work on August 10th, 1952 by placing the coal and steel of the six founder members into a single common market.

(b) *The European Atomic Energy Community (Euratom)* was set up by the Rome Treaty, 25 March 1957, to promote peaceful uses of nuclear energy in the Community.

(c) *The European Economic Community* was set up by a second Rome Treaty, 25 March 1957. It began work on January 1, 1958 with Euratom to remove economic barriers between members and integrate their economic policies. Denmark, Ireland and the United Kingdom joined the three communities on 1 January 1973. The progressive abolition of tariffs between them and the original six was completed by 1977 and the customs union finalized by July 1978. The U.K. introduced freedom for capital movement in 1979.

16.1 INSTITUTIONS OF THE EUROPEAN COMMUNITY

The Community is basically a free trade area with a common external tariff (C.E.T.) on manufactured goods and variable import levies on agricultural products. It has the following institutions:

The European Commission which consists of 13 members, two each from France, Germany, Italy and the UK, one each from Belgium, Denmark, Ireland, Luxembourg and the Netherlands. They are appointed jointly by member governments for four year renewable terms. The President and five Vice-Presidents hold office for two years, renewable.

The Council of Ministers takes final decisions after consulting the *European Parliament* and the *Economic and Social Committee* and after discussion in the *Committee of Permanent Representatives.*

The Court of Justice is the ultimate court of appeal. It is a supreme court of nine individual judges assisted by four advocates-general. They are all appointed jointly by member states for six-year renewable terms, and deal with disputes between all sections of the Community and its members under the Community Treaties.

16.2 ECONOMIC AND SOCIAL POLICIES OF THE COMMUNITY

Member states finance the economic and social policies of the Community from their own resources.

A cutoms-free trading area of over 250m people (more than the U.S.A. or U.S.S.R.) should benefit its members through (a) economies of scale, (b) a guaranteed market and (c) increased competition. Faster economic growth might be expected but, in fact, the G.N.P. of the Common Market is little more than half the U.S.A. figure.

Pioneers of European unity hoped that a common currency would fulfil their economic aspirations more quickly. Their hopes naturally rose when the customs union between the six founder members was completed in 1968, 18 months earlier than the Treaty of Rome had envisaged.

16.3 THE COMMON AGRICULTURAL POLICY AND GREEN CURRENCIES

The Common Agricultural Policy should have been a further unifying force. Its aims included (a) 'a fair standard of living for the farming community. . .' and (b) the stabilization of markets. (Articles 39/40/ and 44 of the Treaty of Rome). In the U.K. before E.E.C. entry, these aims were achieved by (a) deficiency payments to make up the difference between an adequate income for the farmer and the market price of his produce and (b) subsidies to reduce the cost of production.

Such arrangements were administratively too cumbersome for the E.E.C. countries. Intervention payments fixed by the Council of Ministers were therefore devised to provide a 'floor' for farm prices. The farmer who could not get this price in the open market would sell to the intervention agency and so get a guaranteed minimum for his produce. The intervention agencies stored the produce until the price recovered. If it didn't, they were left with 'butter mountains' and 'wine lakes'; or perishable food such as fruit or wheat. These had to be 'dumped' or made fit only for animals or manu-facturing. . .to prevent fraud after subsidies had been paid.

Imports from outside the E.E.C. were subject to a levy. The levy raised prices to a threshold where they did not undercut the price of produce grown in the E.E.C. There was no common currency in the E.E.C. The Council of Ministers invented an artificial pricing unit known as a *unit of account.* They used this to calculate intervention and threshold prices. The unit of account (ua) had the worth of 0.88867088 grammes of fine gold. It could be converted into member states' currencies through their respective gold parities. (Art 2: Regn.129/62)

Examples

French franc

(a) 1 ua = 0.88867088 grammes of fine gold.

1 French franc = 0.18 grammes of fine gold, i.e. $\dfrac{0.18}{0.88867088}$

ua = 0.2025496 ua

1 ua = $\dfrac{1}{0.2025496}$ = $\underline{4.93706 \text{ francs}}$

German mark

(b) 1 German mark = 0.222168 grammes of fine gold, i.e. $\dfrac{0.222168}{0.88867088}$

ua = 0.25 ua

1 ua = 4 German marks.

French franc and German mark

(c) 1 German mark = $\dfrac{0.25}{0.2025496}$ French francs = 1.234655 French francs.

The unit of account system worked well for 5 years but, in 1969, the French franc was devalued from 0.18 to 0.16 grammes of gold. This meant that 1 unit of account was worth 5.55419 francs instead of the 4.93706 (1962) rate. The effect of this change on the pricing system of, e.g. sugar, can be seen as follows. The intervention price for 1 tonne of sugar was 212.30 ua. At pre-devaluation prices this meant 212.30 × 4.93706 French francs (or 212.30 ua × = 849.20 German marks.) = 1048.14 francs. But at the new gold price of 0.16 grammes, the exchange price for 1 tonne of sugar became 212.30 × 5.55419 francs = 1179.15 francs.

Such a price change for sugar (and other farm produce) could have led to massive inflation in France. So the first 'green' currency, the green franc, was introduced. It treated the unit of account as if the franc had not been devalued. There was an obvious complication to this arrangement: what of the German farmer? At the new rate of 0.16 grammes of gold for a French franc, the German mark now equalled $\dfrac{0.16}{0.88867088}$ = 1.3885486 francs, and not as pre-devaluation: 1 mark = 1.234655 francs. French produce (in this case, sugar) became more competitively priced than the German. It exchanged at $\dfrac{1048.14}{1.3885486}$ = 754.84 marks which at the old (green) rate was 931.67965 francs against the intervention price of 1048.14 francs. By contrast, the German farmer had to sell his sugar in France at 1179.15 francs to get the equivalent of the German intervention price of 849.20 marks.

To compensate for these disparities, Regulation 1586/69 established fixed levies on French exports to other E.E.C. countries with fixed refunds for imports from other E.E.C. countries into France. These monetary compensation amounts (M.C.A.'s) were meant originally to be only a temporary measure to phase price changes over a two-year period rather than overnight. But Germany revalued the mark later that year and the 'green mark' then came in. Like the green franc, it temporarily kept the old exchange rate. M.C.A.'s increased German import prices by levy and reduced their export prices by subsidy (for the foreign exchange rate of the mark was above the green rate.)

Thereafter, came many changes in rates: of the gold parity; from fixed to floating, with further complications caused by the entry of three new member states. When the mark floated upwards in 1971, *variable M.C.A.'s* were created. These applied only when the disparity between the spot exchange rate and the green rate of any currency exceeded 2.5%, and were used mainly between the U.K., Ireland and Italy. After the second dollar devaluation in 1973, the *Special Drawing Right* replaced the dollar as an international accounting unit. It was fixed at 0.88867088 grammes of fine gold (the 1962 gold parity of the dollar). The E.E.C. unit of account was expressed in SDR's as were the joint float currencies (see The Snake in the Tunnel).

M.C.A.'s are now recalculated weekly to offset changes in actual exchange rates. But further disparities have arisen with the Community budget. Contributions to this are not based on a country's G.N.P. and so comparatively poor countries by E.E.C. standards may make the biggest net contribution to the Budget. Britain was faced with a net contribution to the E.E.C. Budget for 1980 of £1004m, the largest contribution, though the third poorest EEC country.

16.4 THE GREEN POUND

The market exchange rate of the pound against the joint float currencies fell around 40% over the 5 years to 31 December, 1977. The unit of account was not adjusted to reflect this change, partly because food prices in the U.K. were much lower than in the E.E.C. and it was agreed to phase them upwards in transitional steps over a five-year period. While the market exchange rate fell by 40%, the green pound fell by only 20%.

A depreciating currency normally makes imports dearer and exports cheaper. But if the relative green currency is overvalued, the level of support prices is reduced. This was the case with the 'green' pound. Sterling intervention prices were below those of their German equivalents. U.K. consumers gained; U.K. farmers lost. Harder still for U.K. farmers was the fact that imports of raw materials such as fertilisers and machinery were priced at the spot exchange rate. M.C.A. levies on U.K. prices reduced their competitiveness; M.C.A. subsidies on German/French farm products made them more competitive in other Community markets. The M.C.A. was payable when the cargo passed customs. As it could vary from week to week, forward pricing became difficult.

The Common Agricultural Policy is faced with two basic problems: how to protect (a) consumers in countries with depreciating currencies from the inflationary effects of rising import prices and (b) farmers in countries with strong currencies from the effects of cheap foreign competition. The green currency (pound, lire etc) was used as a representative rate with Monetary Compensation Amounts as taxes on exports and duties on imports. It was hoped that the green rate would protect farmers from cheap imports and consumers from rising food prices.

16.5 THE ADVANTAGES OF E.E.C. MEMBERSHIP

Some writers have tried to assess the cost of E.E.C. membership in terms of food prices. Britain has gained in terms of cheap food, but could Britain have bought more cheaply on world markets? Perhaps E.E.C. prices are too high because they are linked to a strong currency in the Community, and one whose farmers' lobby is politically powerful. By 1980, the Common Agricultural Policy still accounted for 75% of the Community budget, so there is a strong demand for fundamental reform by the British, whose highly efficient farmers account for only $2\frac{1}{2}$% of their workforce. Meanwhile countries with a large farming community such as Germany and France, desire only minor adjustments to the C.A.P.

The Community Budget is another source of British discontent with Common Market policies. The Community raises its revenue from (a) the common external tariff on manufactured goods imported from outside the E.E.C., (b) import levies on food imported from outside the E.E.C. and (c) a proportion up to 1% of member countries V.A.T.

As Britain is a heavy importer of food and manufactured goods from outside the E.E.C., her contribution to the E.E.C. budget is high.

Britain's net contribution to the E.E.C. budget 1973—1980

Year		£m.	% G.D.P.
1973		111	0.2
1974		37	0.1
1975		−45	−0.1
1976		178	0.2
1977		481	0.4
1978		822	0.6
1979	(forecast)	829	0.5
1980	(forecast)	1,199	0.7

Other difficulties for Britain which have made the cost of E.E.C. membership seem high are that Britain's fishing industry interests conflict with those of the E.E.C. Countries' exclusive fishing zones will rise to 200 miles instead of the former 12 miles from their coasts from 1982, unless some compromise is reached. There is no coherent energy policy. Britain is in an advantageous position with regard to oil supplies compared with the rest of the Community.

Nevertheless the aims of the E.E.C are 'to strengthen the safeguards of peace and liberty to establishing this combination of resources.' Britain, along with the other Community members, gains from being a member of a supranational block. Whether this is worth the 1980 price of 0.7% of G.D.P depends on an analysis of the opportunity costs involved.

16.6 EFFORTS AT MONETARY UNION

16.6.1 THE WERNER REPORT

The Werner Report, published in 1971, formed the basis for discussion of economic and monetary union within the Community.

It wanted: (a) Convertibility of currencies.
(b) Fixed exchange rates with irrevocable parities and no margin of flexibility.
(c) Co-ordination of demand policies among governments.
(d) Free movement of capital.

There was little progress towards these aims. National governments, even in a customs union, have different priorities on employment and inflation, as recent German and British statistics show.

The Werner Report's recommendation of a fixed exchange rate assumed a common level of inflation amongst members. This prediction proved woefully false. Rigid exchange rates only work if surplus countries make 'swap' arrangements with their weaker neighbours. Swaps involve the exchange of national currencies at a fixed exchange rate for a short period of time. The exchange rate is fixed at the beginning of the deal; the currency is paid back at the same rate at the conclusion. Such swaps are only feasible if the period of time is short and if the borrowed currency does not fall too precipitately in the foreign exchange market. With different speculative stresses at work in the early Community, 'swaps' (or any other attempt at recycling), might have strained the bonds of membership to breaking point.

The Werner Report, in effect, asked nations to surrender the right to make national policy decisions. Europe was a long way from this ideal, so the Report was never implemented. The emphasis on exchange rate unification did, however, provide the theory for the European 'snake'.

16.6.2 THE SNAKE IN THE TUNNEL

The Smithsonian Agreement of December 1971, brought forth an odd progeny, the European snake. Parties to the Agreement in Washington, had accepted a margin of $2\frac{1}{4}$ % each side of a central rate. But if a country at the top of the band, changed places with a country at the bottom of the band, the actual movement of those 2 currencies against each other (their 'cross parity') would be a fluctuation of 9% (a total of $4\frac{1}{2}$ % down and $4\frac{1}{2}$ % up) (Figure 16.1).

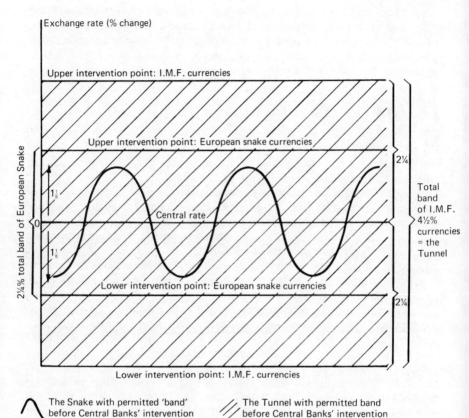

Figure 16.1 The 'snake in the tunnel'.

The E.E.C. countries decided therefore to limit fluctuation between their currencies to $1\frac{1}{8}$ % either side of a central rate: a total band of $2\frac{1}{4}$ %. Within this narrower band, the E.E.C. currencies floated as a group against the American dollar in the Smithsonian 'tunnel'. Britain, Denmark and Norway joined the snake in May 1972. Britain left in June 1972 and floated thereafter. Italy followed Britain in February 1973. In March 1973, the snake soared upwards out of the dollar tunnel.

The European snake worked in the following way: When the parity between two snake currencies appeared as if it would exceed the agreed limit, the central banks intervened. They bought the depreciating currency or lent the appreciating one. If the debtor country could not repay the short-term intervention loan before settlement day, other reserve assets could be used in an agreed formula.

By 1978, the snake had become almost a deutschmark bloc. The French franc came out between June 1974 and July 1975, and again in 1976. The krone from an 'associate' member, Sweden, left in August 1977, and Austria, which had kept in line with the deutschmark from 1976, went its own way thereafter. By 1978, the snake included only the Benelux countries (which originally had even narrower margins than the snake), Denmark, Norway and West Germany. But the wide margins in inflation rates of the different countries narrowed. The trend continued, and, in 1979, those who had dropped out from the snake with the exception of the U.K. returned to give it the kiss of life.

16.6.3 THE TINDEMANS REPORT

In 1976, came a new drive towards E.M.U. (economic and monetary union). The Belgian Prime Minister suggested in a report that the weaker E.E.C. brethren, among whom were included Britain, Italy and Ireland, should be allowed to lag behind the stronger powers. This two-tier Community would have common foreign policies. All nine members should join the snake as a prelude to E.M.U.

Britain, as a potential candidate for the lower class tier, naturally enough rejected the two-tier structure. The other low-rated powers were equally unenthusiastic. They argued that such a two-tier system would break the Community. Those who lost their economic strength, would soon lose their political muscle as well.

16.6.4 A SINGLE CURRENCY: A EUROPA?

Several economists have suggested a single currency for Europe. Regional subsidies could help depressed areas. Others disagree. They point to the fact that national currencies such as the pound or the lira do not help the 'depressed' regions of the U.K or Italy. Subsidies aid the relief of poverty. They do not cure the situations which created the regional poverty in the first place.

Those who want a single European currency like the idea of it being issued by a central bank (B.I.S., E.I.B., I.M.F.?). A 'Europa' could circulate alongside each E.E.C. national currency. Citizens could exchange the Europa for their own currency at a variable exchange rate. This overcomes the rigidities of a fixed exchange rate while allowing the purchasing power of a national currency to find its true rate. Countries with high inflation and who are therefore liable to suffer from severe recession during the transition period, could be helped by regional subsidies.

The depression in world trade, currency crisis within the E.E.C. and the dollar's depreciation all caused E.E.C. to recede as a short-term policy objective. The Cambridge school of economists argued for import controls; the

Mediterranean countries such as Greece and Portugal and Spain wanted to join the Community. Such ideas. . .and expansion might have lessened the impetus towards monetary union.

Roy Jenkins, President of the European Commission in 1978 differed. A vocal protagonist for monetary union, he argued that both Europe and the world must gain from the creation of a common European currency. It provided the opportunity to tackle inflation on a united front. The related problems of economic activity and regional inbalances could be more easily overcome. The centralization of a European monetary authority would be counterbalanced by less centralization in other areas. Finally, greater monetary integration led to greater political integration.

His ideas and those of other monetary unionists eventually won through. The chairman of the E.E.C.'s monetary committee, Mr Jacques van Ypersele, suggested a new snake in April 1978. He wanted intervention to be in E.E.C. currencies and the E.E.C. to double its short-term lending facilities. The Big Four E.E.C. countries should agree on targets for domestic money supply, and co-operate in devising a new unit of account as a European currency, not merely an accounting unit. Issued by the European Monetary Co-operation Fund, it would:

(a) Settle indebtedness between central banks;

(b) Earn interest for holders;

(c) Develop into a new reserve currency.

16.6.5 PROBLEMS OF ECONOMIC AND MONETARY UNION

The major difficulties of monetary and economic integration are firstly, to reach agreement on 'acceptable' levels of unemployment and inflation in each country, and the trade-off between them. The second area of difficulty concerns the different levels of productivity in each country. The solution is to analyse the cause, e.g. lack of capital; cultural attitudes towards work and technical change; towards union power and other types of monopoly; towards private and public ownership. Some kind of consensus must be found. The third type of problem is that of regional poverty such as exists in different national areas. The E.E.C. assists distressed regions with the help of the various Funds at its disposal. Monetary union would continue to provide such assistance.

The European Monetary System was the outcome of the various ideas for monetary integration. The principles were adopted in 1978. It was to include all nine partners of the E.E.C and to begin in January 1979. France suffered a change of heart at the last moment; Ireland needed a little more wooing and Britain, quixotically, wanted to retain her independence, and did not join. The European Monetary System finally began in March 1979 with all the E.E.C. partners except Britain.

The impetus towards the setting-up of the system came from the differential movements of European currencies. Those countries with balance of payments surpluses found that they could not increase sales to countries with balance of payments deficits. The latter were unable to expand their own growth because of constant exchange crises. The weakness of the dollar and the instability of the international monetary system were two other reasons, which, combined with the intellectual debate on the issue, finally led to the E.E.C. taking the plunge into a monetary union.

The European Monetary System is meant to create a zone of monetary stability between the initial joining members: Belgium, Denmark, France, Holland, Ireland, Italy, Luxembourg and West Germany. Non-members might get associate membership and members not participating could join at a later date.

Each currency has a central rate against a new European currency unit, the ecu. Each currency therefore also has a rate against each other based on the ecu. This means bilateral exchange rates on a parity grid system, similar to the old 'snake'. Every country must maintain a margin of + or $- 2\frac{1}{4}$ % on either side of the central rate, except Italy whose intervention margins were 6% either side of the central rate.

The ecu is a weighted average of all E.E.C. currencies. The highest weight is the mark, 33%, the French franc comes next, and third is sterling with a weight of 13.25%, although the U.K. did not join the system. The ecu acts as the denominator for the exchange rate mechanism and for operations in the intervention and credit mechanisms; it acts as the basis for the divergence indicator and as a means of settlement between the monetary authorities of the E.E.C.

When margins of fluctuation against the ecu central rates (known as 'thresholds of divergence') are exceeded, action must take place, e.g. intervention on the exchange markets, changes in domestic policy or changes in the central rate. The ecu is identical with the European unit of account. The reason why the parity grid was adopted rather than the 'basket' system of parities was that the latter would have meant each member maintaining a stable exchange rate with the rest of the system. This could have caused great domestic problems to certain countries in reducing their money supply, inflation and public sector borrowing requirement. On the other hand, stronger countries under the parity grid system have to make no efforts to alter their domestic policies, probably because they are successful enough.

There are three types of support facility: (a) the very short term which provides in theory unlimited amounts of support for periods of up to ten weeks and a further automatic three months if necessary, (b) a short-term monetary support which allows for 14bn ecu for up to nine months. Each country has a borrowing ceiling as well as a 'commitment' ceiling which is twice as high as the borrowing ceiling, (c) 11bn ecu is available for assistance to member countries in difficulties with their balance of payments. Credits extend for 2—5 years but are subject to economic policy conditions imposed by the Council of Ministers of the E.E.C. The first two facilities are extensions of those already established, but are at 25bn ecu compared with 10bn under the old arrangements. The borrowing and lending facilities are to be administered through the European Monetary Co-operation Fund. Member countries deposit 20% of their gold holdings with the Fund and 20% of their dollar holdings, and are issued with the equivalent amount of ecus which can then be used between members in settlement of debts.

16.7 HARMONIZATION AND THE MARJOLIN REPORT

In 1975, a study group produced, under the chairmanship of Mr Robert Marjolin, a report which suggested a short-term programme for concerted effort by the Community in investment, regional and unemployment policy. On the monetary and financial side, the study group wanted more integrated monetary policies, exchange rates; better facilities for inter-community credit, and the development of a European unit of account.

For a time these ideas languished until October 1977 when Mr Roy Jenkins in his role as President of the Commission brought forward the topic of monetary union with his Jean Monnet Memorial Lecture at the European Institute in Florence. A month later, in November 1977, the European Commission submitted to the Council, *a Five Year Plan of Action on Growth, Jobs and Stability* with a view to eventual economic and monetary union.

The substance of the Plan was *convergence*: a gradual co-ordination of member states' economic policies; integration of the common market to ensure progress on taxation; freer movement of goods, services and capital, and the abolition of monetary compensation amounts (M.C.A.'s) which distorted the market in farm produce. Efforts should be made to deal with new economic needs and to improve working life. On the financial and monetary side, further integration was needed and study of the ways by which significant monetary functions could be transferred to Community levels. Joint action should be taken on regional, social, industrial and energy policies, and on new facilities for investment. Above all was the continued need for monetary union to restore order in the international monetary system. In April 1978, the Commission declared that yearly targets would be set and monitored at summit level. Grand words, but action, long delayed, came out of them.

16.7.1 HARMONIZATION OF CREDIT INSTITUTIONS

In November 1977, the directive was finally approved for the harmonization of credit institutions. Although it had originally been suggested and approved in December 1974, member governments could not agree on the exceptions to be permitted. These difficulties were resolved by 1977. A bank can now set up in other E.E.C. countries if it meets the legal requirements of the home country, and the home country accepts responsibility for the bank's operations in the E.E.C. country. Harmonization came into force in 1980 and was one of the ideas which led to the U.K. Banking Act 1979 and the Companies Act 1980.

There are to be some exceptions. Italy and Ireland will be able to prohibit the entry of other E.E.C. banks until 1990 on the grounds of 'no economic need'. Denmark will be able to keep its real estate banks. Giros, central banks and certain kinds of savings banks will similarly be exempted from the new directives. A general escape clause is provided for governments to defer 'the application of this directive to certain types. . .of credit institutions' if this caused insoluble short-term problems.

The directive provides for the setting-up of a committee of banking and government officials from the nine to be in charge of future harmonization policy. New banking legislation has been introduced by the U.K. as presaged in the White Paper*, for licensing is necessary in the E.E.C. Common rules on deposit insurance and common accountancy conventions are likely to be introduced. A pooled credit information exchange system will allow the supervisory authorities to check on the amount of credit which customers are getting. These exchange information systems work in Germany, Italy, Belgium and France, but the other five countries have yet to be convinced of their usefulness.

16.8 E.E.C. FINANCIAL AND MONETARY INSTITUTIONS

16.8.1 THE MONETARY CO-OPERATION FUND

In March 1971, the European Community Council passed a Resolution, re-affirmed by the Heads of State at a meeting in Paris, October 1972, to establish economic and monetary union by 1980. *A Monetary Co-operation Fund* was thought to be an essential preliminary to a community system of central banks.

The Monetary Co-operation Fund (F.E.C.O.M.) was therefore set up under Article 3 Regulation 907/73 of 3 April 1973. The high hopes with which the Fund began, did not materialize. In reply to a written question (527/74) by Mr Glesener, the following information was given (12 February 1975) by the Council:

"The European Monetary Compensation Fund is at present responsible for:

the concerted action necessary for the proper functioning of the Community exchange system,

the multilateralization of positions resulting from interventions in Community currencies by central banks under the intra-Community exchange system, and

the administration of the short-term financing arrangements.

---

*The Licensing and Supervision of Deposit-taking Institutions Cmd 6584.

The Fund has not so far considered it necessary to recruit staff to carry out these functions. It has delegated to its agent, the Bank for International Settlements, responsibility for entering the Fund's accounts transactions by the central banks relating to interventions in Community currencies or in connection with currency transfers by way of short-term support.''

By 1975 then, it can be seen that the European Monetary Co-operation Fund had only a theoretical existence. B.I.S., as agent, was carrying out the Fund's functions. No strengthening of the Fund could really take place without a common economic policy.

16.8.2 THE EUROPEAN INVESTMENT BANK

Difficulties may have beset E.M.U., but one financial development of the E.E.C. has certainly taken root and flourished: the European Investment Bank. Set up under the Treaty of Rome in 1958, it is a non-profit-making public institution. Its aim is to contribute to the 'balanced development' of the Common Market. Towards this end, it makes loans or guarantees for the finance of projects which aid the Community's interests or those of less developed regions.

Finance comes from the E.I.B.'s own capital, subscribed by member states, and from the sale of issues on the world's capital markets. The paid-up capital was raised to 557m units of account in 1975. The U.K.'s share was 124m ua.

Most loans range from 2—16m ua but can be higher. About 40% of the fixed asset cost is provided. The borrower finds the rest. Loans are for 7—12 years but can go up to 20 years. Interest charges (save for the African, Pacific and Caribbean countries which get a cheaper rate) are around market level. Originally, all interest rates were fixed at the time of making the loan and were the same for all types of customer and project. Finance had to be borrowed in several currencies.

In 1976, more flexibility was introduced. Interest rates were modified. Loans could be in American dollars or Swiss francs, in addition to the previous mixture of currencies. Currency cocktails have varying interest rates for different mixtures of yen, deutschmarks, Swiss francs and American dollars. Loan repayments must be made in the currencies borrowed. This can be a disincentive to entrepreneurs in countries with a depreciating exchange rate. In the U.K., public sector borrowing is shielded from such hazards by exchange risk guarantees from the Treasury. There is no such munificence for private industry. Hence, when industrialists borrow, they like short-term money, and preferably from intermediaries such as the Industrial and Commercial Finance Corporation.

Preferred areas for loans are European projects too large for one E.E.C. member to handle (such as the European Airbus); the creation of jobs in undeveloped or depressed regions such as southern Italy, parts of Ireland, Scotland, south Wales and northern England.

16.8.2.1 *External relations in the E.E.C.*

The E.I.B. has now extended its activities. In 1976 13% of its loans went to projects outside the E.E.C. under the Lome Convention or the terms of association with 13 Mediterranean countries. The Lome Convention signed in 1975 by 46 African, Caribbean and Pacific countries, granted them duty-free access for 99.2% of their exports to the Common Market. The majority of agricultural and all industrial products from these countries benefit from the provisions and those (STABEX) to stabilize export earnings. Only certain farm products covered by the CAP are excepted. The concessions cost around £50m—£60m a year.

The *Export Stabilization* scheme guaranteed the 46 countries of the Lome Convention (Title 11) against loss of export income through fluctuations in commodity prices. If those prices fell below an agreed figure by more than $6\frac{1}{2}$ %, Community aid made up the difference. The richer countries repay the sums when their situation improves; the poorer ones do not. Cocoa, coffee, cotton, coconut, raw hides, sisal and iron ore are the commodities covered. Of the total of 3,390m ua for financial aid provided by the Community, 375m ua was for the stabilization scheme.

When the Lome Convention expired in 1979, a new one was signed by the Community and 57 African, Caribbean and Pacific states. It came into force on 14 March 1980 and builds an earlier preferential for the agricultural products of these states into the Community market.

TYPICAL QUESTION

Comment on the significance of the European monetary system.

ADDITIONAL QUESTIONS

1. Write brief notes on The European currency joint float (the 'snake').

2. What steps has the European Economic Community taken towards European monetary union, and how successful have they been?

SUGGESTED ANSWER

All the members of the European Economic Community except the U.K. joined the European Monetary System which came into force in March 1979. The object of the European Monetary System (E.M.S) was to create an area of monetary stability. It was also hoped that there would be greater co-operation on economic and financial policies among the members of the Community.

The E.M.S. is based on a parity grid system, rather like the European 'snake'. Each currency has a 'central rate' in terms of the European Currency Unit (ecu) the value of which is based on an amount of members' currencies weighted in line with their economic importance in the E.E.C. When the

E.M.S. began, the highest weighted currency was Germany with 33%; the lowest, Luxemburg with 0.35%. Sterling is used in the weightings although the U.K. did not join the scheme.

Every country must maintain a margin of + or − 2½ % of the central rate, at which point intervention must take place. Italy was given intervention limits of roughly 6% on either side of its central rate.

Arrangements to support the established parity rates are provided by short-term facilities of 10 weeks; short-term monetary support (ecu 14bn) up to nine months and medium-term financial assistance (ecu 11bn) for up to five years for countries in difficulties with their balance of payments.

The European Monetary Co-operation Fund adminsters the borrowing and lending facilities. Members deposit with the Fund 20% of their gold holdings and 20% of their U.S. dollar holdings against an equivalent issue of ecus which may then be used between members in settlement of debts.

The E.M.S. is a significant step in the E.E.C. because there must be greater co-ordination of economic and financial policies among the member states, and all must surrender some part of their sovereignty for the system to be successful.

Bibliography
Centre for European Agricultural Studies/Wye College, Ashford, Kent *Green Money and the Common Agricultural Policy.*
Grubel, H.G. *The International Monetary System*, 3rd edition, (London: Penguin, 1977) Chapter 9.

17 The U.S.A. Banking System

At first glance, British and American banking systems look very different. But commercial banks in both countries accept deposits, make loans and provide certain financial services. The central banks carry out the Government's monetary policy and hold the reserves of other banks.

17.1 UNIT AND BRANCH BANKING

However, in Britain, the Big Four handle the majority of business through more than 12,000 branches. In the U.S.A., there are very few branches and over 14,000 unit banks. Of these, only 38.5% belong to the Federal Reserve system. This encompasses 12 central (Federal Reserve) banks and 'member' banks. Banks chartered by the *Federal* government are known as *national banks*. They are automatically *member banks*. Banks chartered by the state (*state banks*) can *choose* to become members if they meet the requirements.

Twenty-one states, mostly on the western and eastern seaboards, allow state-wide branching. Where only limited branching is permitted (in 17 states) branch offices may be established in a bank's own county or within a certain radius from the home office. No branching is allowed in the remainder of the states though some permit bank holding companies which control a number of unit banks. Centralized ownership of several banks in this way is called *group banking*.

17.1.1 BANK EXPANSION

17.1.1.1 *Branching and Mergers*
Entry into banking is regulated. Newcomers must prove 'need'. This is partly to prevent the abuse of monopoly power; partly to prevent the bankruptcy of the inefficient. Monopoly power is also the criterion for mergers. Under the Bank Mergers Act 1960, they were only allowed if they had approval from the Board of Governors of the Federal Reserve (for state bank mergers) or from the Comptroller of the Currency for national bank mergers. In 1966, the restrictions were removed. If the Justices Department did not file suit against them within 30 days, mergers could go through.

Branching has, however, provided the principal form of new entry into banking for some years. Using the criterion of 'need' before new banks are allowed, prevents, it is alleged, an excessive number of banks in an area, a situation which could lead the least efficient into insolvency. But rejections of new bank applications on the grounds of 'insufficient need' or 'unfavourable earnings prospects' actually helps to protect the less efficient banks from competition. This illustrates the *Hawthorne Reverse Effect syndrome* where the operation of a law results in the very situation it was intended to prevent.

17.1.1.2 *Holding Companies*

The Bank Holding Act of 1956, amended 1966 and 1970, forbids bank holding companies from acquiring non-bank companies. One exception is allowed. If a holding company holds only one bank, it can acquire other enterprises, including subsidiaries closely related to banking. Banks have used this escape clause to expand and diversify. Many big American banks have holding companies, e.g. Bank America Corporation owns the Bank of America, the largest commercial bank in the world.

Arguments against this kind of diversification are the same as those levelled against German commercial banks holding large shares in industrial companies: that such 'related' companies get credit preference; or the activities of one department may conflict with another. The latter problem should be easy to resolve. The former was remedied by an amendment to the Bank Holding Act, which set out the permissible activities of bank holding companies as follows:
  (a) Data processing and bookkeeping.
  (b) Selling credit-related insurance.
  (c) Industrial banking.
  (d) Loan servicing.
  (e) Investing in community welfare projects.
  (f) Economic forecasting, trust and investment advising.
  (g) Operating a Trust Company.
Financial intermediaries, noting the competition that has developed from the one bank holding company have tried to reverse the tables and enter banking by the same route. Non-financial groups, too, now offer financial services. Thus, the three largest retail chains provide consumer credit, mortgage banking and insurance underwriting.

Commercial banks therefore compete with other financial institutions and with financial subsidiaries of general, commercial and industrial companies. Banking is forbidden to the latter and insurance or land development to the banks.

17.1.1.3 *The Hunt Commission*

Control of the banking system should have three aims (a) the financial stability of banks, (b) the efficient allocation of credit, (c) the implementation of Government monetary policy. It was felt in the latter part of the 1960's that the American banking system was not fulfilling these aims and the Hunt Commission was set up to make recommendations. It suggested that there should be a reduction in the regulation of all deposit institutions, including the savings/loan associations and mutual banks; and that they be allowed to offer more financial services on an equal basis. It further recommended that savings institutions should be able to offer checking accounts to individuals and non-business groups; that commercial and savings banks should be allowed to branch and merge state-wide; and that, because interest rate ceilings on time and savings deposits distorted the flow of credit, they should be phased out of the system.

The Commission's report led to no immediate broad changes. Most intermediaries wished to compete with others, but were not so enthusiastic about others competing with them.

17.1.1.4 Bank Regulation and Overseas Growth

It can be seen from this general picture that American banks are subject to more legal constraints than banks in Britain. The regulations may differ from state to state and involve several kinds of supervision. It could thus be argued that instead of a two-tier type of banking (unit and branch), there are several, differing from state to state, as well as many kinds of financial institutions.

This diversity of law and of institutions has had two important consequences, one good, one bad. The bad was that such diversity softened the rigours of monetary policy. This was the reasoning behind the Monetary Control Act 1980. The good was that banking, deprived of the home climate in which to flourish, took roots elsewhere. As a result, American banks entered a new era of internationalism. Although some of the 'safe' overseas lending before the oil-price explosion looked much less safe afterwards, nevertheless overseas operations provided most of the gilt on the gingerbread for American banks in the later 1970's and partly compensated them for the harsher fare at home.

The provision of international services by American banks has been unintentionally helped both by the Edge Act and by the Voluntary Foreign Credit Restraint Programme. Though most U.S. banks cannot take deposits or open branches outside their home states, they can open Edge Act subsidiaries which offer international banking services. A bank transacting business in one state can open in another for foreign business. One survey showed that the foreign deposits of America's 11 biggest banks grew at an annual compound rate of 25% between 1970 and 1975. The pace slowed down thereafter. Even in Britain, American banks have penetrated the local sterling markets. It was Chase Manhatten which organized a syndicated loan for the firm of Ferranti (penalized in rosier years by the British government for making excessive profits).

The growth in foreign deposits by U.S. banks in the 1970's came partly from the Voluntary Foreign Credit Restraint Programme inaugurated in 1965 (revoked, 1974). Because of a deficit balance of payments a limit was placed on the amount of funds which U.S. banks could transfer abroad. The average annual growth of foreign deposits at the head offices of U.S. banks then declined from 10.1% in 1960—1964 to 3.0% in 1965—1972. By contrast, the number of U.S. banks operating overseas offices jumped from 11 in 1964 to 108 in 1972. The number of foreign branches rose from 181 to 627. By 1973, foreign branch deposits accounted for nearly 30% of total deposits of all U.S. banks operating abroad. In 1964, the total was only 6.3%. The V.F.C.R. programme illustrated yet again the operation of the reverse effect principle, whereby a law has exactly the opposite effect of what was intended. Foreign banks and branches could take in and lend funds without restraint, but increased competition for overseas business drives operating margins inexorably downwards. In February 1978 a group of international banks lent Venezuela $1.2bn at just over $\frac{3}{4}$ of the cost of their funds. Such margins leave little room for manoeuvre, particularly if yield curves flatten. Some countries cannot now repay their debts. Less developed countries in such circumstances cannot get out of the vicious circle of debt servicing and into the virtuous one of investment, take-off and growth. Should such debts be written off? All? If not, whose? And by how much?

In spite of impediments to domestic growth, the American multinational banks may decide that during periods of world recession, home banking is safest. All the necessary spadework has been done abroad. When world conditions improve they will be ready to reap the fruits of their labours.

17.2 THE FEDERAL RESERVE SYSTEM

The Federal Reserve Act of 1913 was one of those rare instances of legislation which satisfies, at least temporarily, all the parties involved. It allayed the fear of the western states that they would be dominated by the financial interests of the east. It gave the eastern states the assurance that their banking influence would still be significant.

17.2.1 THE FEDERAL RESERVE BANKS

This happy situation came about by the creation of 12 districts each with its own central or federal reserve bank. The banks were in Boston, New York, Cleveland, Richmond, Altanta, Chicago, Kansas City, Philadelphia, Minneapolis, Dallas, San Francisco and St. Louis. They each have a nine-man Board of Directors. Three are appointed by the Federal Reserve Board (nominally the seat of power of the Federal system), while the member banks elect the remaining six. Of these, three (Class A) are bankers, and three (Class B) have commercial, industrial or agricultural interests.

Member banks subscribe an amount equal to 6% of their capital and surplus to the capital stock of the Federal Reserve Bank of their district. Half only is called in, and member banks receive a statutory dividend of 6% on their paid up subscription. Earnings of federal reserve banks above these dividends and retained earnings (determined by the Federal Reserve Board) are payable to the Treasury. The federal reserve banks therefore present an unusual blend of public and private ownership.

17.2.2 THE BOARD OF GOVERNORS

The Board is situated in Washington and has seven members. Each appointment which lasts for a 14-year term, is made by the President and confirmed by the Senate. The members retire by rotation, and not more than one member may be appointed from any one federal reserve district. From the seven members, the President designates a chairman and vice-chairman for four-year renewable terms.

The U.S. President and Congress determine fiscal and monetary policy. If the Office of Management and Budget plans a deficit, the Federal Reserve Banks cannot then pursue a tight money policy. Government demands for credit crowd out other borrowing unless the money supply is increased. A deflationary policy can only be pursued if money growth keeps in line with productive growth. In the monetarist view, this means a reduction in government growth and spending.

The Chairman of the Board has great influence in the Open Market Committee. Here his advice may be crucial but he is still only one out of twelve members. The main power of any chairman of the Federal Reserve Board today seems to lie in the importance of his platform and how he uses this platform to persuade and inform.

17.2.3 THE FEDERAL OPEN MARKET COMMITTEE

Originally, it was thought that the Federal Reserve banks would have independent views and the Board of Governors would act merely as a co-ordinator of these views. The emergence of a national money market in New York and of open market operations as a monetary technique, shifted the balance of power so that the Board of Governors and the Open Market Committee have what amounts to dual control.

The Board sets reserve requirements within the statutory limits. Discount rate is supposed to be established by each Reserve bank. It is more often set at meetings of the Open Market Committee with any disapproving federal reserve bank using dilatory tactics to signify its disagreement or displeasure. But that appears to be all. Such open market meetings have helped to make the Committee an important policy-making body. In this direction, its power is probably equal to the Board of Governors.

The Open Market Committee consists of twelve people. Seven are members from the Rederal Reserve Board of Governors. The other five which always includes the New York Federal Reserve bank president, are presidents of the federal reserve banks, who serve in rotation. Though all twelve presidents attend meetings, only members may vote.

When the Committee makes decisions about open market operations, it communicates them to the manager of the Open Market Account, who is always a manager of the New York Federal Reserve Bank. Through a small group of private dealers, he then buys or sells securities, thus altering the level of bank reserves and their ability to create credit. All the federal reserve banks participate according to their relative financial strength.

From 1952—1962, open market operations were confined to short-term government securities. This was found to give too little leverage on the structure of interest rates. The F.O.M.C. now operates on government securities of all maturities. Directives are 'defensive', to offset uncontrolled factors which affect bank reserves, and 'dynamic', which are designed deliberately to change the size of the reserves.

17.2.4 THE FEDERAL ADVISORY COUNCIL

The Council consists of twelve private commercial bankers chosen by the directors of the twelve Federal Reserve banks. It is an advisory body which meets the Board of Governors periodically to express the views of bankers.

17.2.5 MEMBER BANKS

Members include all national banks (chartered by the Federal Government) and all state banks who want membership and meet the requirements.

17.3 FUNCTIONS OF THE FEDERAL RESERVE

17.3.1 HOLDING MEMBER BANKS' RESERVES

The Banking Act of 1935 gave the Federal Reserve authority to vary the amount of cash which banks must hold against their deposits. These reserves are held in the federal reserve bank in the district, and changes in them affect the availability of bank credit. This fact was somewhat belatedly realized, which accounts for the fact that such changes have been used as a monetary control only since the Second World War.

The Board sets the required percentages for two classes of banks (a) reserve city banks which are all member banks with more than $400m of deposits, irrespective of the bank's actual location, (b) country banks. The reserve requirements are based on a graduated scale. It ranges from 7% on the first $2m of total demand deposits to $16\frac{1}{4}$ % for over $400m, but can be changed for purposes of monetary control.

The state banking commissions set the reserve requirements of non-member banks. These may vary from no legal reserves at all to as much as 30% of demand deposits. Certain earning assets (government securities and deposits with other banks) count as part of the required reserves under state law. Federal Reserve member banks can count only deposits with the federal reserve bank, and vault cash which earns nothing. This difference between the reserve requirements of member and non-member banks was yet another deterrent to membership of the system. . .and effective monetary policy, which the Monetary Control Act of 1980 attempted to remedy.

17.3.2 CLEARING AND COLLECTING CHEQUES

All cheques are sent for collection or payment to the federal reserve bank in the district. The bank thus acts as a clearing house for the member banks. Correspondent banks act for other banks in the payment and acceptance of cheques, where no branch exists. In this way correspondent offices offset, to some extent, the disadvantages of the unit banking system.

17.3.3 PUTTING MONEY INTO CIRCULATION

The federal reserve banks issue notes directly, while coins and U.S. Treasury notes are issued by the Treasury and circulated by the federal reserve banks.

17.3.4 SUPERVISING MEMBER BANKS

Supervision is very much stronger in the U.S. than in the U.K.: one bank could be supervised by a number of groups. The supervisory agencies are:

(a) The Federal Deposit Insurance Corporation which supervises all banks insured with it. Insurance is compulsory for member banks and, since 1980, savings institutions. From the time of its establishment in 1932 until 1976, the F.D.I.C. has paid out $2.3bn in insurance to depositors in over 500 banks. Of this, $2bn was recouped, making an overall loss of $300m. Insured banks used to provide finance for the Corporation by paying an annual premium of 1/12 of 1% of assessable deposits. The assessment has fallen since then and, by 1976, it was 0.037% and its total insurance fund stood at $7bn. The Fund's investment income from Government securities exceeds that from its assessment income. There is also a facility for borrowing from the U.S. Treasury. Only a very few banks (around 250) were not insured with the F.D.I.C. The Monetary Control Act of 1980 now covers bank and savings deposits against loss by fraud or insolvency up to $100,000.

(b) The Comptroller of the Currency (Treasury Department) supervises all national banks to ensure that reserve and other requirements are being met. In the Depository Institutions De-regulation and Monetary Control Act of 1980, the office of Comptroller was given greater powers of supervision over the competence of banks.

(c) The State Commission supervises all the state banks which it charters. To avoid too much supervision by too many, the banks are usually seen only by one agency in a year, which then circulates its report to the others.

17.3.5 GOVERNMENT FISCAL AGENT

The federal reserve banks act as bankers for the Federal Government. They hold the government's accounts; handle the issue and redemption of government securities and pay bondholders their interest; act as Treasury agent in gold and foreign exchange dealings, and for the government in the implementation of monetary and fiscal policies.

17.4 FEDERAL RESERVE POWERS

17.1.4.1 OPEN MARKET OPERATIONS
Through the buying and selling of securities the Federal Reserve can contract or expand reserves of member banks and so influence the money supply.

17.1.4.2 REDISCOUNT RATE
Member banks borrow money directly from the federal reserve bank (by contrast with the U.K. system where, except in rare instances, only the Discount Houses may borrow from the central bank). They take customers' commercial paper (which they have already discounted) to the federal reserve bank who discounts it again (hence rediscount rate). The Federal Reserve can discourage borrowing by raising the rate; encourage borrowing by lowering it.

Discount policy is supposed to be a temporary adjustment mechanism, not a privilege. Regulation A states that discounting can be used to meet 'a sudden withdrawal of deposits or seasonal requirements for credit beyond those which can reasonably be met by its own resources. . .or. . .for longer periods when necessary in order to assist member banks in meeting unusual situations, such as may result from national, regional or local difficulties. . .'. Nevertheless banks are rarely refused discounts or advances.

The Federal Reserve often appears to have a schizophrenic attitude to its use of the discount rate as a technique of monetary policy. The rate is the cost to the banks of obtaining reserves, and so influences the amount of reserves borrowed; yet the Federal Reserve seems to want discount rate to be used only to improve liquidity. The discount rate therefore hovers very near to Treasury bill rate, above or below. In the U.K., Bank rate and its successor, Minimum Lending rate, were meant to have a deterrent, even a penal effect. For this purpose, M.L.R. is deliberately set above Treasury Bill rate, though the Bank of England does not commit itself inexorably to this relationship.

The double-edged attitude of the Federal Reserve may be partly due to the new emphasis on monetary policy over the last decades. As the importance of money supply came to be realized (mainly due to the work of Milton Friedman), the technical manager of that supply, the Federal Reserve, came under greater scrutiny. In 1975, both houses of Congress passed a resolution enjoining the Federal Reserve to set the long-term growth of the money supply at a rate 'commensurate with the economy's potential to increase production'.

This resolution was incorporated in an amendment in 1977 to the Federal Reserve Act of 1913. Under this amendment also, a representative of the Board of Governors has to appear regularly before Congress to explain the Federal Reserve's targets and objectives: a form of public scrutiny over monetary policy not previously experienced.

The Federal Reserve has since paid greater lip service to the monetary aggregates. But already in 1974 it was publishing three kinds of targets: (a) a two-month range for the growth in M1 (simple money supply) and M2 (= to the U.K. M3, but excluding large C.D.'s), (b) annual growth ranges for M1 and M2, (c) target band within which the rate on federal funds may fluctuate from one Open Market Committee meeting to another. Federal funds are used for reserve balances. When one bank has an excess, it lends at interest to another who wishes to borrow such funds. (This system matches the U.K.'s London Inter-Bank Offered rate, which is controlled, however, by market forces.)

As interest rate and money supply targets are nearly always mutually exclusive, it is not surprising that the Federal Reserve's management of monetary policy appears somewhat schizophrenic. Throughout the period, January 1974 to November 1977, the Federal Reserve kept within its federal funds rate almost all the time. But the 2-month M1 growth targets were missed 60% of the time. The annual growth rate targets for both M1 and M2 (ranging from 5—7.5% and 8.5—10.5%) were achieved only 50% of the time. This is not surprising. If fiscal policy is bent on expansion, efforts to restrict the money supply will prove ineffectual. As the Quantity theory points out so succinctly: an increase in PT without an increase in M, can only mean an increase in V.

Beginning in 1974 and going on to 1977, the *velocity* of money in the U.S.A. (the ratio to GNP to M1) rose very sharply. An increase in the money supply at this time might have led to rampant inflation, for if M and V go up together, the effect on P and T must be magnified. The money supply target was therefore wisely abandoned for control of interest rates.

17.1.4.3 SELECTIVE CONTROLS

The most important selective controls are:

(a) Regulation A covers the type of paper eligible for discounting.

(b) Regulations T, U, and G covers the minimum margin requirements needed as collateral for the purchase of stocks on credit. . .thus

Regulation U: bank credit for the same.

Regulation G: credit extended by other groups for the same.

Regulation W: imposes minimum down payments and maximum maturities on loans for consumer durables

(c) Regulation X limited mortgage credit by setting minimum down payments and periods of repayment.

These selective controls were introduced during periods such as World War Two and the Korean War when some particular stringency had to be observed. The argument for their use was that general instruments of monetary policy do not affect all types of credit equally. Selective controls must be used to encourage or restrict specific activities and thus make monetary policy more effective.

Regulation Q has had the most effect and least planning. It imposed interest-rate ceilings on commercial bank deposits and grew out of the Banking Act of 1933. This Act gave the Federal Reserve Board the power to regulate maximum interest rates on different deposits in different locations, that could be paid by member banks. The rates were set out in the Federal Reserve Board's Regulation Q. The Home Loan Board was given similar powers in 1966 to establish maximum interest rates on various types of savings accounts.

Regulation Q had some odd results: (a) The growth of Certificates of Deposit, which unlike time deposits could be given up at any time without loss of interest—C.D.'s led to the greater use by banks of the money market, (b) The development of U.S. banks abroad where maximum interest rate restrictions did not exist at least as a policy control, (c) The development and expansion of the Eurocurrency market, (d) Funds were obtained outside the banking system so leading to inefficient allocation of resources. In July 1973, all interest-rate ceilings were abolished on time deposits of $100,000 or more.

Moral 'suasion' has occasionally been used to change the volume and type of lending. Owing to the numbers of individual banks and their individual characteristics, this technique of monetary policy has proved singularly ineffective.

17.1.4.4 MEMBER AND NON-MEMBER BANKS: THE PROBLEM OF CONTROL

The existence of so many non-member banks outside the Federal system posed a problem of effective monetary policy and control, even though member banks held over 70% of the total commercial bank deposits. The problem was exacerbated by (a) the declining membership of the Federal Reserve system, and (b) the activities of foreign banks in America who had a freedom denied the American banks. They did not have to keep reserve balances in the central bank, nor were they subject to the National Banking Act which prohibited multi-state banking by national banks; nor to state laws which imposed the same restrictions on state banks.

However, the International Banking Act 1978, began regulating foreign banks in the U.S.A. It put them on the same plane as domestic banks by making them subject to the central bank's reserve requirements; unable to open branches in more than one state and unable to specialize in commercial or in merchant banking.

17.5 THE DEPOSITORY INSTITUTIONS DEREGULATION AND MONETARY CONTROL ACT 1980

This Act radically altered domestic banking. The general philosophy behind the Act was two-fold: to encourage competition among all the banking and deposit-taking institutions by gradually abolishing maximum deposit and lending rates; and to make monetary control more effective by giving the Federal Reserve powers to impose reserve requirements for all ordinary and time deposits in deposit-taking institutions. U.S. banking should become more competitive. It is also likely to become more efficient with a wider range of services for customers.

The main provisions of the Act were as follows:

(a) Lifting of maximum ceiling rates paid by banks to depositors;

(b) Abolition of state limitations on the maximum rates which banks can charge for certain kinds of loans;

(c) Expansion of the services which building societies (savings and loan institutions or thrift institutions) can offer;

(d) Changes in the methods by which the Federal Reserve provides services to commercial banks;

(e) An extension of the Federal Reserve's powers over all U.S. banks.

The last provision was the one which tackled the problem of monetary control. The Federal Reserve has sought to increase its powers over member banks by increasing the amount of interest-free deposits which members have to place with the Federal Reserve as part of their reserve requirements. But as the amounts have gone up, the numbers of member banks have diminished. They cannot then get Federal Reserve services, but this is a price they have been prepared to pay. Now all banks and deposit institutions come within the Federal Reserve's control, and will have to conform with the reserve requirements.

All banks will now get the facilities of the Federal Reserve which will issue a specific price list for their different services. The physical transfer of funds between banks should be improved under the new law. Banks and building societies were formerly unable to compete in terms of services. Banks were forced to pay maximum time deposit rates of about 5—7%, with building societies offering about 0.25% more. These restraints are to be phased out by 1986. Savings institutions will be able to offer credit cards, loans, and unlimited mortgages. States which wish to keep limits on ceilings will have three years in which to introduce new legislation.

However, the restrictions on branching continue. Commercial banks are still prohibited from opening branches in more than one state. Thus the Bank of America keeps its retail activities in the U.S.A. confined to California and Citibank within the restraints of New York.

17.6 COMPARISON OF THE U.K. AND U.S. COMMERCIAL BANKING SYSTEM: SUMMARY

U.K.	U.S.A.
4 large banks with 11000 branches (but many other types of financial institutions in private and public sectors)	Great variation; 14,000 unit banks, over 5,000 savings banks and 12,000 credit unions.
No interest on current accounts	Free chequing facilities on current accounts (equivalent to interest-free accounts)

U.K.	*U.S.A.*
Until 1980 mortgages, not easy to obtain	Mortgages
Fairly low charges	Costly transmission service; correspondent network
Loans at fixed interest varying with M.L.R., medium-term	Long-term loans on fixed loan accounts at varying rates
Short-term loans or overdrafts	No overdrafts
Current accounts; deposit and Savings Bank give interest at fixed rates	Cheque accounts; time deposits (fixed term) at varying rates; savings accounts
Consumer credit usually only for durables (cars)	Consumer credit easy to obtain

TYPICAL QUESTION

Write an account of central banking in the U.S.A.

SUGGESTED ANSWER

Central banking in the U.S.A. comes within the framework of the Federal Reserve system which comprises twelve Federal Reserve Banks, the Federal Board of seven Governors and an Open Market Committee.

The Federal Reserve Board is at the apex of the system. Its seven members are appointed by the President with the consent of the Senate for fourteen year terms. The Chairman and vice-Chairman are chosen from the seven members also by the President for four year renewable terms.

The operating costs of the Board are financed by assessments on the Federal Reserve Banks which deduct them and their operating expenses from their earnings and then transfer the remainder to the Treasury.

The Board, along with other agencies, is responsible for the supervision of the commercial banks. It also has a monetary policy role which it shares with the Open Market Committee. The Committee consists of the seven members of the Board together with five representatives of the Federal Reserve Banks elected by the directors of those banks.

The Federal Reserve Board sets reserve requirements and the Reserve Banks establish the discount rate though this is subject to review by the Board. The Open Market Committee controls open market operations which is one of the main instruments of monetary policy.

The twelve Federal Reserve Banks each have nine directors, three from banking, business and public sectors. Member banks elect six from the first two groups. The Federal Reserve Board appoints the remaining three. Each of the Reserve Bank elects a member of the Federal Advisory Council. This has very little power and acts mainly as a spokesman for banking interests.

ADDITIONAL QUESTIONS

1. Compare and contrast the techniques used by the Bank of England in implementing monetary policy with those used by the central bank of another country with which you are familiar.

2. Write brief notes on the U.S. Federal Deposit Insurance Corporation.

3. How are the commercial banks in a country affected by the fiscal policy of the government of that country?

4. Compare and contrast the commercial banking systems of the United Kingdom and the United States.

Index